From the Foreword by
Colonel Walter J. Boyne, USAF (Ret.)

"In *Clash of Chariots*, two capable authors, Tom Donnelly and Sean Naylor, chart the remarkable progress of armored warfare over the years, from its debut on the western front in 1917 to its decisive use by United Nations forces against the armies of Saddam Hussein in Iraq in 1991 . . .

"The authors document the past use of the tank with skill and offer an intriguing picture of its future, as the traditional qualities of the tank are mated with the information superhighway that now governs all battle-fields. Their argument makes it seem certain that wars in the twenty-first century will resonate to the sounds of the clash of chariots just as did those of the twentieth century."

The Army Times Publishing Company is pleased to join with The Berkley Publishing Group in presenting this series of books on military history. We have proudly served the military community for over fifty years by means of our independent weekly newspapers, *Army Times, Navy Times,* and *Air Force Times.*

Clash of Chariots represents the fourth book in the series. The first three are *The Army Times Book of Great Land Battles* by Colonel J. D. Morelock; *The Army Times, Navy Times, Air Force Times Encyclopedia of Modern U.S. Military Weapons* by Timothy M. Laur and Steven L. Llanso; and *Generals in Muddy Boots: A Concise Encyclopedia of Combat Commanders* by Dan Cragg (Ret.).

An *Army Times* Book

CLASH OF CHARIOTS

THE GREAT TANK BATTLES

**Tom Donnelly
and Sean Naylor**

Edited by Walter J. Boyne

BERKLEY BOOKS, NEW YORK

This book is an original publication of The Berkley Publishing Group.

CLASH OF CHARIOTS

A Berkley Book / published by arrangement with
The Army Times Publishing Company

PRINTING HISTORY
Berkley hardcover edition / August 1996
Berkley trade paperback edition / June 1999

The Penguin Putnam Inc. World Wide Web site address is
http://www.penguinputnam.com

ISBN: 0-425-16871-9

PRINTED IN THE UNITED STATES OF AMERICA

10 9 8 7 6 5 4 3 2

For Eamonn and Will Donnelly
and
For David and Verney Naylor

CONTENTS

FOREWORD

IN *Clash of Chariots*, two capable authors, Tom Donnelly and Sean Naylor, chart the remarkable progress of armored warfare over the years, from its debut on the western front in 1917 to its decisive use by United Nations forces against the armies of Saddam Hussein in Iraq in 1991.

The tank, championed by that master of the unorthodox in warfare, Winston Churchill, was called into being by the deadly gridlock that had gripped the western front during World War I. Allied generals were unwilling to give up frontal attacks against the strong German defenses, despite the enormity of the casualties being incurred. In battle after battle, it was hoped that sufficient artillery and a determined infantry attack would break the enemy lines and allow the cavalry to thunder through and so end the stalemate. In battle after battle, thousands of Allied soldiers died, sometimes without gaining a single yard of ground. The tank, with its combination of firepower, mobility, armor, and shock value, promised to change the situation and permit, at last, a breakthrough.

Unfortunately for the Allies, typical bureaucratic bungling prevented the tank from realizing its full promise. It was committed to battle too early, before correct tactics for the exploitation of its gains had been developed. The Germans were resilient, and after the initial shock, they devised tactics to blunt the tank's usefulness. The early tanks lacked any means of radio communication and, once launched, operated in the same tactical vacuum as a lone infantry soldier.

In spite of these problems, the tanks held a promise, one realized by the German army in World War II. The Germans perfected the use of the tank as one component of a combined force of aircraft, armor, and infantry; with it they blazed across Europe from September 1939 to December 1941. The successful use of armor by the Germans almost enabled them to win World War II. They were thwarted by the Soviet Union, a nation that surprised the world with the number and the quality of its tanks and, eventually, with the excellent doctrine it developed for them.

By the end of World War II, tank armor, guns, and communications had made a quantum leap, but other new developments—the pervasive use of ground-support aircraft, new antitank weapons, and even nuclear weapons—seemed to spell the demise of armor as a force on the battlefield. The brief but bitter wars in the Sinai and in Iraq proved this to be far from the case. The technology of the tank had developed commensurately with other weapons, and in the deserts of the Middle East, the tank was still a dominant weapon.

The authors document the past use of the tank with skill and offer an intriguing picture of its future, as the traditional qualities of the tank are mated with the information superhighway that now governs all battlefields. Their argument makes it seem certain that wars in the twenty-first century will resonate to the sounds of the clash of chariots just as did those of the twentieth century.

Walter J. Boyne

AUTHORS' NOTE

WHILE THIS STUDY is a history of armored warfare and not a theoretical treatise, it is possible to discern, through the veil of the narrative, how the notions of what popularly has been called *blitzkrieg* have evolved. Looked at as a whole, this book offers glimpses into the tactical and operational ideas and real-world performance of the great practitioners of tank warfare: the German, the Soviet, the American, the British, and the Israeli armies.

To say that these armies were the great practitioners of armored warfare is not to say that all were equally masters of the trade; clearly, some armies were better at it, for a host of reasons, than others. Greatness, for our purposes, has as much to do with scale as with effectiveness. Some armies were better at certain aspects of armored warfare than others: for example, the Germans were probably never equaled as tacticians during World War II, but the Soviets were able to overcome their tactical deficiencies by superior operational art and strategy.

In general, however, our focus has been on the nuts and bolts of armored warfare: tactics and operations. Just what do we mean by these terms? Traditionally, *tactics* has referred to the techniques and procedures soldiers employ in the course of a battle or engagement. These range from how a tank crew functions to how an armored division or corps maneuvers. *Operations* refers to how battles or engagements may be scripted or fit together to attain some strategic purpose within a theater of war. Thus, in the German invasion of France in 1940, the effort to cross the Meuse River or the subsequent race of Guderian's panzers to the sea would, when considered separately, fall under the purview of tactics; but when taken together, as a method of eliminating the main Allied armies as a preliminary to defeating France, they would be considered operational art of the highest order.

In limiting ourselves primarily to operations and tactics, we have, of course, ignored strategy and politics, and these are perhaps the greatest determinants of ultimate victory in war. The British, for example, have never been especially adept at tank tactics or operations. At the same time, they have been superb at geopolitics.

Nevertheless, the tank—along with the airplane—has defined the character of high-technology conventional warfare in the twentieth century. Its primary attributes—armor protection, mobility, and firepower—and its intangible *shock value* promise to be essential qualities required for future warfare as well. As we argue in the epilogue, a new quality, based upon the ability to gather, manipulate, and process information, is being grafted on to the latest generation of American and other Western tanks; added to the traditional virtues of armored vehicles, this promises to extend the life of the tank well into the future.

Although new means of waging high-technology conventional warfare may be created, the promise of *blitzkrieg* remains as alluring as ever: an attacker may win great strategic victories at relatively little cost. The magnitude of the prize is great: not merely punishing an enemy or destroying his military forces, but occupying territory and exerting political control. Similarly, the cost of such victories is decreasing as the disparity between technologically and operationally sophisticated armies and lesser forces grows: the Germans conquered France with some thousands of casualties; the American-led coalition defeated the Iraqis with a few hundred killed, and a substantial number of those resulted from friendly fire.

Our case studies, too, may suggest something about the current military revolution based upon information processing. If the Germans were the master tacticians and operators of World War II, what advantages did they have over their opponents? A close reading of the historical record suggests that they had at least three. First, they created an operational or doctrinal concept—though they did not themselves call it *blitzkrieg*—that gained maximum results from all of the attributes of the tank: not merely its armor nor its firepower nor its mobility, but the advantages of all three. Second, they created military organizations—the panzer division, then the panzer corps, and ultimately the panzer army—that highlighted these strengths while concealing or compensating for the weaknesses of the tank by allowing the other arms to operate at the same tempo as the armor; holding fast to the traditional notion of combined arms, the Germans brought the infantry and artillery and other supporting elements up to the pace of tank elements. Finally, they entrusted these tools—for the most part, at least—to the care and good use of innovative and insightful commanders. In short, the Germans had good blueprints, good tools, and skilled craftsmen. Alas, they were in service to a demented architect, Adolf Hitler, and the story of the *Wehrmacht* is incomplete without considering the vital but terrible spark provided by Nazi ideology—but this is a book about the trade of tank warfare.

Perhaps the armies that learn to apply these general precepts in the age of information will dominate future battlefields, not merely gathering, but collating and distributing information with speed and accuracy; creating an organization to exploit information superiority; and loosing commanders to employ their ideas and tools with verve, skill, and cold-eyed finality. This last, especially, promises to remain essential, particularly for the battle on land, where warfare is most clearly a conflict between the human beings behind the technologies.

This book is very much a joint endeavor, not merely between two authors but between the writers and those who make the writing possible. Special thanks should go to the patient and even-keeled Walter Boyne and to Joe Acerno, whose enthusiasm got things off the ground to begin with. Scott McLallen and Doria Taylor prepared most of the maps (and all of the good ones), enduring endless micro-management from finickly authors. Above all, we have relied on our families and friends and loved ones, who have suffered the tribulations and should share in the satisfactions, such as they are, of this effort. Tom would like especially to thank his wife, Bonnie Benwick, and sons Eamonn and

Will. Sean would like to thank his family and friends who supported him through the creative process, especially his parents, David and Verney Naylor, who never guessed where all those toy soldiers and great battle books would lead.

Tom Donnelly
Sean Naylor

Washington, D.C.
January 1996

The map symbols explained

All the maps in this book use standard military symbols, explained below. Units on opposing sides are shaded in gray and white. Echelons up through division level are referred to using Arabic numerals - 50th Infantry Division, for example. Roman numerals are used to identify corps, and armies have their designation written out - Second British Army, for instance. Army group designations revert to Arabic numerals.

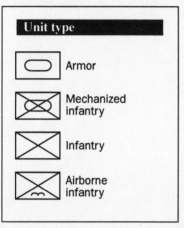

Unit type

Armor

Mechanized infantry

Infantry

Airborne infantry

Echelon of command

I	Company
II	Battalion
III	Regiment
X	Brigade
XX	Division
XXX	Corps
XXXX	Army
XXXXX	Army group

How to read a unit symbol

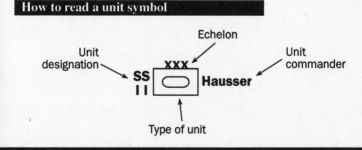

Unit designation

Echelon

Unit commander

SS XXX Hausser

Type of unit

CLASH OF CHARIOTS

PROLOGUE

FRANCE, 1917

Cambrai and the Birth of a Revolution

THE DAWN OF November 20, 1917, broke gray and bitter over northeastern France. Now in its fourth year, World War I had long since halted in a bog of mud, ribbons of trench lines, and a red sea of blood. The new weapons of the industrial age, the machine gun and the rapid-firing artillery piece, outpaced the generals' ability to think: Fire was king! No man could long survive in the open on battlefields swept by steel.

At 6 A.M., near the French town of Harincourt, a desultory barrage from British guns wakened the late sleepers—if there were any—in the German lines. An hour and fifteen minutes later, a more sustained pattern of artillery drove the German infantry into their dugouts, with only a few sentries left topside. These would be ample to give the alert for the attack the veterans knew to expect. By now the pattern was drearily familiar, if still terrifying. "On past experience several hours would now elapse before the enemy infantry attacked," wrote one German veteran of the war, "and the German artillery fired no more than a feeble barrage ahead of our outpost line into the smoke and mist of that pale morning."[1] But then

the outposts were taken by surprise when suddenly indistinct black forms could be discerned. They were spitting fire, and under their weight the strong and deep obstacle belt was cracking like matchwood. The alarm was transmitted to the men in the trenches, and the troops hastened to their machine guns and tried to put up a defense. It was all in vain! The tanks appeared not one at a time

1

but in whole lines kilometers in length! . . . The only alternatives were death or surrender, since nobody could make off to the rear and hope to survive under this fire.[2]

That purple prose describing the opening stages of the battle of Cambrai was the work of Heinz Guderian, the great exponent and practitioner of the Nazi *blitzkrieg* of World War II and, perhaps, *the* greatest visionary of armored warfare. His intent, in 1937 when his tract, *Achtung—Panzer!,* first appeared, was polemical, for the German panzer arm was still in the throes of creation and in need of good publicity, but his description of the infantryman's fear at the close sight of a tank—of a mass of tanks! Lines whole kilometers in length!—was chillingly accurate, and as true in the barren desert of southern Iraq in 1991 as on the sodden fields of Flanders in 1917. For, in addition to the firepower of their menacing main guns, the daunting armor protection of their glacis, and their intimidating cross-country mobility, tanks possess another quality, particularly in large numbers: shock effect.

This shock effect was something only dimly perceived by a few in 1917. Though soldiers had been desperately searching for a way to break the stalemate of the trenches since the mobile phases of the western front had all but ended in 1914, it took some time for senior generals to turn to massed tanks; indeed, the tank had made its first appearance on World War I battlefields more than a year before Cambrai, but those primitive, snail-paced machines had been unreliable and had been employed as support for infantry attacks in what tank enthusiasts derisively called "penny packets." Had not that quixotic warrior, Winston Churchill, then First Lord of the Admiralty, persisted in pursuing the adaptation of Henry Holt's Caterpillar tractor for the purpose of creating a landship, it is arguable that tank design would have languished indefinitely in Britain, though the French, too, had begun work on a tracked combat vehicle as early as 1914.

Beyond the technological problems involved, no military man seemed at first to know what to make of this new creation; in the midst of a war the likes of which no one had anticipated or bargained for, the question became: What existing arm is the tank most like? Was it a mechanical horse, and therefore to be used in traditional cavalry roles? Did its large-caliber main gun make it a piece of artillery? Should it be used independently or in support of infantry? These were profound questions. As more tanks were produced and tank tactics refined, there emerged a cadre of tank enthusiasts who saw the armored combat vehicle as unique and therefore, of course, due its own branch bureaucracy to protect it against the acquisitive desires of the cavalry, gunners, and infantry. Thus these questions remained unanswered for decades.

Not until after the murderous losses at Passchendaele and the French folly of the Nivelle offensives of early 1917 did the Allies, simply short of manpower, attempt to substitute technology for troops. The Germans did not take to the tank. The German armies always seemed to be tactically one step ahead of the Allies. They were the first, for example, to realize the utter futility of infantry charges in the face of massed firepower, so they developed sophisticated defenses and then infiltration tactics for attack, and were not interested in changing the rules of a game they felt they were winning.

The attack at Cambrai was the design of Colonel J. F. C. Fuller, chief staff officer and visionary of the British Royal Tank Corps. He began his planning a month in advance, capitalizing on lessons learned from the intensive training the Royal Tank Corps was carrying out with infantry units for the purpose of a large-scale armored offensive. Fuller's first plan envisioned an attack in two phases.

> The first phase [would employ] five divisions that had trained with tanks for at least two weeks. The attack formation for tanks, worked out by Fuller, called for sections of three tanks each to assist one another in crossing entrenchments, using fascines [bundles of wood linked together to create a platform]. Infantry was divided into three groups. Trench clearers would accompany the tanks to reduce the trenches and dugouts. Trench stops were other infantry assigned to eliminate enemy infantry emerging

after the initial shock of the assault. Finally, the trench garrison would occupy the trenches conquered.[3]

The second phase would revert to traditional tactics, including the never-realized but never-relinquished dream of all World War I strategists: the cavalry exploitation; five divisions were to be on alert. Fuller demanded that surprise was essential: there was to be no predictable, prolonged artillery preparation, only smoke screens and supporting barrages to protect the flanks, and the buildup to the attack was to be conducted as secretly as possible. Tanks and artillery were to be moved to their lines of departure just the night prior to the attack and kept in laager areas until then. Indeed, the secrecy was so complete that the supporting aircraft were left without a clear role.[4]

The overall plan of attack, according to the draft of October 25, was to "break the enemy's defensive system by a coup de main, with the assistance of tanks; to pass cavalry through the break."[5] Tanks were also to participate in the exploitation operation. The offensive was to be commanded by General Sir Julian Byng, head of the British Third Army, a formation comprised of two corps of two infantry divisions with three two-battalion tank brigades of the Royal Tank Corps attached, artillery support of about 1,000 guns plus a great number of aircraft.

These forces were to be concentrated against the German 54th Jäger Division and smaller flank units in front of Cambrai. The British III Corps would strike along the eastern half of the eight-kilometer-wide attack corridor, IV Corps in the west. Though the plans for the use of armor were worked out in meticulous detail, and the concentration of tanks was greater than theretofore tried, they were still parceled out to the infantry divisions; that is, the brigade had the highest concentration of tanks. Furthermore, British tank brigades were really administrative units for the care and feeding of the steel beasts and the training of crew members more than fighting, tactical units; they certainly were not combined arms formations.[6]

The ground chosen for this operation, running generally northeast from the town of Havrincourt toward Cambrai, was "predominantly open ground [that] descended gently to the

River Schelde, which secured the right flank of the attack. . . . In front of the left wing the villages of Fontaine-Nôtre-Dame and Bourlon, together with the intervening Bourlon Wood, formed a kind of bastion which posed potential difficulties for the tanks."[7]

The goal was to seize Cambrai and surround the German forces in the area. To ready its forces for the attack, the British Third Army began to train infantry to accompany tanks and to work on some logistical problems, such as how to supply the troops to sustain the attack and how to move artillery, especially heavy siege howitzers, forward. On November 11, General Douglas Haig, the senior commander of the British forces in France, observed the final training of the infantry and armor, grasping that "the object of the operations of Infantry aided by tanks is to break through the enemy's defenses by surprise and so permit the Cavalry Corps to pass through and operate in open country."[8] The attack was meant to crack the trench lines and introduce mobile warfare where, since 1914, it had been so long absent.

THE ATTACK

The night before the attack, Brigadier Hugh Elles sent orders to his tank crews: "Tomorrow the Tank Corps will have the chance for which it has been waiting for many months, to operate on good ground in the van of battle." At 6 A.M. the next morning, the brigadier, riding in his tank Hilda, participated in that battle with the 2d Tank Brigade, 8th Tank Battalion. The early phases of the attack were spectacularly successful. The tanks crossed their lines of departure just after 7 A.M., tucked in behind a rolling barrage of mixed smoke and high-explosive shells. Though the smoke shielded the tanks, it also limited their already poor visibility, and some of them navigated by compass.[9] Indeed, command of even the smallest tank unit—even a single tank—was a chancy business; the means of controlling larger formations, as future tank commanders were to do by radio, did not exist. Still, as Guderian later wrote, the Germans were quite overwhelmed. The British infantry had little to do but round up prisoners.

The wooden fascines enabled the lumbering Mark IV tanks to cross the first line of German trenches as planned, breaking the barbed wire and routing the German infantry and scouts. However, the Germans had perfected the arts of trench warfare, building deep defenses with several lines of trenches, machine-gun nests, and infantry strong points supported by artillery. As the British prepared to assault the second line of trenches, the attack slackened measurably; the accompanying infantry and artillery were slow to take advantage of the opportunities created by the tanks. From fortified villages, the German guns began to range the British tanks, and the 4th Battalion, in particular, ran into fierce resistance, losing ten tanks as well as eight breakdowns and two ditched out of a total of thirty-five.

Though other units fared better, tank tactics still were very much in their infancy, especially for the handling of larger formations. No one knew, really, what the correct spacing between vehicles on the battlefield should be to ensure mutual support as well as support to and from the infantry and artillery.

By noon, the British were within sight of the breakthrough they had hoped for. They held a bridgehead across the Schelde Canal. Yawning gaps had been torn in the German lines both in the western sector, between the villages of Cantaing and Flesquières, and in the east between Crèvecoeur and Masnières. However, the British lacked the combat power, the will, and the insight to finish the job: the Third Army and its tanks had been used up in creating the breach, and Byng had few tactical reserves at his direct disposal; just the 29th Infantry Division and its twelve tanks. The cavalry might have completed the breakthrough, but only a single squadron reached the battlefield late in the afternoon, and it was shredded by a handful of machine guns and remnants of the 54th Jäger Division.[10] Still, the day had been a huge success. As Guderian summarized the attack's progress:

> By the evening of 20 November the first tank battle in history had come to an end. In a few hours the strongest position on the West-

ern Front had been broken on a frontage of 16 kilometers and to a depth of nine kilometers. Eight thousand prisoners and 100 guns had been captured, for a British loss of 4,000 men and 49 tanks. Cambrai was a great British victory, and the bells rang out in London for the first time in the war. The tanks had achieved a breathtaking success, and fully justified their existence.[11]

The British still could not capitalize on the opportunity their tanks had won. The Germans rushed reserves into the gap as fast as they could, in piecemeal fashion; it was all they could do. The Allies were unprepared for success and unable to reinforce it: Byng received two divisions that were bound for Italy, and the French volunteered a reserve group of two infantry and two cavalry divisions, but these forces arrived in driblets or not at all.

Byng renewed his attacks on November 21, but they were poorly coordinated and, with just forty-nine tanks, achieved diminishing returns. Cooperation between infantry and armor began to fray, as those units trained to operate together were used up; tanks pushed through Cantaing and into Fontaine-Nôtre-Dame, but infantry failed to follow up, and the Germans again held the line. The British continued to attack until November 27, but always with less strength and success than the day before; a week after the attack, the momentum was lost entirely and the tanks withdrawn for refit, some units even departing the operational area by train.[12] Through the first week in December, the Germans counterattacked in great strength, even pushing their lines past the original positions of November 20 by the time their offensive petered out.

THE LEGACY OF CAMBRAI

As World War I passed from 1917 to its final year and the great German Michael offensive campaign faltered, the British and French gradually improved their ability to use tanks in combination with other arms and with aircraft; indeed, German generals accepted that they were defeated by "General Tank," not their Allied opponents. Nonetheless, none of the advanced thinkers of the time believed that the armored vehicle had reached maturity in the Great War, except for perhaps those officers, particularly in the cavalry, who blindly clung to tradition.

Still, much of the potential and many of the problems of this new form of mechanized air-land battle were visible in these earliest glimmerings at Cambrai and at Soissons and other battles in 1918. A number of questions needed to be answered, questions that persist to this day. First, what were the proper characteristics of a tank, and what was the correct balance of these characteristics? Armor protection gave tanks survivability in intense combat; powerful engines and steel tracks gave them mobility cross country; powerful main guns gave them great destructive power. Which of these was most important?

These and other technological questions were intimately related to the tank's proper battlefield role. Was a tank a moving fortress to protect infantry? If so, armor protection—and the weight it entailed—was more important than mobility and speed. Was the tank a mobile artillery piece, striking at enemy artillery and covering the infantry's advance by firepower? If so, a large gun was to be preferred. Was the tank the cavalry successor to the horse, capable of daring raids and exploitation of fleeting openings? If so, mobility, speed, and automotive reliability were paramount. Finally, was the tank a new sort of weapon altogether, properly combining these attributes to achieve something new—the shock effect that Guderian attempted to describe in *Achtung—Panzer!*—and requiring new formations, new operational doctrine and new methods of command?

On the answers to such questions turned all the important issues, from tank design through tactics and organizational innovation. Did, for example, a tank require a turret that rotated 360 degrees? Yes, if it was to support infantry or to equip the cavalry; emphatically yes if it was a new arm of land warfare; but perhaps not if it was an assault gun, a mobile artillery piece. Conversely, what chores could each member of the tank crew be expected to perform? The French, for example, believed that tanks should be used almost exclusively in support of infantry; they made the best-armed, best-gunned tanks prior to World War II. However, they neglected to equip their tanks with radios and relied upon the tank commander to also aim and fire the main gun. French tanks were ill designed for mobile warfare that required initiative, command on the move, situational awareness, and quick firing; they were also slow. The German armor they faced in 1940 were thin-skinned and lightly armed, but a high proportion contained radios, were agile, and were manned by well-trained crews who could see and shoot very rapidly.

In the decades following World War I, the great powers and their armies wrestled with these revolutionary possibilities; but the road from Cambrai and the battles of 1918 to the Ardennes in 1940 was long and winding, and each of the major combatants in both wars—Great Britain, France, the United States, the Soviet Union, and Germany—would follow quite different directions along that journey. Struggling with new technologies and new concepts of warfare, these nations and their armies would find their methods of armored warfare shaped by their internal politics and industrial development, foreign policies, military strategies, and traditions. How each army came to terms with this technological revolution in the two decades between the world wars did much to determine the course of the epic tank battles of World War II. They also did much to discover the design principles, tactical philosophies, and operational rules that govern modern land warfare to this day.

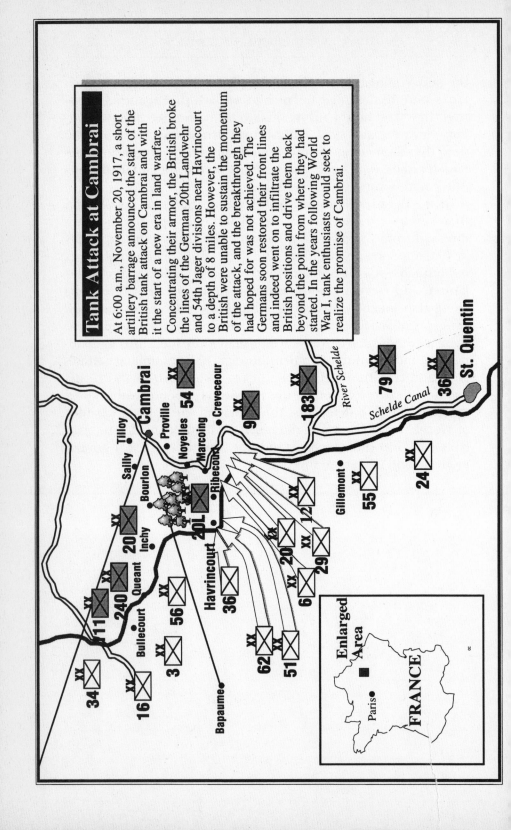

Tank Attack at Cambrai

At 6:00 a.m., November 20, 1917, a short artillery barrage announced the start of the British tank attack on Cambrai and with it the start of a new era in land warfare. Concentrating their armor, the British broke the lines of the German 20th Landwehr and 54th Jäger divisions near Havrincourt to a depth of 8 miles. However, the British were unable to sustain the momentum of the attack, and the breakthrough they had hoped for was not achieved. The Germans soon restored their front lines and indeed went on to infiltrate the British positions and drive them back beyond the point from where they had started. In the years following World War I, tank enthusiasts would seek to realize the promise of Cambrai.

Cambrai

Tilloy
Sailly
Proville
Bourlon
Inchy
Queant
Bullecourt
Havrincourt
Ribecourt
Noyelles
Marcoing
Creveceour
Gillemont
Bapaume
St. Quentin

River Schelde
Schelde Canal

34
16
111
240
20
54
9
183
79
36
3
56
36
6
29
12
55
24
20
62
51

Enlarged Area
FRANCE
Paris

∞

CHAPTER ONE

FRANCE, 1940

The German *Blitzkrieg* Stuns the World

THE BATTLE OF France began on May 10, 1940, and lasted a brief six weeks, but its first five days revealed the tank as the dominant weapon of land warfare and the German *Wehrmacht* as its masters. In less than a week, the fate of France was all but sealed. Although the previous fall's swift conquest of Poland was written off as the inevitable defeat of a second-rate army, the thrust through France came against the force generally thought to be the finest in Europe. As the German Army's chief of staff, Colonel General Franz Halder, noted in his diary: "Techniques of Polish campaign no recipe for the West. No good against well-knit Army."[1]

Moreover, the battle for France was a struggle between two quite distinct concepts of warfare: the French held fast to their doctrine of the methodical battle, and the Germans were animated by what has come to be known as *blitzkrieg,* the rapid application of overwhelming force to the decisive point on the battlefield and the ruthless exploitation of tactical success to achieve larger, operational goals. The tank, massed in the form of the panzer division and aided by effective close air support, was the agent of the German victory. While the French sprinkled their armor equally across their front in battalion-sized units in support of slow-moving infantry operations, the Germans balled their best and most modern units, combining not only tanks but mobile infantry and artillery as well as timely air support, into a fist of seven divisions under General Ewald von Kleist, a cavalryman brought out of retirement. This punch was aimed at the

weakest point in the French line, just north of the Maginot line
of fortified defenses and to the south flank of the main body of
French and British troops. In thus unhinging the allied defenses,
the German attack relied upon the speed, firepower, and above
all, the shock effect of armor appearing in their opponents' rear
areas, confusing communication and spreading panic as the attack penetrated deeper.

THE GERMAN AND FRENCH PLANS

Though the German invasion seemed bold, successful, and sure-
footed in retrospect, the *Wehrmacht* high command was plagued
by doubt that the attack would succeed; it was impressed by the
size and capabilities of the French army. After the defeat of
Poland, the German generals preferred to remain on the defensive in the west. Adolf Hitler, on the other hand, feared, as German rulers had for centuries, a long war in which the strength of
her allied opponents, especially the economic strength of the
British Empire, would wear Germany down. The quick conquest
of Poland had convinced Hitler that a similar victory was possible
in the west. On October 10, 1939, Hitler directed his senior commanders to prepare for the invasion of France and the final defeat of the West. While claiming that he would not dictate
invasion planning in detail, he went on to tell his generals:

> The German attack is to be mounted with the object of destroying
> the French army; but in any case it must create a favorable initial
> situation which is a prerequisite for a successful continuation of
> the war. In these circumstances the only possible area of attack is
> the sector between Luxembourg in the south and Nijmegen in the
> north, excluding the Liège fortress. The objective of the two at-
> tacking groups thus formed is to attempt to penetrate the area of
> Luxembourg-Belgium-Holland in the shortest possible time, and
> to engage and defeat the opposing Belgian-French-English
> forces. . . . An offensive which does not aim at the destruction of
> the enemy forces from the start is senseless and leads to useless
> waste of human life.[2]

Hitler thus wanted not only to set the goal for the campaign in the West—the destruction of the allied armies—but to tell his commanders how to accomplish the goal, by a broad frontal attack through the Low Countries. This notion merely reinforced the reservations of the German military staff concerning an attack in the West, but within ten days, it dutifully produced an initial draft for *Fall Gelb*—Case Yellow—following Hitler's outline. As Robert Allan Doughty has pointed out, this plan was not, as is popularly believed, a recycling of the famous World War I Schlieffen Plan; the Schlieffen Plan placed the main weight of attack on the right wing and sought a decisive victory by driving through the Low Countries into France, while *Fall Gelb*'s goal was to eliminate the threat to the industrial Ruhr and to form a base for further operations, including operations against England.[3]

This broad-front attack would have met French expectations almost precisely. From the mid-1920s, the French defense against the prospect of a German attack, which they fully expected in the course of time, was built upon the Maginot line, whose fortifications would require relatively few troops, and a large field army to defend against an attack through Belgium and Holland, as in 1914. The Maginot line was meant to cut down the Germans maneuvering room, funneling an invasion toward the north, where the French army would dig in and annihilate the attacker by the use of superior firepower. The French doctrine of the supremacy of massed fires, especially artillery fires, over maneuver, encapsulated its lessons of World War I and resulted in its notion of the methodical battle, a slow-moving, tightly controlled manner of fighting meant especially to minimize casualties.

Oddly, however, the French supreme command adopted a war plan that was out of synch with its fighting doctrine. Despite concerns about Belgian neutrality and little coordination between the two countries' armies, the French planned to hold the Maginot line while pushing forward its own best armies in Belgium to stop a German attack there as far from French soil as possible. This maneuver, dubbed Plan E or the Escaut Plan, for the river in central Belgium that was to form the main defensive line, was meant not only to keep French soil from being invaded but to protect the industrial northeast of France, from which the vital matériel for a long war would be produced. There were a number of variants of this plan, depending on the amount of warning time of a German attack and cooperation between Belgium and France.

The success of the German attack in Poland, and especially the speed of the panzer thrusts there, disposed the French command, led by General Maurice Gamelin, toward caution. However, during the long pause—the phoney war—after the September 1939 invasion of Poland and the clear preparations of the Belgians to defend their northern frontier, the French generals began to think they could win a race with the panzers; they now considered that they could advance farther east yet still have time to prepare adequate defenses. By the end of the year, Gamelin had been convinced that the Allied armies could execute Plan D, the Dyle River variant, over the objections of General Alphonse Georges, the commander in chief of the French Northeast Front, who had overall command of the sector. In the spring of 1940, Gamelin went farther still, proposing the so-called Breda variant that would link French forces with Dutch forces in the north. In the months prior to the German invasion, the primary French concerns were thus defending as far forward as possible, and the concerns of Gamelin, Georges, and 1st Army Group commander General Gaston Billotte were with their extreme left wing.

The French commanders were obsessed with maintaining an unbroken line of defenses, as their reading of World War I and their doctrine of the methodical battle required. Even allowing for the economy of forces permitted by the Maginot line defenses, this was a strategy that needed huge numbers of soldiers and required the French to be strong everywhere along the line; it exacerbated the traditional advantage of the attacker—his ability to choose where to strike. The French had no desire to fight a mobile defense behind thin covering forces, using the mobility of armor to block and counterattack; to the French, tanks were moving pillboxes for supporting infantry. What few mobile formations they had went for nought under Gamelin's plan. The Dyle River maneuver would prove to be a roundhouse punch that missed its mark entirely. The Germans countered with a knockout blow from an unexpected angle.

Based upon the lessons they drew from the September 1939 invasion of Poland that began World War II, the Germans made a number of adjustments to the organization of their armored and mechanized divisions and to the quality of their training overall; the consensus of senior leaders was that the infantry had performed relatively poorly, even in the campaign that had brought the term *blitzkrieg*—lightning war—into common usage. The German light divisions—motorized infantry units with a sprinkling of tanks—were changed into full-fledged panzer divisions, numbered 6 through 9. Also, the motorized infantry divisions were shorn of one regiment of infantry, being thought too slow and unwieldy. The Germans realized the prime requirement for mechanized warfare was the ability to *move;* the *Wehrmacht* wanted units that could not only create opportunities through firepower, but could exploit opportunities and permit the German style of command, based upon quickly taken decisions, to flower. However, the Germans were not able to increase dramatically the number of late-model panzers—Panzer III and IV—in the armored units. Many of the new organizations went to war against France in older tanks or with captured Czech models.

However, all the tactical improvements in the German army were set against larger developments that shaped the Battle of France and the subsequent Nazi war effort. As was reflected by the specificity of Hitler's planning directive for the invasion of France, success in Poland had emboldened him to assert greater authority over military matters; as Field Marshal Erich von Manstein wrote in his memoirs, *Lost Victories*, the traditional German army war planning staff had been eclipsed by Hitler.[4] The *führer*, preferring to rule by playing potential rivals for power against one another, created a second strategic planning organization, the High Command of the Armed Forces, which would be his own agent. As Manstein put it: "The Commander-in-Chief of the Army had been demoted from the status of military adviser to the Head of State to that of a subordinate commander pledged to unquestioning obedience."[5]

Although the relationship between the army leadership and Hitler is a complex subject, the immediate upshot was to confuse planning for the invasion of France. The army leadership did not like Hitler's plan; even less they liked the fact of Hitler's supremacy. The senior German generals questioned the wisdom of taking on the French and Allied armies—the memories of World War I were strong in Germany, as well—and hoped for a negotiated end to the war. The army, a highly conservative organization unable to fathom the deep and powerful political roots of Nazi ideology, naively misunderstood Hitler's larger war aim: complete conquest. For the German general staff, war was a tool of statesmanship; disciples of the great strategist Carl von Clausewitz, for whom war was a continuation of politics—a rational act—the senior army leadership did not understand Hitler's radical politics.

There were technical problems with Hitler's plan, and the army seized upon these to play for time. Expecting a long war against France, the German military command thought it would be necessary to wait for the spring to have good weather for campaigning. As mentioned above, they also were concerned about the quality of army training. However, the staff originally produced a plan that met Hitler's specifications but had little chance of producing a decisive victory; not even Hitler imagined that. It called for an attack by three army groups: Army Group B in the north, with the armor and mechanized infantry formations attached and a total of forty-three divisions, under Colonel General Ludwig von Bock; with a supporting attack by Army Group A under Colonel General Gerd von Rundstedt, with twenty-two infantry divisions; in the south, opposite the Maginot line, Army Group C, under Colonel General Ritter von Leeb, was to conduct a tertiary attack.

As this plan was disseminated among the senior leaders and staffs, and war games were conducted, the list of problems began to accumulate and the invasion was delayed several times. Opposition to the plan coalesced around Rundstedt and Manstein, his chief of staff, who drafted a memorandum in December 1939 outlining an alternative solution that shifted the weight of the German attack into Army Group A's sector. His main argument for the switch was that the aim of any attack against France should be to force a quick decision, especially given the threat of the Soviet Union to the east. "The offensive capacity of the German Army was our trump card on the Continent, and to fritter it away on half-measures was inadmissible," wrote Manstein.[6] His plan called for adding a third army to Army Group A's troop roster, but, more importantly, concentrating the panzer and motorized divisions in a surprise attack through the Ardennes. This would be the point of main effort, the *schwerpunkt.*

Initially, Manstein's proposal was strongly rejected by the German high command, even by Guderian, who thought that Manstein was dispersing the strength of the panzers. However, when the two met to discuss the plan and the feasibility of pushing armor through the Ardennes, Manstein drew Guderian's attention to the real object of the campaign: cutting off the main Allied forces along the Somme River. Recalled Guderian:

> After a lengthy study of maps and making use of my own memories of the terrain from the First World War, I was able to assure Manstein that the operation he had planned could in fact be carried out. The only condition I attached was that a sufficient number of armored and motorized divisions must be employed, if possible all of them.[7]

Slowly, Manstein's plan began to win more converts; though Manstein himself was shunted off to command an infantry corps, Rundstedt continued to champion the notion of a rapid thrust through the Ardennes. With the army high command balking, Rundstedt tried a bureaucratic end run, requesting that his plan be submitted to Hitler's High Command of the Armed Forces. The impasse was broken finally by sheer luck and by the German army leadership placing Manstein in corps command. First, an operations staff officer of the German 7th Airborne Division had to make a forced landing in Belgium; he was carrying a part of the operations order for the attack in the west. The Germans had to assume that the Allies believed the main weight of a German attack would come in the north. Then, in February 1940, Manstein was summoned, along with all other corps commanders, to dine with Hitler in Berlin. Manstein used the opportunity to brief the *führer* on his concept of operations. "Shortly afterward," wrote Manstein, "the new and final Operation Order was issued."[8]

Issued on February 20, this order called for four related attacks by three armies and three panzer and motorized corps—the overwhelming bulk of German armored strength—under Rundstedt's Army Group A. Attacking through Belgium, Colonel General Gunther von Kluge's 4th Army had three infantry corps and General Hermann Hoth's XV Panzer Corps; his main mission was to tie down the French First Army, preventing it from displacing to the south and reinforcing the weak French armies opposite the Ardennes. The sharp spear of the *schwerpunkt* were the three corps of *Panzergruppe* von Kleist, reporting directly to Rundstedt and comprised of Major General George-Hans Reinhardt's XLI Panzer Corps, attacking toward the Meuse River around Dinant; Guderian's XIX Panzer Corps, the strongest of the panzer corps, with three divisions and the elite *Grossdeutschland* Infantry Regiment, targeted at Sedan; and General Gustav von Wietersheim's XIV Motorized Corps, with fewer tanks but the bulk of mobile infantry to rush through behind Guderian and allow the tanks to continue to exploit opportunities in the French rear. Despite the initial resistance to Manstein's proposal, in the end the Germans planned and organized their forces for decisive success, adopting novel command relationships—the *Panzergruppe* was an ad hoc creation, a battle grouping on a very large scale, indeed—and ensuring that the focus of the attack, Guderian's attack toward Sedan, had sufficient follow-on forces behind it to allow the panzers to conduct deep operations.

THE SCHWERPUNKT

The decisive phase of the Battle of France engaged a mere twelve German divisions, but this small, mechanized force was able to confound completely French and Allied expectations and thereby achieve surprise at every level of warfare: strategic, operational, and tactical. The two sides' plans dovetailed together in perfect harmony, pitting two diametrically opposed conceptions of modern warfare; one would be supremely successful, the other disastrously mistaken. The French and Allied lines were strong on the wings, with fifty-seven divisions in the north and thirty-six divisions holding the Maginot line in the south, and weak in the center, where the French Second Army, commanded by General André Corap and the Ninth Army, under General Charles Huntziger, mustered sixteen divisions of suspect abilities. By contrast, the Germans were strong in the center, where Rundstedt's Army Group A totaled forty-five divisions, including *Panzergruppe* Kleist, a fully mechanized army of eight divisions grouped in two corps. Another twenty divisions waited in reserve behind Army Group A. The Germans economized on their flanks: Army Group B, in the north, opposed the Allied main force with twenty-nine divisions, including two armored divisions; in the south, Army Group C would demonstrate in front of the Maginot line with just nineteen divisions.

Similarly, there was a mismatch of armored forces. The French distributed their 3,776 tanks fairly evenly along the front, as did the British with their 631 tanks. The French did have some armored divisions—four organized by the infantry to help in the methodical reduction of strong points, and four divisions designed by the cavalry, called *Divisions Légères Mécaniques* to conduct traditional cavalry covering force and exploitation missions—but the majority of the French tanks were spread in World War I–style penny-packets among forty-two independent tank battalions. These were tightly controlled by army-level headquarters to be sent forward to assist in division operations; the French had almost no thought of concentrating their armor for a deep attack or mobile defense, except the two light divisions grouped together in a cavalry corps.

The Germans packed their 2,479 tanks into nine combined-arms panzer divisions, each capable of independent operations on the battlefield and long-range movements. As indicated above, the bulk of these were clenched together in the armored fist of *Panzergruppe* Kleist, under corps commanders Reinhardt, Guderian, and Wietersheim's motorized infantry. The remaining two panzer divisions, under Army Group B, were to attack the French First Army directly, both to reinforce the desired perception that the main attack was from the north, as the French anticipated and the Germans wanted the French to believe, and to prevent the First Army from moving to block the true main effort through the Ardennes.

The Germans' operational and strategic success was based upon the outcome of four tactical battles at, from north to south, Gembloux, Dinant, Monthermé, and Sedan. These four engagements saw increasing degrees of German success. Taken together, they permitted the *Wehrmacht* to pry open the French and Allied defenses at the hinge between the Maginot line and the main body of the Allied armies, and to trap the Allies in a giant encirclement, mitigated only by the failure to close the trap at Dunkirk and the heroic evacuation from its beaches.

The battle at Gembloux actually was a French tactical success, for it halted the attack of the 3d and 4th Panzer Divisions of Colonel General Erich Höpner's XVI Panzer Corps. However, it was an operational defeat, for it allowed the Germans to pin down the French First Army and thus prevent it from reinforcing the weaker French defenses to the south. This was a strategic loss, for the largest and best Allied forces were then nearly encircled in north France and Flanders.

The German invasion of France began in the north, and the stunning airborne assault on the Belgian fortress at Eben Emael, the seizure of bridges over the Albert Canal, the collapse of the Belgian forward defenses, and the heavy air attacks in Army Group B's sector cemented the belief of the French high command that the Germans were indeed committing their main forces in a reprise of the 1914 Schlieffen Plan. The French prepared to execute the Dyle Plan, rushing forward through Belgium to the Dyle River, where their main defensive line was to be anchored. A key element of the plan was to allow the best Allied armies, the French First Army and the British Expeditionary Force, enough time to set their defenses properly; in front of the First Army, Lieutenant General René Prioux's Cavalry Corps was to fight a covering force battle. His mission was to delay the advancing Germans along two lines east of the Dyle until at least the fifth day of the war, preventing the First Army from having to fight the kind of fluid meeting engagement the French dreaded. The French wished to fight according to their doctrine of the methodical battle.

Prioux's Cavalry Corps, comprised of the 2d and 3d *Divisions Légères Mécaniques,* was one of the finest formations in the French army. Its SOMUA S-35 tanks were fast and fitted with a high-velocity 47 mm main gun. Its Renault R35 tanks had just been made faster and their main guns improved, its Panhard armored cars were quick and well armed, and its infantry rode in cross-country vehicles. The corps' scouts had new motorcycles. Prioux, one of the French army's brightest senior officers, had super-vised its training. On May 10, the Cavalry Corps roared across its starting line on the 150-mile march to the Dyle. In his memoirs, Prioux wrote: "Among those around me there was only ardor, the desire to march, relief at seeing the long period of waiting be-hind us."

However, the French ardor began to dim when they reached the Dyle to find that the Belgians had done next to nothing to construct obstacles or fortifications to slow the German attack. The Belgian frontier forces had offered only token resistance and the Germans, as Prioux feared, enjoyed superiority in the air. On May 11, he cabled his superiors that holding the Ger-mans for five days would destroy his forces. In response, First Army Group commander Billotte came forward and told Prioux that he need only hold his position until May 14, and that the First Army would speed its march to the Dyle.

The next day, at 9 A.M., Höpner's panzers attacked the center of Prioux's line, but were driven back; losses were heavy on both sides. Smaller attacks continued through the day and into the night, when a sizeable force of panzers followed air and artillery preparatory fires and pushed back Prioux's right flank. Again, the French counterattacked, and SOMUA-equipped units pinned the panzers in a small village. On May 13, Höpner's men came again, this time in greater strength: a 200-tank attack in the center was supported by three secondary probes all along the front. Again, French armored counterattacks halted the Ger-mans, but by afternoon, Prioux's reserves had all been committed and he began to withdraw to the second line of defenses after dark. This second delay line was just a few kilometers from the Dyle. On May 14, the Germans swept through the weak obstacles in the delay line and by 9 A.M. had penetrated in the center to the Dyle. Though the Cavalry Corps still held on the wings, French First Army commander General Blanchard ordered Prioux's forces to withdraw, breaking up the corps and distributing its tanks and other assets to the infantry corps of the First Army; it never again operated as an integrated, massed armored striking force.[9]

Looked at from Prioux's perspective, the Cavalry Corps had more than accomplished its mission, and in so doing, conducted the single successful tank operation by the French army during the Battle of France. However, from the German view, all was going well: Höpner's panzers were still more than capable of sustained combat operations. As the lone force equipped and organized for large-scale armored operations, Prioux's force could perhaps have accomplished more. Its equipment was, if anything, superior to the Germans' in armor protection and penetration, but Prioux believed the Dyle maneuver overcommitted the French forces. He also was paralyzed by the German command of the air.

Indeed, even as Höpner's tanks tore through the final positions of the French Cavalry Corps, Stuka dive-bombers were executing deep attacks on First Army positions west of the Dyle. At 6 A.M. on May 15, the Germans massed 300 tanks against the First Army's 1st Moroccan Division; two hours later, the Stukas came again. Throughout the day, the Germans probed and penetrated, and the French counterattacked. In large measure, the French held and imposed heavy casualties on the Germans; the French fought in their slow, methodical fashion, with ferocious artillery fire support, killing a German tank regiment commander and wounding a brigade commander, but the French, too, suffered mightily. One counterattack combining one infantry and one tank battalion resulted in the loss of more than one-third of the infantry—and half its leaders—while the tank battalion lost forty of forty-five tanks. The exhausted French withdrew from the Dyle on May 16, but the Germans were too badly bloodied to pursue until the next day. By then, the French stand on the Dyle had proved itself to be a blunder, for farther to the south, the front was collapsing.

THE PANZER THRUST

Lieutenant General André Corap's Ninth Army guarded the First Army's flank directly to the south, its front extending about 115 kilometers from Namur nearly to Sedan. Corap's zone was divided into two parts: the north part was open country, and the southern half was blocked by the Ardennes forest. Corap thus had two missions, which taken together would make his front swing like a door hinge: in the north, his 1st and 4th Light Cavalry Divisions, each with forty-four tanks and fourteen armored cars and the rest mounted on horses, were to move forward with the First Army; in the south, II, XI, and XLI Corps, primarily infantry formations, were to defend behind the line of the Meuse River. Corap retained a reserve of two infantry divisions and three tank battalions.

From the perspective of the French high command, particularly Billotte and Gamelin, the Ardennes could not be penetrated rapidly by large armored forces. Consequently, the Ninth Army was likely to see little action and thus could make do with second-rate troops. Corap's three-star rank is an indication of the French view; he was not raised to the full four-star grade of *général d'armée* and remained a dependency of General Charles Huntziger's Second Army to Corap's south.[10] Supply problems slowed training, as did the French emphasis on fortifying the line of the Meuse. Few reservists called to duty had fired their weapons and peacetime restrictions on practice ranges were kept in effect; the army was short of ammunition and fuel. When the alert came to move forward to the Meuse on May 10, Corap's cavalry halted there and did not push forward to make contact with the Germans—or the Belgians—or make any attempt to shape the battle or conduct reconnaissance. This was particularly unfortunate, for the Belgian cavalry, by tough resistance in delaying actions, was able to slow the attacks of the 1st and 7th Panzer Divisions until, realizing that the French were not coming to their aid, they withdrew. However, neither the Belgian nor the French cavalry did a very good job of covering the obstacles with fires, either from artillery or direct-fire weapons. The cavalry was to keep the Germans from reaching the Meuse until May 15.

The hinge in the French lines manned by the Ninth Army would be the focus of the main German effort. Seven panzer divisions, along with forty-five infantry divisions in Twelfth and Sixteenth Armies and part of the Second Army thrust at Dinant and Monthermé. The northernmost of the panzer forces was Colonel General Hermann Hoth's XV Panzer Corps, with the 5th and 7th Panzer Divisions; 7th Panzer was commanded by Major General Erwin Rommel. Hoth attacked in the northern Ardennes, where there was no cavalry cover at all, and was quickly able to advance to within about forty kilometers of Dinant on the Meuse by May 11. There, at Marche on the Homme River, the French 4th Light Cavalry Division blocked Rommel's path, holding the line of the river throughout the day.

However, the light cavalry divisions were no match for the panzer divisions. As Rommel's strung-out forces began to gather at Marche, they began to overwhelm the French, who were suffering irreplaceable losses. The front began to break in places, some units withdrawing early and exposing their neighbors' flanks, and on May 12 Corap ordered the cavalry back behind the line of the Meuse, but left the armor to fight a delaying action. This it did poorly, outmaneuvered in the open country east of Dinant, uncomfortable in a fluid meeting engagement action. As in the First Army, the armor was dispersed among the infantry holding the river line.

The Germans were close on their heels. "From the high ground we could see the valley and, on its western side, further heavily wooded hills," recalled Hans von Luck, who served as Rommel's chief scout. "We could also see, however, the broken bridges, which Rommel would have liked to take intact. We felt our way down into the valley, but at once came under well-directed gunfire and were straddled by heavy artillery."[11]

In the night, the Germans attempted to cross the river; the

French line was slow in establishing its front, since the French timetable was for the line to be fully manned only on May 14. Also, the line was much thinner, the force-to-space ratio perhaps one-third of that in the First Army sector at the Dyle River line. However, some of the first German attacks were beaten back, and only a few small units managed to make it across the water.

In the morning, Rommel renewed his attacks, but again the French defenders gave stubborn resistance. The panzer division commander came forward to size up the situation.

"What's going on?" asked Rommel, wondering why his attack was halted.

"Held up by artillery fire," responded Luck and his men.

"Show me. Where is it coming from?"

For several minutes, perched on his command car, Rommel surveyed the French positions on the far bank through binoculars; his decision was quick: "Stay put. This is a job for the infantry."[12] He called forward the 7th Panzergrenadier Regiment, the mechanized infantry that was part of Rommel's 7th Panzer Division. They dismounted from their vehicles, and with engineer support and cover from the smoke of houses that had been set afire, crossed the river in rubber dinghies. The French successfully beat off the first attack, and French General Boucher of the 5th Motorized Infantry Division effectively organized a counterattack despite the pressure of constant German air attacks. Rommel remembered in his memoirs:

> On arrival at [infantry] brigade headquarters on the west bank [of the Meuse] I found the situation looking decidedly unhealthy. The commander of the 7th Motorcycle Battalion had been wounded, his adjutant killed and a powerful French counterattack had severely mauled our men . . . . There was a danger that enemy tanks might penetrate into the Meuse Valley itself.[13]

Again, the French were weakening as the Germans were gaining strength. With the second infantry wave, the 7th Panzer Division had established a bridgehead on the west bank of the river. Boucher's subordinates did not understand as he did the need for infantry and armor with speed; their abilities to adapt to a

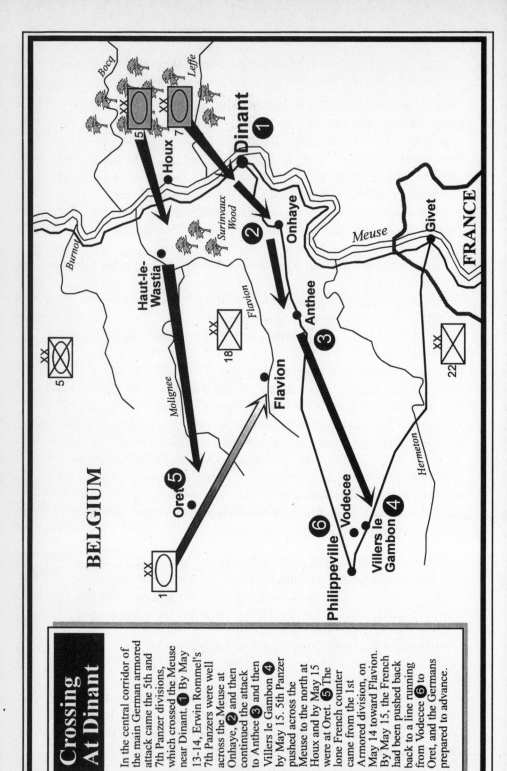

Crossing At Dinant

In the central corridor of the main German armored attack came the 5th and 7th Panzer divisions, which crossed the Meuse near Dinant. ❶ By May 13-14, Erwin Rommel's 7th Panzers were well across the Meuse at Onhaye, ❷ and then continued the attack to Anthee ❸ and then Villers le Gambon ❹ by May 15. 5th Panzer pushed across the Meuse to the north at Houx and by May 15 were at Oret. ❺ The lone French counter came from the 1st Armored division, on May 14 toward Flavion. By May 15, the French had been pushed back to a line running from Vodecee ❻ to Oret, and the Germans prepared to advance.

BELGIUM

FRANCE

Bocq
Leffe
Houx
Dinant
Surinvaux Wood
Onhaye
Meuse
Givet
Burnot
Haut-le-Wastia
Flavion
Anthee
Molignee
Flavion
Hermeton
Oret
Vodecee
Villers le Gambon
Philippeville

5
7
18
5
22
1

fight that was anything but a methodical battle failed them. In the night, the first tanks were ferried across, and on May 14, Rommel renewed his attack, again led by infantry and with close air support. The action was desperate; Rommel's radio car was hit by antitank shells and fell over a steep slope, but the French were hanging on by their fingernails. On Corap's south, the German 32d Infantry Division turned the flank and jeopardized the whole position around Dinant. Desperate, Corap ordered a counterattack by the French 1st Armored Division, but the tanks did not have sufficient fuel for an attack that night. The next day it was too late.

On May 15, the French position at Dinant gave way entirely. At 2 A.M., General Bouffet of French II Corps ordered his troops to establish a new defensive line about fifteen kilometers west of the Meuse, but Rommel had broken out of his bridgehead. "Keep going, don't look left or right, only forward," Rommel told von Luck's reconnaissance battalion. "I'll cover your flanks if necessary. The enemy is confused; we must take advantage of it."[14]

The second of the three German panzer spearheads was Reinhardt's XLI Panzer Corps, with the 6th and 8th Panzer Divisions, aimed at the French 102d Fortress Infantry Division at Monthermé on the Meuse. The fortress infantry division had some additional firepower, by comparison to a standard infantry division, but next to no tactical mobility. Monthermé was at the southern end of the large Ninth Army sector, and the situation was much the same as at Dinant. On the afternoon of May 13, with a small number of close air strikes and limited artillery support, Reinhardt's lead elements, part of Brigadier General Werner Kempf's 6th Panzer Division, succeeded in gaining a foothold on the western bank of the river. Crossing in rubber dinghies, the leading German infantry attack stalled, with forces too weak to push farther on, but the French also were too weak and too lacking in mobility and spirit to eliminate the bridgehead.

Reinhardt had the narrowest attack corridor of the three panzer corps. This was a mixed blessing: he would be sandwiched between Hoth and Guderian later in the campaign, but at the Meuse, the threat from Guderian's 2d Panzer Division just

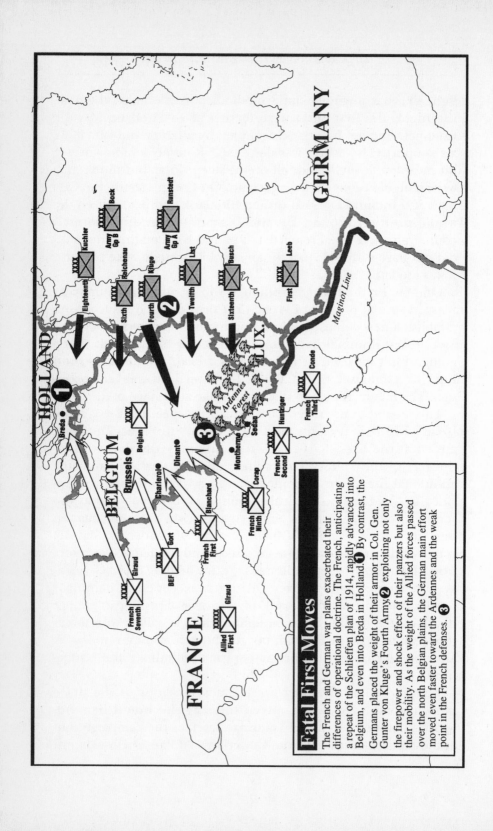

Fatal First Moves

The French and German war plans exacerbated their differences of operational doctrine. The French, anticipating a repeat of the Schlieffen plan of 1914, rapidly advanced into Belgium, and even into Breda in Holland. ❶ By contrast, the Germans placed the weight of their armor in Col. Gen. Gunter von Kluge's Fourth Army, ❷ exploiting not only the firepower and shock effect of their panzers but also their mobility. As the weight of the Allied forces passed over the north Belgian plains, the German main effort moved even faster toward the Ardennes and the weak point in the French defenses. ❸ to the south at Sedan put the French flank at Monthermé in jeopardy and the French position there caved in. Again, Corap was too slow to reinforce the threatened position; he dispatched the 53d Infantry Division to seal the gap, but confused orders and poor traffic management in the Ninth Army rear delayed the French movement. The Germans quickly probed Corap's southern flank, with Major General Adolph Kuntzen's 8th Panzer and the 2d Panzer Division picking off the thinly spread French positions one by one. As the Germans got their tanks across the Meuse, they were vulnerable while infantry lagged behind, but the French could not organize their defenses, especially the seam between Corap and Huntziger's Second Army to the south.

Rapidly, the Germans tore an eight-mile hole in the French front. Panic spread throughout the French lines, and their leaders, who believed in a continuous front above all else, also lost heart. At midnight on May 14, the French XLI Corps and 102d Fortress Infantry Division were ordered to retreat to the secondary defense line west of the Meuse, but the infantry, with nothing but their own foot power against the speed of the panzers, were bypassed in large numbers while moving slowly across the country. Moreover, Corap's men had far too much front to defend with far too few troops. Even though the Germans could not bring the full weight of their main thrust to bear at once— moving through the Ardennes was difficult, as the French generals had believed—they could keep up the pressure on French units that had little hope of reinforcement, no air cover, few tanks, and no large, mobile counterattack force. When Reinhardt's lead units reached Montcornet on the evening of May 15, he was eighteen kilometers *west* of Corap's headquarters.

Still, despite the desperate situation in the French Ninth Army sector, neither Hoth's nor Reinhardt's attack was the decisive thrust of the campaign. Indeed, the greatest contributions of XV and XLI Panzer Corps were in supporting the attack of Heinz Guderian's XIX Panzer Corps near Sedan, about eighty kilometers to the south of Monthermé. Here was the place where the French lost the war, not only because the line of the Meuse was penetrated, but because Guderian would be able to exploit the opening by driving all the way to the sea and cutting off the First Army, the British Expeditionary Force, and the heart of the Allied armies. Guderian's attack was perhaps the prototype of all armored operations, and it is arguable that it never was surpassed for tactical prowess, operational boldness, and strategic effect. Tactically, Guderian used every tool at his command; his attack was not a wild tank charge but a highly synchronized and choreographed campaign utilizing close air support, special operations troops, and tanks in all kinds of roles from destroying French pillboxes to exploiting fleeting opportunities with rapid and deep penetrations. Operationally, Guderian shocked the French and even his own superior commanders, seeing from the outset a chance to leverage initially slight, momentary advantages in battle into a successful campaign. Strategically, the campaign exposed the weakness of the French army. In this, the Germans were aided by the folly of the Allied plan to rush forward into Belgium. Beyond the purely military mistakes, the *blitzkrieg* applied just the kind of force the French were intellectually and emotionally unprepared to accept. Fragile France shattered from the shock.

THE APPROACH MARCH TO THE MEUSE

One of the truly great achievements of the German attack was the approach march to the French border; its size and weight took the French entirely by surprise. That is was accomplished so rapidly speaks volumes about the superiority of German staff work, planning, discipline, and flexibility; the tactical prowess of the *Wehrmacht* is often portrayed as the product of inspired improvisation, and though senior German combat leaders often thrived in chaos, their real genius lay in imposing order on chaos.

No operation reveals that genius better than the advance to the Meuse. The Germans used the full gamut of their ground forces, including air mobile and special operations troops, to secure vital choke points along the planned routes through the Ardennes. The following panzers were meticulously scheduled as to their order of march and expected timetables. Detailed reconnaissance identified and described obstacles and terrain, and produced technical information about the capacity of bridges and other features.[15] Two examples of the care with which the *blitzkrieg* was planned are the seizing of the steel gate at Fouhren and the Diekirch railroad bridge in Luxembourg at the outset of the attack. The gate straddled an important route, with a sheer gorge on one side and a face of bedrock on the other; unless it was seized intact, it would halt the march of the 2d Panzer Division.

At 3:15 A.M. on May 10, two Luxembourgois gendarmes closed the gate and returned to the town of Fouhren, stopping at the local café. A short time later, they noticed a group of four men coming their way:

> It seemed strange to the Gendarmes that anyone would be out walking at this late hour. The four had yellow [scarves] protruding from their pockets or tied around their necks. When the strangers were within five meters, they threw open their overcoats and confronted the Gendarmes with submachine guns. Simultaneously, they ordered them to raise up their hands and turn over the keys to the Fouhren steel gate.

As it happened, the gate still required demolition, but it was seized in time to allow the 2d Panzer Division to pass rapidly the next day. The bridge at Diekrich was seized in similarly stealthy fashion, and the 1st Panzer Division passed over it less than twelve hours later.

Guderian's XIX Panzer Corps crossed into Luxembourg in three columns: in the north came the 2d Panzer Division; in the center, 1st Panzer; in the south, 10th Panzer. The *Grossdeutschland* Infantry Regiment also was assigned to the corps. With thousands of vehicles and tens of thousands of troops, the possibilities for a traffic jam through the winding roads of the Ardennes were quite real. Even the most glancing aerial attack would have snarled the tank columns and slowed the attack to permit the French to reinforce the threatened sector.

Guderian designated 1st Panzer as his main effort, with the corps artillery, air defense units, and the main corps command post following in its wake. He also gave Brigadier General Friedrich Kirchner the four best main attack routes. Its first-day objective was to sprint through Luxembourg and then penetrate the Belgian border fortifications. While little if any fighting was anticipated in Luxembourg, the Belgian *Chausseurs Ardennais*—lightly armed cavalry units—were expected to delay back to the Our River that marked the border, while other Belgian units committed to the defense.

The key to a quick progress lay in the success of the division's advance guard, led by 1st Infantry Regiment commander Lieutenant Colonel Hermann Balck, and especially the advance guard's forward detachments of bicyclists, scouts, and engineers; reconnaissance aircraft also scouted for the lead ground units. At about 5:30 A.M. on May 10, in heavy fog, an assault group stormed the border bridge over the Our and disarmed the Belgian customs agents while the rest of the detachment forded the river. Guderian, as always commanding from the front, rode with the division as it crossed the frontier near Wallendorf.[16]

However, despite the initial successes of the advance guard, the dense Belgian belts of obstacles soon slowed the attack. The Belgians, however, were indifferent about covering the obstacles with fire: in some places, troops held firm and forced the Germans to dig them out; in others they resisted weakly. The *Chausseurs Ardennais* planned to withdraw to the west and so attempted no serious defense nor counterattack. The Belgians, like the French, anticipated a slow-moving battle and thus relied on telephone communications rather than radio; when the airborne troops of the *Grossdeutschland* Regiment cut the telephone wires, Belgian command and control fell apart.

As important as the progress of the advanced guard was, so, too, was the ability of the Germans to keep their rear areas in good order, to keep compact formations. This was a struggle. Beyond the inevitable traffic jams, overexcited commanders of infantry formations supporting Guderian's panzers seized upon any openings to push their troops forward. Keeping reasonable order over the tight Ardennes roads required the harshest discipline; on May 10, panzer commander Kleist issued an order that "any unauthorized persons using Tactical March Routes and using rank to usurp Military Police authorities risked immediate field court martial proceedings resulting in the severest possible punishment," not excluding execution.[17] German commanders used their Fieseler Storch reconnaissance aircraft not just to scout the French lines but to keep watch on their march routes. However, even the meticulous German staffs had overlooked some problems: MP officers were young, inexperienced, and low-ranking, and their troops were insufficiently trained or briefed on the needs of panzer formations. Discipline suffered as a result.

Guderian spent most of the day in the front of the action, visiting each division by early evening to gain an impression of their progress; none had reached its objectives. Nonetheless, when Guderian called a halt to operations at 10:30 P.M. on May 10, he had achieved much; the French had reacted slowly as anticipated, and Kleist's operations order for the next day, issued at 2 A.M., was essentially unchanged. However, an hour later, the *Panzergruppe* commander and his staff began to have second thoughts: they expected an attack from the south, from the vicinity of Longwy, by French motorized troops, and ordered Guderian to halt the 10th Panzer Division and conduct a hasty defense. "I asked for the cancellation of these orders," wrote Guderian in his memoirs. "The detachment of one third of my force to meet the hypothetical threat of enemy cavalry would endanger the success of the Meuse crossing and therefore of the whole operation."[18]

This incident set a pattern of continuing confusion and conflict between XIX Panzer Corps and its higher headquarters, with Guderian and his division commanders inclined to use every inch of freedom allowed by the German concept of *auftragstaktik,* or mission tactics, to continue their mission as they saw fit. On May 11, Kleist himself came forward to Guderian's command post and suggested to Colonel Walter Nehring, Guderian's chief of staff, that 10th Panzer be directed to attack southward. During the day, however, the corps made strong advances toward the Meuse. 1st Panzer Division captured Neufchâteau and its tank brigade drove back the French 5th *Division Légère Mécanique* at Bertrix; overall, the division made up for slow progress in the first day, having advanced about 100 kilometers from the German border in all, and halted just 5 kilometers from the French border and 20 kilometers from Sedan. In the north of the corps sector, 2d Panzer was just a hair behind, its forward elements halting at Paliseul. In the south, 10th Panzer, taking a longer and less direct route, stopped at Straimont and Suxy. Guderian's command post was at Neufchâteau, right behind 1st Panzer. The Belgians had never had much chance to occupy their second defensive line; the German attack was too swift. Guderian ordered his troops to press on the next day.

May 12 saw XIX Panzer Corps close upon the Meuse, although 2d Panzer in the north, struggling against terrible road conditions and French artillery fires, stopped at Bosseval, seven kilometers from the river. General Ferdinand Schall's 10th Panzer marched all through the night of May 11–12 and reached the river at midnight. 1st Panzer swept the remnants of the French light cavalry division off the heights east of Sedan, although the French artillery made progress a halting matter, requiring constant attention from the *Luftwaffe*. However, the Germans could not seize Sedan, though Guderian rode his subordinates hard all day long.

At about 6 P.M. on May 12, a Fieseler Storch plane bearing Guderian took the XIX Panzer Corps commander to a rendezvous with Kleist at *Panzergruppe* headquarters at Ebly. With the crucial Meuse crossing in prospect for the next day, the two panzer generals were at loggerheads over how the operation was to be conducted. The crucial issue was close air support for the crossing; German intelligence had confirmed that the French had taken the bait offered in the form of Army Group B and Höpner's panzers and that the weight of Stuka dive-bomber activity could safely be shifted to the Meuse crossings.

Guderian had long maintained that he was willing to sacrifice a very heavy bombing for constant harassing air cover. His aim was to have the Stukas substitute in part for artillery, suppressing French artillery and supporting the exposed German infantry as they assaulted across the Meuse into prepared positions. Late in the afternoon, he met with General Lörzer of the 2d Air Corps and General von Sutterheim, commander of the 2d Close Air Support Group, to confirm the planned list of targets and timing of the attack and to coordinate and synchronize the air attacks with the ground fire support. Separately, Kleist had met with Field Marshal Hugo Sperrle, commander of the 3d Air Corps. Together, Kleist and Sperrle had agreed on a massive bombardment of the whole area rather than specific targets or a search for French artillery. The confusion, along with the fact that Guderian had repositioned his divisions for the Meuse crossings away from Kleist's original intended crossing sites, made for a rather unpleasant meeting. Guderian told his superior that to reposition his divisions would delay the crossing until May 14, so Kleist agreed to the new crossing sites. However, Kleist refused to modify his orders regarding the air attacks, though Guderian protested:

> My whole attack plan was thus placed in jeopardy, since if such an attack were carried out the long-drawn-out neutralization of the enemy batteries could no longer be achieved. I argued strongly against this and asked that my original plan, on which the whole attack was founded, be followed. General von Kleist refused this request too, and I flew back in the Fieseler Storch, with a new pilot, to my corps headquarters. The young man maintained he knew where the landing strip from which I had set off was located, but he could not find it in the fading light and the next thing I knew we were on the other side of the Meuse, flying in a slow and unarmed plane over the French positions. An unpleasant moment.[19]

The Germans spent the remainder of the night of May 12 clearing the east bank of the Meuse of French resistance and preparing for the river crossing the next day; artillery struggled forward over the congested roads, engineers confirmed crossing sites, and infantry recalled the lessons they had learned in many rehearsals. Corps chief of staff Nehring updated the operations orders from a war game conducted on the Moselle eight weeks earlier and disseminated it to the panzer divisions.[20]

For their part, the French tried at the last to bolster their defenses in a sector they never imagined would be attacked in force. The assessment of General Charles Huntziger, the French Second Army commander, was that the most dangerous avenue of approach was toward Carignan and Mouzon, not Sedan.[21] Even so, the French had made many improvements to the static defenses around the town, adding blockhouses and preparing a second line of defenses about fifteen kilometers to the west. What they did not do as well was to train: for example, French soldiers only received instructions on how to use their machine guns for air defense on the morning of May 13; in general, about half a day each week was spent on training.

In preparing his defenses, Huntziger counted on General Grandsard's X Corps of three infantry divisions, the 55th Division around Sedan and the 3d North African Division, which had relieved the 71st Division in April, to the east, allowing 71st Division to become the corps reserve, and the separate 147th Fortress Infantry Regiment. As elsewhere along the French line, Huntziger's troops prepared to fight a static defense from bunkers, blockhouses, and modestly fortified houses. After the Germans invaded on May 10, Grandsard sent some of his corps artillery assets forward to help the divisions in their fight, and the 71st Division had been ordered back to reinforce the corps front, marching forty miles in two days. The results of this activity were as much confusion as reinforcement, especially for the lower-grade troops of the Second Army.

The French positions opposite Sedan on the east bank of the Meuse were in three lines, with very modest and not-very-mobile reserves. In front were the fortified bunkers and houses, located at the river's edge and overlooked by artillery and a second line on the heights to the west. In general, the west bank of the river is more open ground than that on the east bank, although the Germans would have to uncover themselves in the final assault to the river.

THE CROSSING OF THE MEUSE

Guderian and Kleist had worried about the river-crossing mission since the creation of XIX Panzer Corps and the reworking of the German invasion plan early in 1940. After their curt meeting on May 12, Guderian returned to his command post, and, with Nehring, modified the previously arranged river-crossing plan: XIX Panzer Corps would attack with all three divisions abreast, 2d Panzer in the west and north, at Donchery; 1st Panzer in the center at Sedan; 10th Panzer in the east and south, at Wadelincourt.

1st Panzer had the main attack—really, the absolute tip of the German spear aimed at France—and for it, the *Grossdeutschland* Regiment was brought forward from corps reserve for added infantry and the two heavy artillery battalions stripped from the 2d and 10th Panzer Divisions.[22] 1st Panzer's mission was to seize the heights of La Boulette and the Bois de la Marfée, then turn south. Indeed, the whole corps was to parallel this move after crossing the Meuse, in preparation for an exploitation attack to the west. After the all-night approach march, the attack was scheduled for 3 P.M. on May 13.

Before the ground attack was to begin, however, a saturation air bombardment was to soften the French positions, as Kleist had ordered, at noon. The air attacks were to cover three pairs of large areas around the crossing sites, one near the river and one deeper in the French rear. As the anxious Guderian waited for a fleet of Luftwaffe dive-bombers to plaster the target areas and then depart, he was surprised to see just a few aircraft on station at noon. Kleist's order for a massive raid had arrived too late; Lörzer simply followed the original plan for constant aerial coverage. Throughout the day, about 1,000 aircraft flew missions in the XIX Panzer Corps zone, primarily around Sedan.[23]

The rush to bring forward as much combat power as possible for the crossing had left Guderian's divisions with little time to create original plans; as did its parent corps, the 1st Panzer Division merely updated a previous plan from a war game. There was also confusion about the time of the attack, which 1st Panzer originally set as 9 A.M. Also, because the ground near the riverbank was open to French artillery fire, the Germans needed to remain hidden several kilometers from the water's edge, hampering final preparations.

The 1st Infantry Regiment, led by Lieutenant Colonel Hermann Balck, perhaps the most brilliant German tactical commander of the war—he would rise to command an army group by the war's end—would lead the division's attack. Balck was a highly decorated veteran of World War I, and the Germans could have asked for no better man to lead the way in the invasion's most crucial attack. Despite the detailed preparations, the attack ran into problems from the start: the engineers who were to operate the rubber boats to ferry Balck's regiment across the Meuse failed to arrive at the line of departure on time, nor would the engineers of the *Grossdeutschland* Regiment, to Balck's left, pilot the 1st Infantry Regiment's boats; Balck was forced to improvise with his own men. Supported by tank main-gun fire and direct-firing artillery to silence the French bunkers and machine guns, the 1st Infantry Regiment made for the river beginning at 3 P.M., as scheduled, led by the 7th and 8th Companies of its 2d Battalion. The division's journal described the action.

> The first obstacles are overcome in a rapid advance, and the first bunkers rolled up. Despite this, French resistance comes back to life. Enemy artillery begins to shoot at the crossing point. The crews in the bunkers desperately defend against the advancing infantrymen. One bunker after the other, antitank guns, machine guns and field fortifications are taken in individual combat and through the personal example of all the leaders who advance in front of their men. Antitank and anti-aircraft [weapons] also play a tremendous role in the reduction of the enemy, and they destroy the French in relentless actions, sometimes at point-blank range.[24]

Slowly, Balck's infantry infiltrated the French defenses. By 5:30 P.M., they had worked their way about a kilometer and one-half toward the high ground overlooking the river; half an hour later, Guderian himself came across and up to the front. Balck insisted upon pressing the attack, over his subordinates' objections, in order to enlarge the bridgehead and maintain the advantage they had won. The French defenses, linear and static, had been pierced, and Balck and Guderian sensed the opportunity for a breakthrough. Driving his battalions until midnight, Balck was able to push forward elements into the Bois de la Marfée and to cut off the French artillery positions overlooking the river. The 2d and 10th Panzer Divisions, on 1st Panzer's flanks, did not enjoy as much success, but Balck's infantry had driven a wedge into the French line that would unhinge the entire position at Sedan.

During the night, Guderian jammed as many tanks and artillery across the bridgehead as time and space would allow. By nightfall, he had nearly 300 armored vehicles and a battalion of 105 mm guns over one bridge, but German engineers were unable to construct a second span; most of their bridging had been used to move through the Ardennes and could not yet be brought up.[25] The corps commander wanted to use the 2d Panzer Division in a flanking attack to roll up the French defenses along the Meuse, but traffic jams—rear echelons were pressing harder than ever to get into the action—forced 2d Panzer to share the bridge at Gaulier with 1st Panzer.

The French, too, were aware of how the situation hung in the balance. Huntziger and his division commanders were trying to shore up their infantry, which had performed poorly on May 13. From the south and southwest, German scout planes had spotted elements of the French 3d Armored and 3d Motorized Infantry divisions thrusting toward the German bridgehead and the positions of the 1st Panzer Division at the Bois de la Marfée. At last, the French were mounting a counterattack. Allied planes began to strike the bridge at Gaulier. Guderian renewed his efforts to get his armor massed on the west bank of the Meuse, but neither the 1st nor 2d Panzer Regiments fully crossed the river until early morning on May 14.

The French tanks attacked at first light, forcing the Germans to commit their armor piecemeal, one company at a time. By 8:30 A.M., the two sides were in heavy contact near the towns of Connage and Bulson. The French had some initial successes, pushing back the forward elements of the German infantry, but the panzer attacks stopped the French in their tracks. The Germans were tactically superior to the French, and they pressed their advantage in an attack toward Maisoncelle. As one panzer company commander recorded:

> Suddenly, 10 French . . . tanks, grouped together closely in a column, appeared on the edge of Maisoncelle on the road to Raucourt. In a flash, [my] company opened fire with every gun tube. The enemy was completely surprised. He did not fire a single round. Three vehicles turned toward the south and, although hit, managed to escape. Four tanks remained in place, one of them burning in a fiery blaze. They were nevertheless so badly damaged that their crews abandoned them.[26]

The Germans had caught these French tanks in column, not in a tactical formation, and had gotten off the first shots. In tank engagements, victory often goes to those who shoot first. Also, Guderian's troops did not wait to methodically assemble a large force. General Kirchner, commander of the 1st Panzer Division, was willing to accept the risk of a hasty attack, mixing elements of his 1st and 2d Panzer Regiments, in order to seize a fleeting opportunity and to keep the French off balance. The Germans were ruthless about pressing their advantage. By 10 A.M., the fight was all but gone from the French units, and they retreated toward Chémery. The German tanks, especially the lightly armed Panzer IIs, were inferior to the French armor in main guns and armor protection, but their automotive systems were reliable and the higher proportion of radios in the panzer units permitted good command and control of a confused, hectic, fast-moving engagement.

This hasty attack and its success in beating off the French also allowed Guderian's corps some breathing room to assemble the rest of its combat power for a synchronized, coordinated major attack. Both 2d and 10th Panzer Divisions were able to expand their bridgeheads, attacking southward in parallel with 1st Panzer. However, early in the afternoon, despite the progress, Guderian was becoming concerned that his corps was headed not west, but south. Even while these battles raged, Guderian wanted to turn his attack ninety degrees to the right and begin to break out, again leading with 1st Panzer Division.

This was a highly risky operation, for it would expose the division to flank attacks, particularly from the south, where strong French forces, including tanks, remained. By 2 P.M., he was nearly ready to take his chance, meeting with Kirchner and his operations officer, Major Walther Wenck, at the 1st Panzer command post. Guderian wanted above all else to maintain the momentum of the attack and keep the French reeling. Turning to Wenck for his final thoughts about the proposed maneuver, the operations officer quoted back Guderian's favorite motto, *"Klotzen, nicht kleckern:* The general taught us to hit with a fist and not feel around with our fingers."[27] Guderian retired to his command car to dispense the necessary warning orders; then, later in the evening, he returned to his command post to settle the details with Nehring for the next day's operations. XIX Panzer Corps halted major operations just before midnight to allow the Panzers to rearm and refuel.

If Guderian was sure the French were nearly beaten, Kleist remained tentative. At 6:30 P.M., in a radio conversation, the *Panzergruppe* leader agreed with Guderian's aims, but four hours later, he changed his mind. Concerned with the exposed southern flank, Kleist ordered Guderian to halt until the bridgehead could be secured by the following 12th Army infantry. After thirty minutes' debate, Kleist was persuaded of Guderian's arguments, though not without some heated exchanges and a not-so-gentle reminder by Guderian of the World War I French Miracle of the Marne that had halted the German advance in 1914. The headstrong Guderian, flushed with the prospect of a major operational victory and sure of his own reading of the battle, was willing to use just about any tool to maintain his freedom of operation, but his superiors to the rear were less sure and wished to keep him on a tight rein. Kleist was far from the most conservative in this respect; other army-level commanders in Army Group A, and Rundstedt himself, were even more nervous.

Still, the stage was set for a breakthrough, if the panzers could be refueled and rearmed and combat power massed for a thrust westward—no mean feat, given that 1st Panzer had paid a stiff price for its progress—and the *Grossdeutschland* Regiment could hold the southern flank. At this point, only a major French counteroffensive, in far greater strength than on May 14, could stem the rising German tide.

THE BREAKOUT AND THE RACE TO THE SEA

Even as Guderian was plotting his attack west and arguing with Kleist, the 1st Panzer Division was pivoting to attack toward Singly. May 13 had seen the division's infantry play the central role in the river crossing, while on May 14, the panzers had played the lead in driving back the French. On May 15, the Germans would adjust their tactics to take advantage of the hard lesson learned: in less than two days of hard fighting, the Germans had discovered the limits of what tanks could achieve in restricted terrain, and now they modified their doctrine to mix infantry and armor together in task forces, called *Kampfgruppen*—battle groups. The division combined tanks and infantry into Battle Group Krüger, after the 1st Infantry Brigade commander, and Battle Group Nedtwig, named for the 1st Armor Brigade commander.

The morning saw renewed heavy fighting. The division logistics troops had worked through the night to rearm and refuel the tanks—and to recover and repair as many damaged tanks as possible—and at 5:45 A.M., the division again pushed forward, its goal the town of Rethel. Battle Group Krüger, with a preponderance of infantry, attacked in the north, through the village of La Horgne, while the tank-heavy Battle Group Nedtwig advanced along the southern corridor, through Chagny.

Desperate to hold their fraying defenses, the French fought hard in both sectors. For the first time in the operation, Balck's First Infantry Regiment was stopped around La Horgne by the French 3d Spahi Brigade, a horse-mounted cavalry unit with two Moroccan and Algerian regiments. Manning barricades and trenches along the narrow roads leading into the village, the Spahis held Battle Group Krüger from early morning until late

afternoon, suffering horrendous casualties.[28] The first frontal attack by Balck's 3d Battalion failed. He then ordered his 2d Battalion to circle around the town through the dense woods to the
north, where the Germans surprised the staff of the 2d Spahi
Regiment, killing many including the commander, but still the
defenders held the town. Balck's men, exhausted from days of
heavy fighting, began to flag; only by Balck's personal example
and determined leadership was the regiment willing to move forward. A third attack on the town, employing frontal and flanking
maneuvers, finally succeeded in clearing the way; Balck once
more drove his man onward toward the next town, Bouvellement. More than 600 Spahis were killed defending La Horgne.[29]
The next day, Guderian came forward to Balck's position. In his
memoirs, he wrote:

> In the main street of the burning village I found the regimental
> commander, Lieutenant Colonel Balck, and let him describe the
> events of the previous night to me. The troops were overtired, hav-
> ing had no real rest since the 9th of May. Ammunition was run-
> ning low. The men in the front line were falling asleep in their slit
> trenches. Balck himself, in wind jacket and with a knotty stick in
> his hand, told me that the capture of the village had only suc-
> ceeded because, when his officers had complained against the
> continuation of the attack, he had replied: "In that case, I'll take
> the place on my own!" and had moved off. His men thereupon fol-
> lowed him. His dirty face and red-rimmed eyes showed that he had
> spent a hard day and a sleepless night. For his doings that day he
> was to receive the Knight's Cross.[30]

Battle Group Nedtwig was likewise stalled at Chagny. The
panzer brigade commander, concerned about the French armor
to his south, retained a substantial reserve and thus his tanks
could not force their way through the village. Using his small
force of attached infantry, he, too, attempted a flanking maneuver to the south, but a French counterattack threatened to flank
the German infantry in turn. Although exhausted—he later collapsed and was replaced in command by Balck—Nedtwig turned
his force to the northwest and assumed a defensive posture.
When the infantry of Battle Group Krüger broke through to

Bouvellement, the French at Chagny felt themselves in an untenable position and withdrew, allowing Nedtwig's tanks to advance. In the night, the two battle groups established contact, rested, reorganized, and established a security perimeter.

The French Second Army had collapsed; an expanding hole now lay open for an exploitation attack westward, as Guderian and his troops knew. As the log of the 1st Panzer Division explained:

> Reconnaissance initiated during the night report [the villages of] Louvergny and Sauville along the southern flank clear of the enemy. Reconnaissance carried out in the early morning hours at Chagny reports this village unoccupied. The penetration of Battle Group Krüger and the capture of Bouvellement appear to have had their effect. Now it is important to thrust. *Now it is time to thrust forward without consideration of casualties and exhaustion before the French have the opportunity to set up again. There is no time for half-stepping now.* [Italics added.][31]

However, the view from higher headquarters was quite different. During the night of May 15, Guderian had yet another heated exchange with Kleist, during which he won another day's freedom. Kleist was caught in a vise between his corps commanders—Reinhardt's XLI Panzer Corps, to the north, also had broken through and demanded freedom of operation—and the army high command, which, bowing to pressure from Hitler, on the night of May 16 ordered the *Panzergruppe* to halt its westward drive and wait for the infantry of the 12th and 16th armies to secure the beach in the French lines and protect against a counterattack from the south. At Army Group A, Rundstedt, too, was concerned about the unprotected flank.

Guderian and Reinhardt had established a two-corps front that combined tremendous combat power with great mobility. The Germans had the opportunity to turn their tanks loose. Guderian would not be restrained, and he issued orders by radio to continue the march on May 17. Unfortunately, Kleist's headquarters overheard the transmission; Guderian was once again summoned to be reprimanded. Guderian again flew to *Panzergruppe* headquarters, but this time the two leaders were at loggerheads and Guderian impetuously submitted his resignation. Kleist would not be intimidated and accepted the resignation. Rundstedt and the 12th Army commander, Colonel General Wilhelm von List, had to finesse the situation by permitting Guderian to carry out a "reconnaissance in force," which the XIX Panzer Corps commander interpreted as he pleased. Soon, his panzers were on the road bypassing French troops and headed for the sea and the encirclement of the Allied forces in northern France and Belgium.

At last, the Allied high command had tumbled to the fact that the Germans had broken through. As the Panzers roared through the Allied rear, they brushed aside several counterattacks that were too late in coming and too weak to stem the tide of the German advance, as Hoth's XV Panzer Corps, to the north of Reinhardt, also linked up with Reinhardt and Guderian. On May 18, the French 2d Armored Division was swept aside, primarily by the 6th Panzer Division near Saint-Quentin. Further north, Rommel's 7th Panzer Division advanced through Cambrai, near the site of the World War I tank battle.

In Guderian's sector, only two British reserve divisions lay between the panzers and the sea. The French mounted a stronger counterattack of about 150 tanks—an assortment of heavy Char Bs, Somuas, and D2s—under General Charles de Gaulle and attacked toward Crécy into Guderian's southern flank. At Crécy, Guderian had prepared an ambush of infantry antitank guns while the main body of his own armor pressed westward. French light tanks and then heavier D2s assaulted the German positions without infantry support and suffered heavy losses, causing Northeast Front Commander Georges to call off the attack. The Allies, their main forces trapped in northern Belgium and their rear areas clogged by refugees and sown with panic by the panzer breakthrough, were unable to mass sufficient forces to halt Guderian's advance.

By May 19, all three panzer corps, except for the 9th Panzer Division, were no more than fifty miles from the sea, and by midmorning the next day, Balck's division had reached Amiens, destroying the British Royal Sussex Regiment. The 2d Panzer

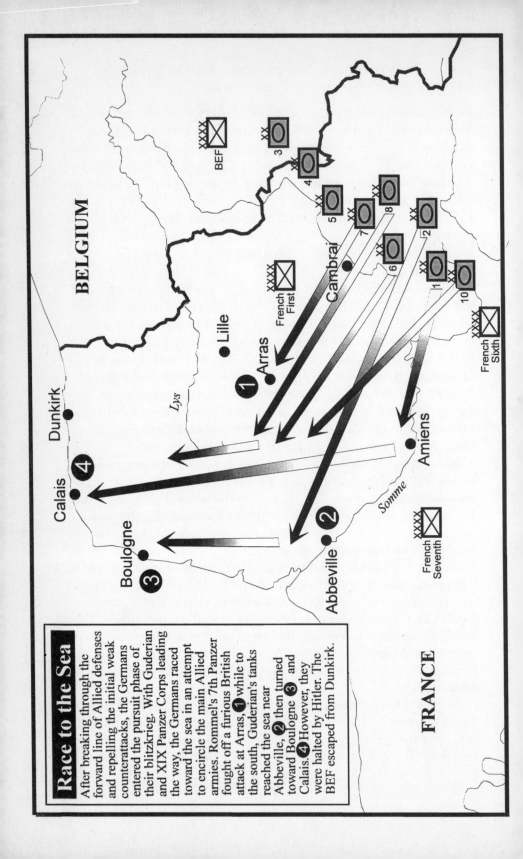

Race to the Sea

After breaking through the forward line of Allied defenses and repelling the initial weak counterattacks, the Germans entered the pursuit phase of their blitzkrieg. With Guderian and XIX Panzer Corps leading the way, the Germans raced toward the sea in an attempt to encircle the main Allied armies. Rommel's 7th Panzer fought off a furious British attack at Arras, ❶ while to the south, Guderian's tanks reached the sea near Abbeville, ❷ then turned toward Boulogne ❸ and Calais. ❹ However, they were halted by Hitler. The BEF escaped from Dunkirk.

Division bypassed the fight to tackle the British 35th Brigade at Abbeville, on the Somme River estuary. By the end of the day, First Lieutenant Spitta's battalion of 2d Panzer reached the coast near Noyelles.

A day later, the British tried one last time to cut off the German spearheads, counterattacking at Arras against Rommel's 7th Panzer. Advancing in two columns, the British created trouble for Rommel initially; the German antitank guns and the light Mark I and II panzers were no match for the heavily armored British, but the overall weight of the attack was not enough to put the Germans in any operational jeopardy. In the evening, Rommel returned to the attack, driving the British back from Arras.

On May 22, Guderian struck for the Channel ports in strength, with all three of his panzer divisions. Despite furious fighting on the part of British units at Boulogne and Calais, the French senior commanders were beaten, mentally as well as physically; the Allied forces were all but encircled inside the Dunkirk pocket. On May 24, Hitler halted the ground advance: Dunkirk was to be left to the *Luftwaffe*. For all the equipment abandoned there, the bulk of the British Expeditionary Force escaped, leaving the Germans with an implacable enemy relatively safe in its island fortress where the panzers could not reach them and the *Luftwaffe* could not achieve victory. France was defeated, but the war in the West was not settled.

Still, the German armor had succeeded beyond all but the zealots' imaginings. A superior concept of land warfare, what we still refer to as *blitzkrieg,* had enabled the Germans to capitalize on the mistakes of the Allied high command—as embodied in their war plans—to create an operational opportunity and a strategic success. That it was not a complete success—the Battle of Britain was still to be fought—would return to haunt the Germans in many ways, not only in the West, but also, and perhaps most importantly, in the East.

CHAPTER TWO

NORTH AFRICA, 1940–1942

Battles in the Western Desert

GERMANY NOT ONLY invented the *blitzkrieg*, it depended upon it, for its economy was geared to winning a series of brief wars. Yet, after the victories in western Europe, the concept was fatally diluted in the vastness of the Soviet Union and in the trackless waste of the North African desert, where German forces were summoned to rescue the Italian army.

The great surging tank campaigns along the Mediterranean coast of Africa can be roughly divided into three periods. The first brief period saw the British establish ascendancy over the Italians, who had assumed initial responsibility for the theater. Throughout World War II, the Axis powers fought parallel rather than coordinated wars. The Japanese were of course too far distant for effective coordination, but in the Mediterranean theater, Mussolini unwisely conducted independent campaigns in Greece and North Africa, apparently more concerned with impressing Hitler than with winning the war.

The second period began with the arrival of the Germans, sent to rescue the Italians, and was dominated by the legendary Desert Fox, then-Lieutenant General Erwin Rommel. The third period saw the British reestablish superiority by means of better intelligence and the allocation of vast resources to the theater. The essence of the struggle was reduced to a contest between Rommel, the tactical genius working with minimal resources, and General Bernard Law Montgomery, a painstaking man who did not move until his strength was overwhelming. The latter's methods were proven by the battle of el Alamein in 1942.

ARMORED WARFARE

North Africa ultimately became far more important to Churchill than it was to Hitler, and this importance was reflected in the amount of resources each man devoted to the battle. Churchill wished to defend North Africa not only for obvious reasons such as the control of the Mediterranean and the protection of the Middle East oil fields and the Suez canal, but also because it was the only place where he could place British ground troops in action against the Germans. Hitler, preoccupied with the invasion of the Soviet Union, was content—until it was too late—to provide his North African commanders with a minimum of forces.

The series of desert battles began in September 1940, when Marshal Rodolfo Graziani, much against his better judgment, was forced by Mussolini to launch an invasion of Egypt with the Italian Tenth Army. The halfhearted attempt ground to a halt before reaching Mersa Matruh, a coastal town 140 miles east of the border between Libya and Egypt.

Graziani halted, complaining to Rome that his army was suffering from battle fatigue and needed to be refurbished with better equipment before further advances could be made. Graziani, no Caesar by anyone's measure, nonetheless had a point. Italy had rearmed before Germany or Great Britain. Consequently, it was saddled with obsolete weapons systems it was unable to replace with new equipment because of its inferior industrial capacity.

On paper, the Italian force in North Africa looked imposing: three corps comprised of a dozen divisions. In reality, the Italians presented a hollow challenge to the British waiting behind their defenses in Egypt. The vast bulk of the Italian troops were poorly trained infantry, next to useless in desert terrain when outflanked by mechanized forces. The Italian armor consisted of about 60 obsolete M11 and obsolescent M13 medium tanks, and roughly 240 L3 light tanks. The latter were described by one senior Italian officer as "little more than pretty mechanical toys from six to ten tons, to be offered as targets to the enemy antitank guns."[1]

In marked contrast, the British Western Desert Force forces

had some 323 tanks for which the Italian armor was no match, just as Graziani was no match for the British commander, Lieutenant General Richard O'Connor, a dashing leader too often overlooked by historians. O'Connor, like Rommel, liked to lead from the front; he did this once too often and was captured. He escaped from a prisoner of war camp and returned to battle late in the war; but for his period of incarceration, he probably would have become a field marshal.

O'Connor had at his disposal 200 light tanks for reconnaissance, 75 cruisers, the A9, A10, and A13 medium tanks for rapid armored thrusts, and 48 heavy tanks—the famous Matildas—to be used in infantry support roles. These were organized according to the prewar British philosophy of armored operations. Unfortunately, the designers of the cruisers, which formed the backbone of the British armored divisions, had traded the weight of sufficient armor protection and firepower for speed and range. Their resulting vulnerability to enemy tank and antitank fire was to prove fatal to many of their unfortunate crews.

The A9 cruiser model had a maximum speed of twenty-five miles per hour, but weighed just 12.5 tons and it was only protected by armor 14 mm thick. The Matilda, by contrast, had a full 78 mm of armor shielding its crew, but it weighed a whopping 26.5 tons and crawled along at only fifteen miles per hour, although in the desert this was often reduced to about eight miles per hour. Both the cruisers and the infantry tanks had another Achilles' heel, however: their 40 mm two-pounder main gun, which the Battle of France in May 1940 had revealed to have neither the range nor the velocity to take on German armor.[2]

The light tanks and cruisers belonged to the 4th and 7th Armoured Brigades of the 7th Armoured Division, O'Connor's main striking force. The Matildas were the property of the 7th Royal Tank Regiment, which formed part of the corps troops, units that came under O'Connor's direct command, rather than that of his division commanders.

Thus, though the Italians outnumbered the British, the British enjoyed a preponderance of armor. More importantly, they had leaders itching for the opportunity to test their theories of modern armored warfare on real live opponents. O'Connor himself had participated in the mechanized experiments of the early 1920s, and was a keen believer in the potential of mobile armored forces to achieve decisive victories. He shared the enthusiasm of Major General Percy Hobart, the erstwhile 7th Armoured Division commander who had trained his outfit for a mobile striking role since 1938, and who had been sacked by General Sir Archibald Wavell, the overall British commander in the Middle East, after a row with Lieutenant General Maitland Wilson, the commander of British forces in Egypt. Hobart was a superb trainer and stamped the beliefs of the Royal Tank Corps—especially the belief in the tank as an independent and dominant arm—on the division. Both the early British victories in the desert and the defeats that followed must be considered part of his legacy.

OPERATION COMPASS

O'Connor's riposte to Graziani was so dramatically successful by any measure—ground covered, enemy prisoners captured, casualties taken—that for a while the British had good reason to believe that, in the desert at least, they had no masters in armored combat. O'Connor's offensive, code-named Operation Compass and originally conceived as a five-day tank raid, began December 9, 1940, with a three-pronged assault against Italian forces in Egypt.

One prong was the 1,800-man force under Brigadier A. R. Selby, which moved west along the coast to engage the Libyan garrison at Maktila, about fifty miles east of the border, while a second prong, the infantry of the 4th Indian Division with the Matildas in support, made a short wheel southwest into the desert and then headed straight north to attack the Italians at Sidi Barrani, ten miles west of Maktila but still on the coast. The 7th Armoured Division, meanwhile, made a far wider hook to strike the Italians deeper in the rear at Azziziya and Buq Buq, thirty miles east of the frontier on the Mediterranean. These tactics—fixing the enemy on the coast with infantry and artillery while outflanking him with armored sweeps into the desert—were to become the hallmark of nearly every battle in the theater.

Within three days, the entire Italian invading force had been destroyed or captured—a haul of over 38,000 prisoners—at the cost of fewer than 700 British casualties. The defeat turned quickly into a rout, as O'Connor chased the Italians across Libya's Benghazi Bulge, capturing Bardia, Tobruk, and Brace in turn. While the 6th Australian Division, which had replaced the 4th Indian Division, pursued the Italians along the coast road, O'Connor sent the 7th Armoured Division across the desert to cut off the Italians south of Benghazi. After a furious two-day dash, the division's vanguard, led by Lieutenant Colonel J. F. B. Combe of the 11th Hussars, reached the coast at Beda Fomm less than two hours before the Italians, who were in pell-mell retreat south from Benghazi.

Even after these stunning maneuvers, the British still were greatly outnumbered by the Italian Tenth Army, which retained four intact divisions, but the Italians were defeated in a series of engagements during which they repeatedly violated a cardinal rule of armored warfare—never to split up the mass of one's armored force—by throwing small packets of M13 tanks against the fire of British cruisers, antitank guns, and artillery. As they saw their armor being destroyed piecemeal, the Italian infantry gave up the fight. In all, O'Connor's Western Desert Force, now renamed XIII Corps, had advanced 500 miles in ten weeks and had captured 130,000 prisoners, almost 500 tanks, and 845 artillery pieces, while suffering less than 2,000 casualties.[3] It was a stirring achievement for the British army, which had had precious little to celebrate so far in the war, and was achieved by the skillful integration of armor with infantry and artillery in well-executed all-arms engagements. However, as at least one author has noted, "Beda Fomm was the last battle fought by Britain's pre-war professional army."[4] As the British army expanded, the tactical values demonstrated during these weeks were forgotten, at great cost.

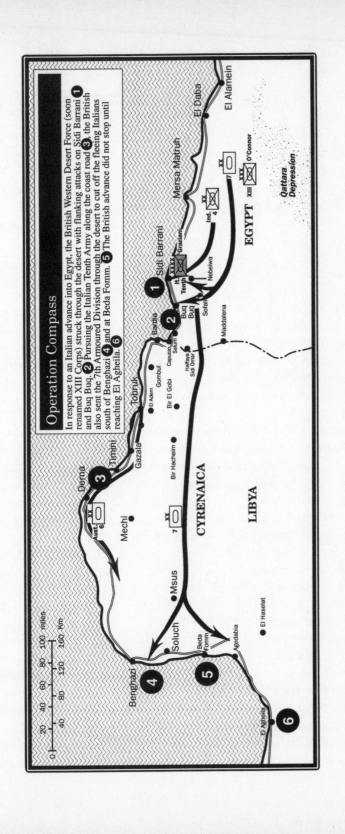

Operation Compass

In response to an Italian advance into Egypt, the British Western Desert Force (soon renamed XIII Corps) struck through the desert with flanking attacks on Sidi Barrani **1** and Buq Buq. **2** Pursuing the Italian Tenth Army along the coast road **3**, the British also sent the 7th Armoured Division through the desert to cut off the fleeing Italians south of Benghazi **4** and at Beda Fomm. **5** The British advance did not stop until reaching El Agheila. **6**

ROMMEL SEIZES THE INITIATIVE

The political effects of the Italians' dramatic reversal reverberated through the corridors of power in Rome and Berlin. On February 12, five days after the Italian collapse at Beda Fomm, Hitler dispatched Erwin Rommel, one of the panzer heroes of the invasion of France and now promoted to colonel general, to stiffen the Italians' spine and prevent any further setbacks that might jeopardize the entire Axis southern flank.

Within forty-eight hours of Rommel's arrival at Castel Benito, the advance elements of his *Deutsche Afrika Korps* landed at Tripoli, and the desert war entered a dynamic new phase. The events of the next two years in North Africa would make Rommel one of the true household names to emerge from the ranks of World War II commanders and would create a legend around the *Afrika Korps* enjoyed by no similar military organization involved in the conflict. Rommel's tactics would make case studies for the U.S. Army sent to fight a desert tank war in 1991.

Rommel arrived in Africa with strict orders from Berlin to do no more than conduct a defensive campaign, at least until the end of May, when both *Afrika Korps* divisions were to have arrived, but the bold and energetic German commander, fresh from exhilarating success with the 7th Panzer Division in France, had little patience for such a cautious strategy. As his tanks were unloaded onto Libyan docks, they were immediately sent east, as Rommel, always instinctively looking for a chance to go on the offensive, probed the British front lines at El Agheila. What he found delighted and excited him: the British force had become a paper tiger. Ironically, the battle-hardened British army commanders considered themselves skilled practitioners of armored warfare, their prewar philosophy having been apparently validated by the crushing victory over the Italian forces. Unfortunately for the British, they had learned exactly the wrong lessons in their encounters with the Italians, and they were forced to spend one and one-half years of painful reeducation at the hands of the Germans.

The British advance had halted at El Agheila, on the frontier

54

between Cyrenaica and Tripolitania in central Libya at the base of the Gulf of Sidra, and the leaders of XIII Corps were anxious to press on and exploit their opponents' weakness. O'Connor was of the opinion that his forces could seize Tripoli by the end of February, but his superiors took a very different view.[5]

Italy had also suffered a humiliating debacle in its invasion of Greece, forcing the Germans to retrieve the situation there by an invasion of first Yugoslavia and then Greece itself. Churchill decided to give the highest priority to sending a British Expeditionary Force to go to the aid of Greece rather than capitalize on the successes in the Western Desert. Thus Wavell, himself in two minds about what to do, was forced to hold the line at El Agheila and shift his attention to the action in Greece, which was also in his theater of command. Under the new plan, not only would XIII Corps not be reinforced for an advance on Tripoli, but it was to be denuded of many of its most experienced troops, now needed for the campaign in Greece. The 7th Armoured Division was withdrawn to Egypt to rest up and be reequipped. It was replaced by the inexperienced 2d Armoured Division. At this stage, Wavell and his staff had little inkling of the arrival of a sizeable German force in Tripolitania, and it was not until March 8 that Rommel was identified as the German commander.[6]

The desert fighting had taken its toll on British equipment. Any hopes to fight a mobile defense lay with the fifty-two cruiser tanks the 2d Armoured Division (really a brigade, for two brigades had been deployed to Greece) had inherited from 7th Armoured, and these were thoroughly worn out from the exertions of the previous month. The balance of the division's eighty-six tanks were Italian M13s captured at Beda Fomm. Nevertheless, the British were not immediately concerned by the weaknesses of their forces in Cyrenaica. They were more impressed by the difficulties the Germans faced ferrying supplies the 650 miles from Tripoli to Benghazi; Wavell and his staff concluded a German offensive was out of the question until May.

Rommel operated on a less conservative timetable, however. Bursting with his characteristic energy and enthusiasm, his first action upon arriving in Africa was to make an aerial reconnaissance of the territory to his east. His superiors in Berlin had ordered him not to engage the British in anything more than a limited offensive to recapture Agedabia, and perhaps Benghazi, and that was to wait until the *Afrika Korps* reached its full two-division strength with the deployment of the 5th Light and the 15th Panzer Divisions.[7] This plan did not sit well with Rommel, whose natural affinity for the offensive was reinforced by intelligence reports indicating the British were overstretched in the theater. He lost no time in ordering each German unit to the front immediately upon its arrival in Tripoli, and on March 24, he launched a preliminary attack against the weakly defended British forward position at El Agheila. This was quickly overrun, and the British withdrew to Mersa el Brega, a choke point on the coast twenty miles to the east.

Not for the last time, Rommel chafed at the restrictions Rome and Berlin tried to place upon his freedom of maneuver.

Paul Carrell asks in *The Foxes of the Desert*:

> Was he supposed to wait? To wait until his opponent had built up a strong defense position against which an attack in May might fail or succeed at the cost of enormous sacrifice, simply because Hitler and the German High Command in Berlin had a completely false concept of the desert war and because Mussolini and his generals in Rome were still quaking with fear after the devastating "sixty-two days campaign"? No. Mersa el Brega and perhaps even Agedabia must be taken at once and he must certainly not wait until the end of May.[8]

Rommel's strength was growing, and he seized every initiative. A week after taking El Agheila, he launched a concerted, combined-arms attack on the British infantry and guns at Mersa el Brega. Infantry from the 3rd Reconnaissance Battalion and 5th Panzer Regiment tanks, supported by *Luftwaffe* Junkers Ju 87 Stuka dive-bombers, pounded the position, which was defended by the 2d Armoured Division's support group. When the desperate British commander on the scene requested help in the form of armor, he was turned down by the division commander, Major

General M. D. Gambier-Parry, on the grounds that not enough daylight was left. British armored forces were traditionally reluctant to engage the enemy after sundown.[9]

Rigid adherence to outmoded methods often decides battles; here Gambier-Parry's decision was crucial, because it ceded all initiative to Rommel. After taking Mersa el Brega and noting the hectic nature of the British retreat, he decided to exploit apparent British confusion to the fullest extent possible. Mersa el Brega was one of the few defensible positions in Cyrenaica, and its collapse left the rest of the British-occupied province extremely vulnerable. It was for this reason that Rommel had told the German high command that the absence of easily defended positions meant Cyrenaica had to be held in full or not at all.[10]

The *Afrika Korps,* with Italian units mixed in, proceeded to roll up British positions all the way along the coast. A mere forty-eight hours after the capture of Mersa el Brega, Rommel's troops were in Agedabia.

It was there that Rommel made a decision of the sort that marks great generals; although the British were in headlong retreat, they had not been defeated in detail. The orthodox rules of war proscribe splitting a force in the face of an undefeated enemy who retains his mass. Like General Robert E. Lee during the American Civil War, Rommel had made a career out of discarding the rule book when it suited him, and with the British in disarray this seemed to him an appropriate occasion to do so again. He divided his force into three self-supporting, combined-arms *Kampfgruppen,* or battle groups, each containing panzers, infantry, and artillery. The contrast between the earlier British attacks, where tanks performed one role—the cruiser tanks for mobile operations, the heavy Matildas in infantry support—and the other arms other, separate roles, was marked. Each of Rommel's battle groups would operate with mobility and independently, in accord with their commander's general wishes but seizing the opportunities of the moment, rather than in an elaborately orchestrated attack.

One battle group was to follow the coast north and then east; a second was to retrace 7th Armoured Division's steps through the

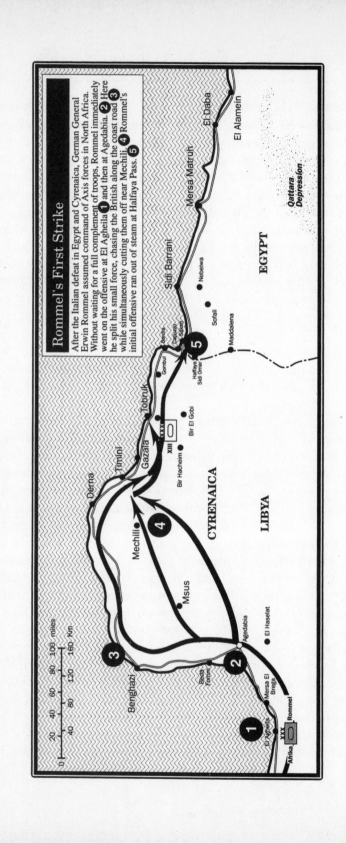

Rommel's First Strike

After the Italian defeat in Egypt and Cyrenaica, German General Erwin Rommel assumed command of Axis forces in North Africa. Without waiting for a full complement of troops, Rommel immediately went on the offensive at El Agheila ❶ and then at Agedabia. ❷ Here he split his small force, chasing the British along the coast road ❸ while simultaneously cutting them off near Mechili. ❹ Rommel's initial offensive ran out of steam at Halfaya Pass. ❺ desert to Mechili, by way of Msus; while a third was to make an ever wider sweep through the desert to Mechili. Rommel's gamble paid off handsomely. The British, dazzled by this display of virtuosity, retreated in disorder, their formations disintegrating into ever-smaller pockets of easily outflanked infantry and armor. By April 10, the *Afrika Korps* had coalesced at Mechili, having captured several senior British officers, including O'Connor's replacement, Lieutenant General Philip Neame, Gambier-Parry, and, most unfortunately for the British, O'Connor himself, whom Wavell had sent forward in an attempt to retrieve the situation. Rommel urged his units on relentlessly, and on April 25, German troops returned to Egypt, taking the Halfaya Pass.

STALLED AT THE BORDER

There they stopped; as so often would be the case in the desert war, logistics now trumped tactics as the determining factor in armored operations. Rommel's swift advance, despite meeting relatively little opposition, had taken a toll on machines and men. The *Afrika Korps* was getting its first harsh lesson in desert operations; these were not the fertile fields of France, laced with hard-packed roads where tanks could fill up at civilian service stations, and linked to a modern industrial base for quick repairs. Instead, the only fuel, food, and water was that brought laboriously over hundreds of miles of empty desert; instead of service stations, the tanks found only the sand and dust that swirled around their columns, reducing engine life by two-thirds.[11]

The Germans were also outrunning their tenuous supply lines. The British, however, being closer to their burgeoning stocks of matériel in Egypt, had fewer logistical challenges to overcome. It was an ironic axiom of mechanized desert warfare in World War II that the farther a side was pushed back toward its rear area, the more forces it could put into the field, and vice versa. Success bred weakness.

Rommel's logistical problems were exacerbated by his separation from Axis matériel stocks in Italy and Germany. The Royal Navy, aided by superior intelligence, which became so refined that it could identify which ships in a convoy were carrying the highest-value cargo, had turned the Mediterranean into a British lake. Again and again, to Rommel's immense frustration, Italian convoys bringing supplies to the *Afrika Korps* were sent to the bottom, while German aircraft had to hug the waves to evade the attentions of the Royal Air Force.

Much of the problem lay with the Axis failure to capture or neutralize the island of Malta, the hub of British operations in the Mediterranean. From there the British were able to hamstring Rommel by interdicting his supplies; the ensuing shortages would contribute mightily to his eventual defeat.

Stalled at Halfaya, Rommel had another problem with which to contend: the port fortress of Tobruk, where the retreating infantry of the 9th Australian Division had dug in, supported by disparate armor and artillery outfits and even some aircraft from the British Desert Air Force. Rommel was determined to rid himself of this thorn in his side and during April launched several assaults on the fortress. They were the sort of attacks that had paid off for him in France: a narrow front of tanks and infantry bringing as much fire to bear as possible as they moved forward, supported by an artillery barrage. Whereas the *blitzkrieg* campaigns in Europe had allowed the Germans wide room to maneuver around enemy strong points, the siege of Tobruk forced them to confront for the first time the challenges of a head-on armored assault against strongly held defensive positions.

The British mounted a flexible defense at Tobruk, combining armor, artillery, and antitank fire behind thirty miles of ditches and minefields. On April 14, a Stuka raid preceded the first German attack, but did little to soften up the entrenched defenders. Australian Major General Sir Leslie Morshead, Tobruk garrison commander, had ordered his infantrymen manning the perimeter to concentrate on stripping the Axis attack of its infantry, while the Allied artillery, tanks, and antitanks guns to their rear dealt with the advancing panzers. His plan worked to perfection.

When the German infantry advanced under cover of night to breach the minefields and antitank ditch, they were able to do so only with considerable losses. Then two panzer battalions surged through, with more infantry riding on the backs of the tanks. The Australians wiped out most of the panzers' luckless passengers, while the four regiments of British twenty-five-pounder field guns, supported by antitank guns and Australian infantry manning captured Italian artillery pieces, hammered the German armor. The all-too-predictable assaults became bogged down, and Rommel was forced to call a halt with the loss of seventeen panzers and 400 German troops dead or captured. Subsequent attacks in the following days met with little more success.[12]

Wavell launched an abortive attempt, code-named Operation Brevity, to relieve the beleaguered garrison on May 15, but he only succeeded in recapturing Halfaya Pass. British possession of this vital terrain feature rendered all of Rommel's territory around Tobruk insecure, so twelve days later, he was forced to assault and retake it with a tank-heavy attack. In both engagements the German crews were intimidated by the British Matilda infantry support tanks. The Matilda's 78 mm armor proved impervious to anything the German tanks could throw at it, and during the May 27 action, a counterattack by the tiny Halfaya garrison's nine Matildas actually caused the Germans temporarily to retreat.[13]

There was, however, one weapon in the German arsenal to which the Matilda's armor offered scant protection: the much-feared 88 mm flak gun, an antiaircraft weapon that the Germans had discovered was equally proficient at destroying tanks. Capable of firing up to twenty armor-piercing rounds per minute, the 88's only drawbacks were its limited protection, high profile, and the time needed to prepare it for action, which meant its six-man crew liked to fight with it from prepared positions, if at all possible.[14] During the next six weeks, a battery of 88s was added to German defenses at Halfaya, and they were to have their say when Wavell attempted another effort to break through to Tobruk in the ill-fated Operation Battleaxe.

Just as Mussolini had pressured Graziani, so now did Churchill pressure Wavell, who launched his next attack on June 15. Both sides had spent the past two months reequipping their forces with new tanks, and the British now slightly outnumbered the Axis forces in tank strength, 200 to 170. This advantage was wasted when the British split their force into three groups and sent the middle column of Matildas along the Halfaya escarpment straight into the sights of the 88s, which made short work of them. It was a tactic Rommel's troops would use time and again, allowing British armor to throw itself upon the sword of German antitank guns.

Further south, near Fort Capuzzo, the Matildas of the 7th Royal Tank Regiment had better luck against the 8th Panzer Regiment. Supported by antitank and artillery fire, the British tanks knocked out fifty of 8th Panzer's eighty tanks in a few hours.[15] A furious and confused fight raged for two days before Rommel, in a move that typified his tactical elan, sent the 5th Light Division and the remnants of the 8th Panzer Regiment on a wide sweep to the south and east, toward the escarpment east of Halfaya pass. The British again found themselves retreating in haste before the onrushing panzers, and only the desperate rearguard action of a handful of Matildas enabled the British forces to escape encirclement.

THE LESSONS OF BATTLEAXE

Operation Battleaxe was important. It marked the last British attempt to relieve Tobruk and led to the sacking of Wavell and his senior commanders. It also highlighted so many of the weaknesses that were to dog British armored forces in North Africa until the arrival of Montgomery over a year later. First among these was the British commanders' tendency to ignore the principle of mass and split their armored force, as well as their artillery and antitank guns, into small, separate formations. This practice frequently allowed an outnumbered but unified German panzer force to destroy each of the quasi-independent columns in turn, achieving local superiority during each engagement.[16] The Germans were also much more adept at combined arms warfare.

Their panzer formations rarely engaged the enemy without support from infantry, artillery, and, most importantly, a screen of antitank guns. In addition, the *Luftwaffe* was much more responsive to ground commanders' requests for close air support than the Desert Air Force, which was controlled from corps headquarters far in the rear.[17]

Another principle of war recklessly flouted by the British was unity of command. Senior British commanders often found their orders being questioned rather than obeyed by subordinates, and a habit developed whereby important decisions were made only after extensive, almost collegial, discussion among commanders and staff. High-level British leaders also tended to direct the battle from the rear and thus often found themselves out of the loop when events on the battlefield required immediate decisions to be made. Rommel, by contrast, was always to be found in the thick of things, so much so that he only narrowly avoided death or capture on several occasions. As he overflew laggardly columns in his Fiesler Storch aerial command post, he would drop written messages to the effect that unless they did not quicken their advance, he would be down soon to shake things up. There was never any doubt where command lay in the *Afrika Korps*.

The Germans also excelled in the recovery and repair of armored vehicles. This was a crucial advantage, because relatively few tanks left on the desert battlefield in the wake of combat had suffered catastrophic kills. Often they had been hit in their tracks or running mechanism or had simply broken down or run out of fuel. Either side, therefore, could considerably offset its losses so long as it controlled the battlefield long enough to tow away the disabled tanks, and while it possessed the technical expertise to fit them. The superior German repair shops even became adept at fixing captured British tanks, which were then fed into the German line. This was a useful skill, as British tanks were very prone to break down, a trait that often led to the abandonment of an otherwise undamaged tank in the middle of the battlefield. Crusader cruiser tanks, just arrived for Battleaxe, were notoriously unreliable, breaking down at the rate of one every ten miles when traveling in column. Radio security was another

British failing. They made no serious attempt to talk in code, and German intelligence officers gleaned much vital information about British movements and plans simply by monitoring unguarded radio traffic. Radio intercepts gave Rommel plenty of advance notice of Operation Battleaxe, for instance.[18]

THE BRITISH LICK THEIR WOUNDS

Something of a lull in the desert war followed Battleaxe, as both armies busied themselves in reorganizing and refitting. On the British side of the frontier, supplies and reinforcements poured in and were reflected in an expansion of the allied forces. The Western Desert Force, as the British-led force in North Africa had been called, was renamed the Eighth Army. The new organization included two corps: XXX Corps, comprising the 7th Armoured and 1st South African Divisions, 22d Guards Brigade, and the 4th Armoured Brigade Group; and XIII Corps, which included two infantry divisions—the 4th Indian and the 2d New Zealand—and 1st Army Tank Brigade. Wavell was replaced as commander in chief in the Middle East by General Sir Claude Auchinleck, previously commander in chief in India, who in turn appointed Lieutenant General Sir Alan Cunningham to command the Eighth Army. Fresh from a string of victories in East Africa, Cunningham was a well-known and popular figure in Britain, but events were to prove him a poor choice to lead the increasingly mechanized Eighth Army. For a start, he was an artillery officer, not a tanker, and his victories in Abyssinia and British Somaliland had been won with infantry forces.[19] This inexperience with armor was compounded by what one writer has called a lack of the intellectual depth necessary to adapt his tactics to the unique demands of desert warfare.[20]

Thus, as they prepared for a major offensive in the autumn, the Allied troops were being led by men with little experience in either armored combat or desert warfare. Opposing them was a man who had spent most of the war leading armored formations, and who had been in the desert far longer than either of them.

This gave the Axis forces an often-overlooked advantage: while British commanders were constantly being replaced by officers who had to learn the rules of armored warfare from scratch, the Germans were led by a general so thoroughly grounded in the rules he knew just how to bend them.

However, the British operational deficiencies were made up in intelligence and logistical prowess and by the superiority of the Royal Navy and Royal Air Force. As the British built up their stockpiles in Egypt, they also enjoyed considerable success in preventing similar supplies from reaching Rommel. Operating from its base at Malta, the Royal Navy sent thousands of tons of Italian shipping to the bottom every month, climaxing on the night of November 8, when it sank all seven ships of a heavily defended Italian convoy, plus one of its destroyer escorts. This and other disasters put such a strain on Rommel's logistics operation that he was forced to introduce fuel rationing.

Nevertheless, enough men and machines reached *Afrika Korps* to allow his organization also to be significantly expanded. Rommel was given command of a large staff brought over by Lieutenant General Alfred Gause, who had originally been appointed German liaison officer to the Italian North African Command. Instead, Gause found himself named Rommel's chief of staff, and his staff became the headquarters for *Panzergruppe Afrika*, the new highest level of German command in the theater. The Afrika Korps, now commanded by Major General Ludwig Crüwell, comprised only two panzer divisions, the 15th and 21st. The latter had been upgraded and redesignated from the 5th Light Division, a common German practice. Throughout the war, the Germans tinkered with the structure of the panzer division—often reducing the number of tanks in response to Hitler's passion for creating more formations—but each division remained a combined arms organization.

The two armored divisions in the *Afrika Korps* each included a panzer regiment with two tank battalions, an artillery regiment, a motorized infantry regiment of three battalions, an antitank battalion of thirty-six guns, and a reconnaissance battalion, plus engineer and administrative units.[21] Together, the panzer divisions could muster 139 Panzer IIIs, 35 Panzer IVs, plus between 50 and

60 Panzer Is and IIs.[22] In addition, Rommel formed another division, the 90th Light, from disparate units already in Africa under his command. Despite having no armor and only four infantry battalions, this division's three field artillery battalions, one antitank battalion, and one dual purpose antiaircraft and antitank 88 mm battalion gave it a lot of firepower.

Rommel used the summer months to train his troops vigorously in an attempt to correct the faults he had noticed during his failed assault on Tobruk and operations Brevity and Battleaxe. The German forces were taught new tactics that emphasized even closer cooperation between armor, antitank guns, and artillery.[23] In September, Rommel decided to try his theories out in practice and launched Operation Midsummer Night's Dream, a reconnaissance in force by the 21st Panzer Division, which penetrated deep into Egypt. The raid was intended to detect and disrupt any British preparations for an offensive aimed at relieving Tobruk, but it ended up being counterproductive.

Not only did the raiding party suffer the indignity, not to mention the risk, of having its panzers run out of fuel, it was forced to return to Cyrenaica under pressure from the RAF and British mobile forces, having completely missed the large British dumps established near the frontier to support the offensive planned by Auchinleck.

OPERATION CRUSADER

When the British launched their next attempt to relieve Tobruk, dubbed Operation Crusader, on November 18, they took Rommel by surprise. Convinced that no British offensive was imminent, he was instead on the verge of launching his own attack on Tobruk, the taking of which he considered essential before he pressed ahead with his plans to invade Egypt and strike at the heart of British power in the Middle East.

The heavy rains that grounded the *Luftwaffe* ensured the level of surprise was total, but Auchinleck and Cunningham chose tactics that initially prevented their exploitation of this advantage.

Cunningham had recognized that the destruction of the German armor, concentrated in the *Afrika Korps*, was the key to victory, but beyond this basic insight, he had little idea how to achieve this aim. The use of other arms in combination with armor to wreak havoc upon German tanks was not explored in detail, and as General Sir William Jackson noted perceptively, "Cunningham's formula for 'Crusader' was to win the great armoured battle in true Nelsonic style by 'engaging the enemy more closely,' and depending upon superior British fighting qualities to win the day."[24]

Unfortunately for the British troops, their German opponents not only possessed similar superior fighting qualities, but were also blessed with commanders who understood the principles of mass and maneuver as they related to armored warfare to a far greater extent than their British counterparts. Although Cunningham focused on the destruction of *Afrika Korps*, his plan of attack split the British armor force into several disparate pieces.

The British plan was similar to most offensives scripted by either side during the North African war. The bulk of the British infantry, concentrated in XIII Corps, was to fix and then encircle the Axis garrisons on the coast before advancing toward Tobruk to join up with XXX Corps, which circled south to seek out and destroy the German armor. In broad brush strokes, there was little wrong with the plan, but the devil was in the details. Cunningham's principal tank formation was the 7th Armoured Division, but instead of keeping this vital outfit intact until reconnaissance elements had found the *Afrika Korps'* location, he cast it to the winds. The division's three armored brigades were each assigned a separate objective, and rather than the mailed fist so beloved of tank warfare aficionados, the Eighth Army's offensive resembled nothing so much as fingers feeling their way in search of the enemy. What followed was three weeks of confusion.

Once the Germans realized what was happening, the *Afrika Korps* descended upon each isolated British armored element in turn. None of the British brigades came to each other's help, and it was left to the tankless 7th Support Group, which combined infantry and artillery and was brilliantly led by Brigadier "Jock" Campbell, to conduct some of the most spirited fighting on the British side. This action took place at the Sidi Rezegh airfield and showcased the Germans' tactical and technical advantages. The *Afrika Korps'* troops displayed their usual skill in combining panzer thrusts with a screen of antitank guns—both 88s and the new long-barreled, towed 50 mm—to confound British tank units.

Much of the credit for the success of the Germans in this and similar engagements was due to their superior technology and, especially, tactics. Of the Germans' 249 tanks, 174 were Panzer IIIs and IVs, the most modern tanks in the *Wehrmacht* arsenal of the time. The Panzer III was armed with a 50 mm main gun, slightly inferior to the 40 mm two-pounder mounted by most British tanks. However, the Germans were adept at masking the weaknesses of their Panzer IIIs by combining them with the more capable Panzer IVs, as they would later combine the Mark IVs with successor models. The Panzer IV, which was the most successful tank design of the early war years, until bested by the Soviet T-34, boasted a 75 mm gun capable of firing both high explosive and smoke rounds at ranges up to 3,000 yards. However, the Germans' greatest skill was in translating any technological edge into a tactical advantage. For example, the British twenty-five-pounder antitank guns outranged the Panzer IVs, but once the Germans got within firing range of the British antitank screens, the unprotected gunners were forced to stop shooting and withdraw, leaving the British nothing effective to throw against the advancing panzers until the German tanks were within the two-pounders' 500-yard range, a distance easily closed.[25]

The Germans eventually overran the Sidi Rezegh position, but Rommel, eager to make the sort of bold thrust into his enemy's rear for which he was renowned, overplayed his hand. Instead of destroying the scattered remnants of XXX Corps in detail, he opted to mass what remained of *Afrika Korps'* armor and make a wide sweep through the desert toward the Egyptian frontier. He intended this audacious action to relieve the invested German garrisons at the border posts of Halfaya and Sollum, plunder the unprotected Allied logistical trains, and cut XIII Corps off from its base of operations.

Had it been executed by fresh, fully equipped units, this plan might have stood some chance of success, but its execution got off to a poor start and never recovered. The exhausted men of the *Afrika Korps* failed to meet Rommel's deadline to be ready to move east by 10 A.M. on November 24. Rommel impatiently set off at 10:40 A.M. at the head of the 21st Panzer Division, which had readied itself first, and reached the frontier wire less than six hours later. Trailing behind were the 15th Panzer Division, with the Italian *Ariete* armored division a long way in the rear. Not only were Rommel's units now strung out, rather than concentrated, but his decision to remove *Afrika Korps* from the decisive battlefield around Sidi Rezegh had allowed what remained of XXX Corps to gather themselves, and these elements clung to the German flanks during the "Dash to the Wire" and so harried them that by the end of the afternoon, Rommel had only sixty panzers left at his disposal. Moreover, the Germans had failed to spot and loot the huge British logistics depots lying well camouflaged in the desert. Their problems were exacerbated by poor radio communications, because the New Zealanders had overrun *Afrika Korps'* headquarters at Gambit earlier in the battle.

During November 25 and 26, Rommel's position on the frontier grew progressively weaker. He had dispersed his units to fight a series of uncoordinated actions along the frontier, none of which resulted in a decisive breakthrough. Meanwhile, unknown to him, XIII Corps' drive westward was proceeding apace, and on the night of November 26, the New Zealanders finally linked up with the Tobruk garrison's breakout at El Duda.

Alarmed by the increasingly frantic cells for assistance from the *Panzergruppe Afrika* staff he had left behind at El Adem, Rommel reluctantly called off the action on the frontier, frustrated in his desire to relieve the besieged German garrisons, and ordered both panzer divisions to return toward Tobruk. There, after some hard fighting, they squeezed the New Zealand infantry out of its positions at El Duda and Sidi Rezegh, forcing the 2d New Zealand Division to retire from the battlefield and resealing the Tobruk perimeter in the process. However, the Axis victory was a

Pyrrhic one. Rommel's forces were now too weak to continue the investment of Tobruk and simultaneously defeat the Eighth Army in the field, and he knew it. When the Italians informed him that no sizable resupply could be expected from Europe before the end of the year, Rommel decided to withdraw his forces. On December 8, the *Afrika Korps* headed west from Bir el Gubi, and the withdrawal continued through Gazala and Benghazi, finally stopping at El Agheila. The last German rear guards retreated across the frontier into Tripolitania on January 6, 1942.[26]

At every stage, Rommel's troops conducted their retreat with the professionalism that had become their hallmark. The withdrawal began with a mere fifty panzers, but transports arriving at Tripoli and Benghazi delivered a further forty-five; the Germans immediately went to the offensive. On December 26, sixty *Afrika Korps* tanks struck the 22d Armoured Brigade outside Agedabia, destroying thirty-seven British tanks at a cost of only seven panzers. Three days later, a similar engagement resulted in a further destruction of twenty-three British tanks for another seven panzers lost. Since the British brigade had brought only ninety tanks to Western Cyrenaica to begin with, the losses effectively neutralized it as an armored strike force.[27]

ROMMEL RECOVERS

There then followed yet another pause in the desert war, as both sides underwent another round of refitting and reorganizing. The *Afrika Korps* was to emerge more revitalized than its opponents. Its tank strength had risen to eighty-four, and that of its Italian allies to eighty-nine. The British failure to deliver as crushing a blow to the Germans in retreat as they had against the Italians at Beda Fomm a year previously was to prove telling. Meanwhile, the Axis forces in the Mediterranean were finally putting enough pressure on the Royal Navy and Royal Air Force to improve communications with North Africa. Consequently, supplies were reaching Tripoli at last, including more panzers as well as vitally needed fuel and ammunition. As usual, Rommel used the spare time to train his units ever more thoroughly in desert warfare.

In contrast, the British again frittered away a hard-won advantage. Men and supplies that should have been destined for a final assault by the Eighth Army on Tripoli were instead diverted to the Far East. There were also problems at the higher levels of command. Auchinleck had relieved Cunningham for losing his nerve during Operation Crusader and replaced him as commander with Major General Neil Ritchie, the deputy chief of his general staff. Nevertheless, the British continued their debilitating practice of reaching decisions via debate and treating orders as items open to discussion.

New, half-trained units appeared in the desert to take the place of those worn down during Crusader. The exhausted 7th Armoured Division was withdrawn from the front and sent to Tobruk to be reequipped. From there its battle-hardened 7th Armoured Brigade was dispatched to Burma. Replacing the division on the front lines was the 1st Armoured Division, new to the theater and under optimal strength. The move exemplified the different approaches to the question of reinforcement and battlefield replacements adopted by the British and Germans. The British would withdraw an experienced, battle-tested formation such as the 7th Armoured Division in its entirety and replace it with a new unit whose commanders and troops had little or no experience of mobile warfare in the desert, but the Germans tended to replace troops on an individual basis. Therefore, even in units that had taken many casualties and therefore received many fresh replacements, there remained a hard core of experienced warriors to impart vital lessons to the new arrivals. Institutional memory was not lost.

It did not take long for the Rommel's chief of intelligence, Major F. W. von Mellenthin, to realize his commander not only enjoyed temporary local superiority in men and matériel, but also that the forces opposing Rommel across the frontier were dispersed and lacked unity. The confused state of mind that gripped many of the British commanders in the forward area was easily divined by Mellenthin, as the British still spoke openly to each other over the radio without the slightest attempt at using code. Mellenthin's calculations indicated *Panzergruppe Afrika* would enjoy superiority in Western Cyrenaica until January 25.[28] On January 21, Rommel attacked.

Taking the British completely by surprise, Rommel pushed his mobile forces forward in two columns. On the left, the mobile elements of the 90th Light Division and some tanks from the 21st Panzer Division advanced along the Via Balbia, the main coast road. This assault group was called Group Marcks. To their right, the *Afrika Korps* advanced through the desert.

The offensive ran into very little organized opposition from the Eighth Army. The British retreated in haste, allowing the panzers to shoot up their supply columns. An attempt by Rommel to encircle the 1st Armoured Division east of Agedabia was only thwarted by the 21st Panzer Division's failure to close the circle in time, allowing most of the British armor to escape. Nevertheless, Rommel was determined to destroy the 1st Armoured Division, and on January 24, he gave orders to advance to Msus in pursuit. The next day, Panzer Regiment 8 of the 15th Panzer Division ran into what Mellenthin described as "very superior tank forces."

> These were overwhelmed by Panzer Regiment 8, closely supported by antitank guns and artillery; it soon became apparent that the British tank units had no battle experience and they were completely demoralized by the onslaught of 15th Panzer. At times the pursuit attained a speed of 15 miles per hour, and the British columns fled madly over the desert in one of the most extraordinary routs of the war.[29]

By the end of January 25, 15th Panzer had reached Msus airfield, capturing a dozen aircraft on the runway, and had amassed 96 tanks, 38 guns and 190 trucks in war booty taken from the British. Only lack of fuel prevented the Germans from further exploiting the disarray of the British forces. On January 29, Rommel captured Benghazi, after taking personal command of Group Marcks and leading it on what Mellenthin describes as "a brilliant march through pouring rain and over very difficult ground." A thousand prisoners from the 4th Indian Division fell with the town into Rommel's hands, after he had misled Ritchie into diverting his remaining armor into the desert to meet a nonexistent threat, an Afrika Krops feint in the direction of Mechili.[30]

Realizing his position in Western Cyrenaica was now untenable, Ritchie withdrew his forces to Gazala. Rommel's exhausted troops, now collectively known as *Panzerarmee Afrika,* lacked the strength to do anything more than follow, and on February 6, their astonishing advance halted before Gazala. For four months the two sides waited, glowering at each other across vast minefields while they replenished their depleted stocks of men, vehicles, and supplies. The *Luftwaffe* mounted increasingly heavy attacks on Malta, which had the twin effects of hampering British resupply operations in the Mediterranean while covering Axis ships and aircraft ferrying matériel to Rommel.

On their side of the front, the British were engaged in a methodical buildup of supplies that could only mean they were preparing to go on the offensive. Sensing this, Rommel's natural instinct was to preempt the British attack. At the end of April, Hitler authorized an offensive against the British positions in Cyrenaica, on the condition that once Tobruk fell, the attack would halt. Rommel decided to attack in May, before the British preponderance in matériel became insurmountable. Even so, he was still heavily outnumbered by an experienced, confident enemy.

INTO THE CAULDRON

On the even of his offensive, the Axis forces had 560 tanks in North Africa. Of these, 228 were Italian M13s, and 50 were Panzer IIs, which were armed with a 20 mm main gun and useless against Allied armor. The rest were an assortment of Mark IIIs and IVs, including 19 Mark III Specials, boasting heavier armor and the new long-barreled L/60 50 mm guns, and 40 Mark IVs with 75 mm guns.[31] Opposing the panzers was a British

inventory of almost 1,000 tanks. Pride of place among these belonged to the recently arrived Grant, a British adaptation of the
American M3 Lee medium tank. The Grant was armed with a
turret-mounted 37 mm and a 75 mm gun in a side sponson. Together, these conferred upon it the attributes of both the German Mark III and Mark IV. Its 37 mm gun fired good capped
ammunition to be used in an antitank role similar to the Mark
III's, and the 75 mm gun fired a high explosive shell for use
against soft targets at long ranges, just like the Mark IV. The
Grant also had 57 mm frontal armor and a reputation for reliability. Its weaknesses lay in its awkward design: the low mounting
of the 75 mm meant it could not engage from a hull-down position, and it had a very limited traverse.[32]

The two British armored divisions, the 1st and the 7th, had
167 Grants between them, in addition to 149 Stuarts, or "Hon-
eys," as the British called the light tanks, and 257 Crusaders. The
Eighth Army's two separate tank brigades shared 110 Matilda
and 166 Valentine infantry tanks, while a third armored brigade
was given 75 Grants and 70 Stuarts. In the antitank arena, the
British had begun to receive limited quantities of the six-
pounder gun, which were distributed to the Royal Artillery antitank units, and the antitank units in turn gave their less-effective
two-pounders to the infantry brigades of the two armored divisions. German antitank screens were bolstered by more 88s, as
well as some captured Russian 76 mm guns, which were more effective than the German 50 mm pieces.

Auchinleck also completely revamped British military organization in the theater. The brigade group replaced the division as
the principal combat unit. Brigade groups came in three types:
armored, with three tank regiments; motor, with three motorized
infantry battalions; and infantry, with three dismounted infantry
battalions. Each group was self-sufficient in field artillery, antitank and antiaircraft guns, engineers, and supply troops. The armored divisional support groups were broken up to provide the
armored brigade groups' infantry and artillery.[33]

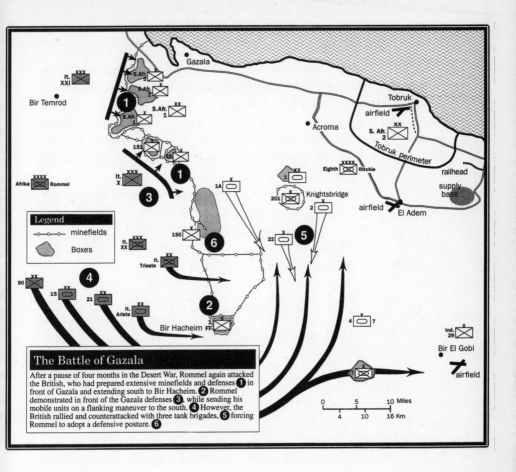

Gazala

It.
XXI

Bir Temrod

S.Afr.
3

S.Afr.
2

1

S.Afr.
1

S.Afr.
1

XX

Tobruk

airfield

Acroma

S. Afr.
2

XX

Tobruk perimeter

railhead

supply
base

It.
X

XXX

Afrika   Rommel

XXXX

3

151

69

1

1A

XX

Eighth   Ritchie

XXXX

201

XX

Knightsbridge

2

El Adem

airfield

Legend

minefields

Boxes

It.
XX

XX

150

6

22

X

5

X

It.
Trieste

XX

90

XX

4

15

21

It.
Ariete

XX

2

1

Bir Hacheim   FF

XX

4   7

X

Ind.
29

XX

Bir El Gobi

airfield

X

The Battle of Gazala

After a pause of four months in the Desert War, Rommel again attacked
the British, who had prepared extensive minefields and defenses ❶ in
front of Gazala and extending south to Bir Hacheim. ❷ Rommel
demonstrated in front of the Gazala defenses ❸, while sending his
mobile units on a flanking maneuver to the south. ❹ However, the
British rallied and counterattacked with three tank brigades, ❺ forcing
Rommel to adopt a defensive posture. ❻

0   5   10 Miles

4   10   16 Km

When Rommel launched his attack on the night of May 26, he did so against an opponent that believed itself well prepared to meet whatever the Desert Fox might throw at it. The Eighth Army had built an impressive system of fortifications. Extensive minefields formed the first layer of the British defenses, behind which their brigade groups were each installed in heavily defended areas called boxes.

At first, Rommel's attack went as planned. *Afrika Korps* and the 90th Light Division's route skirted the British via the by-now-familiar southern hook and began to dispose of British formations as they offered themselves up for destruction, one by one; but by midafternoon of May 27, the attack had ground to a halt. Three British armored brigades, the 22d, the 2d, and the 1st Army Tank, rallied and inflicted damaging casualties in uncoordinated but effective attacks on the *Afrika Korps* from the north, east, and west. During these attacks, the Grant showed itself to be one of the most potent weapon systems on the battlefield. This came as a nasty shock to the Germans, whose intelligence had failed to reveal its presence in the theater. A chaotic situation developed, and by the end of the day, the German position was very unstable.

German tank strength had been reduced by over a third, and the Allies had cut their supply route, which ran south of the Free French Brigade box at Bir Hacheim that marked the bottom of the British defenses. Desperately low on fuel and water and hemmed in by British armor on three sides and minefields to the west, *Afrika Korps* laagered in a patch of desert that became known as the Cauldron. Rommel tried to clear a path west through the minefields along which to pass his logistics trains but was interrupted by the British 150th Brigade Group.

Still, the British failed to take advantage of the opportunity, lapsing into command by committee just when a firm hand was required. Auchinleck and Ritchie failed to commit their armor to a coordinated attack on the Cauldron during any of the last three days of May, when such an assault would probably have wiped out the *Afrika Korps*. Instead they dithered, letting Rommel launch a ferocious attack, backed by Stukas, against the

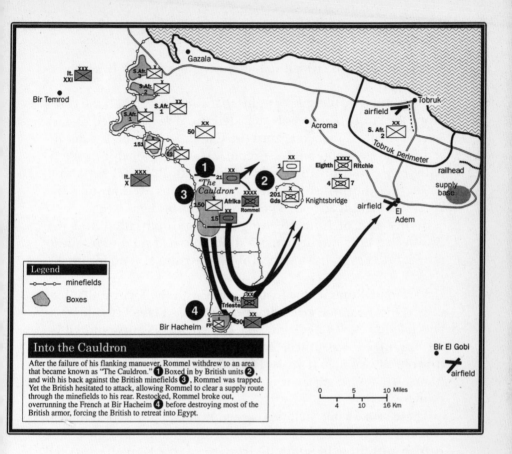

Bir Temrod

It. XXI

Gazala

S.Afr. 3

S.Afr. 2

S.Afr. 1

S.Afr. 1

50 XX

151

69

It. X

1

21 XX

"The Cauldron"

3

2

1 XX

Acroma

Eighth Ritchie

4 X 7

201 Gds X

Knightsbridge

Afrika XXXX Rommel

150

15

It. Trieste XX

4

1 Fr

90

Bir Hacheim

airfield

Tobruk

S. Afr. 2 XX

Tobruk perimeter

railhead

supply base

airfield

El Adem

Bir El Gobi

airfield

Legend
—o—o—o— minefields

Boxes

Into the Cauldron

After the failure of his flanking manuever, Rommel withdrew to an area that became known as "The Cauldron." **1** Boxed in by British units **2**, and with his back against the British minefields **3**, Rommel was trapped. Yet the British hesitated to attack, allowing Rommel to clear a supply route through the minefields to his rear. Restocked, Rommel broke out, overrunning the French at Bir Hacheim **4** before destroying most of the British armor, forcing the British to retreat into Egypt.

0   5   10 Miles

4   10   16 Km

150th Brigade box, which fell after several hours of heavy fighting on June 1.

Invigorated by the supply trains that could now reach the Cauldron, the *Afrika Korps* easily defeated the uncoordinated attacks Ritchie finally launched against the Cauldron on June 5. After investing Bir Hacheim until the remnants of the French Brigade finally broke out on the night of June 10, Rommel set about destroying the British armored brigades clustered around the 201st Guards Brigade box known as Knightsbridge.

By the end of June 13, Knightsbridge had fallen and the British had only seventy tanks left. Ritchie had no option but to retreat into Egypt, leaving the Tobruk garrison to fend for itself.

This time, Rommel made no mistake with the fortress that had caused him so much grief the previous year. A concerted June 20 attack led by *Afrika Korps* infantry and engineers encountered little organized resistance. The Commonwealth troops fought bravely as usual, but in isolated groups. Within twenty-four hours, the entire garrison of over 30,000 Allied troops had surrendered.

These remarkable victories earned Rommel promotion to field marshal on June 22, and left him at the gateway to Egypt. The British withdrew in some disarray to Mersa Matruh, pursued doggedly by the *Afrika Korps*. Luftwaffe Field Marshal Albert Kesselring, in charge of German operations in the Mediterranean, suggested that Rommel wait for an Axis invasion of Malta before launching an invasion of Egypt that would stretch his logistics tail to the breaking point. However, Rommel now had the bit between his teeth and, buoyed by vast amounts of captured British supplies, had no intention of letting his quarry slip away to regather its strength.

At Mersa Matruh he was again able to capitalize on British command and control failings to force *Afrika Korps*, now down to fifty tanks, between XXX Corps and XIII Corps on the night of June 26.[34] As British units formed up to repulse the attack the next evening, XIII Corps commander General "Strafer" Gott, believing the situation far worse than it was, ordered a retreat, and to Rommel's astonishment and delight, the British pulled back.

The victory at Mersa Matruh left both sides mentally and physically exhausted. For the high-spirited Axis troops, the abortive battle marked the apex of their fortunes in Africa. The British and Commonwealth troops, in contrast, retreated headlong before a German commander they had come to view as invincible. Their retreat finally came to a halt on June 20 at a forty-mile-wide gap between the Mediterranean and the impassable salt marsh of the Qattara Depression. The gap was named after a small, dusty station astride the coastal railroad: El Alamein.

THE EL ALAMEIN LINE

The British had been preparing a linear series of defenses—chiefly minefields—along what became known as the El Alamein line, and now they fell back upon them in the knowledge that failure to hold the Germans here would mean the probable loss of Egypt and give Rommel and Germany access to the oil fields of the Middle East. In Cairo, smoke could be seen above the British Embassy and GHQ as the staffs there burned documents to prevent them falling into German hands.[35]

But 140 miles to the northwest, Auchinleck was about to stem the tide, if not immediately turn it. He had relieved Ritchie prior to the Mersa Matruh debacle and had taken personal command of the Eighth Army. Now he set about putting some of its more obvious wrongs to right. His overriding imperative was "to keep Eighth Army in being,"[36] even if territory had to be sacrificed to do so. To this end, he refined the brigade group concept, keeping only as much infantry in the front lines as could be carried by available transport. Brigade battle groups now centered around artillery and fully motorized infantry, greatly reducing the risk of units being caught flat-footed and encircled due to lack of transport. Unfortunately, this also entailed breaking up units and command relationships at a crucial time.[37]

Auchinleck's new approach also emphasized the traditional British strength in artillery. From now on, indirect fire (i.e., fire brought on a target that is not in the direct line of sight of the artillery) was to be concentrated at the highest possible level, and brigade groups' actions were to be coordinated with this aim in mind.[38]

These and other steps were necessary because the Eighth Army lacked the manpower to station troops along the length of the El Alamein line. Instead, Auchinleck positioned units in prepared boxes, diminishing in size from the sea to the depression.[39] The brigade battle groups were to rely on their mobility, the Eight Army's armor, in which they lacked confidence because of recent beatings, and its powerful artillery for their salvation. All combined to give the complex defenses an enormous strength.[40]

To the relief of all British concerned, the concept worked. Rommel spent the first few days of July trying to find a chink in Auchinleck's new suit of armor, but each German offensive was met with a fearsome artillery barrage, while the 1st Armoured Division got the better of the 15th Panzer Division in encounters on the Ruweisat Ridge on July 1 and 4.[41]

The initiative now passed to the British. They again were able to enjoy the advantages of operating close to their rear area stocks, and troops and equipment destined for the Eighth Army continued to arrive at Egyptian ports. For their part, the Germans again faced the challenge of operating with worn-out vehicles at the end of a very long supply train. Auchinleck launched a series of attacks against the Axis lines, all directed at those parts of the defenses manned by the Italians. To counter these, Rommel began to corset Italian units, stiffening his line by placing German outfits among them.

In general, British armor, which a year previously had sought contact with *Afrika Korps'* tanks, now was much less inclined to tangle with German armor. However, the 23d Armoured Brigade, fresh from England and completely inexperienced, lost over 100 tanks and 200 men in two attacks supporting first the New Zealanders on Ruweisat Ridge and then the Australians on Miteiriya Ridge.[42]

After several weeks of tussling, the line stabilized, and both sides concentrated on building up their forces and planning for the climactic encounter to come. When his intelligence staff told him that the British would not be able to replace their June losses until mid-September, Rommel made one final attempt to seize the initiative. On August 30, he launched *Afrika Korps* and the Italian XX Corps in one of his patented armored sweeps around the south of the British defenses, hoping to establish himself in the British rear, thereby breaking up the British defenses and giving him another chance to push toward the burgeoning British depots in the Nile Delta.[43]

On this occasion, however, Rommel's judgment failed him. The armored thrust spent itself breaking through thick minefields while it was harried by British screening forces on its flanks and bombarded by the RAF. Rommel was forced to adjust his planned route, bringing the armored divisions north face to face with the heaviest British defenses on the Alam Halfa Ridge. Unable to close with the British armor there because of fierce fire from the six-pounder antitank guns on the ridge, the Axis attack ground to a halt, and the long columns of German and Italian vehicles found themselves parked in an RAF killing ground from which there was no escape but whence they came.

ROMMEL IS FORCED TO DEFEND

Rommel was very ill at the time, and it took him two days to reach the decision to withdraw. His men were thus needlessly exposed to prolonged aerial bombardment. When he did give the order to pull back, his troops carried out the order with characteristic professionalism, holding off British counterattacks as they retreated. Eventually, the front stabilized on September 6, the Axis forces having withdrawn to positions they seized from the British at the start of their foray. Rommel now knew he was left with no alternative but to prepare his forces to fight a desperate defensive battle against an enemy able to choose the time and place of attack and whose material superiority grew greater by the day. Supplies were also reaching the Axis troops, but not of the type or in the quantity required. Instead of fresh armored formations, Rommel was sent the 164th Light Africa Division, which arrived in Tobruk from Crete in July, to be followed by the Ramcke Parachute Brigade. The Italians sent over the Folgore Parachute Division and the Pistoia and Friouli Infantry Divisions.[44]

All these units lacked their own transport, and as such they were "as good as useless in the open desert," according to Rommel.[45] However, they did constitute thousands of extra mouths needing food and water, which, like everything else except German courage in the face of adversity, were in short supply behind the Axis lines. His shortage of supplies, particularly of fuel, forced Rommel to adopt static, attritional tactics that were otherwise anathema to him. Rather than concentrate the *Afrika Korps'* armor to deliver a decisive counterattack, lack of fuel and overwhelming Allied air supremacy necessitated keeping it in six Italo-German groups close behind the front lines, concealed to the greatest extent possible, so it could react to any Allied penetrations of the Axis infantry. Rommel knew that only if his armored units were fighting a close battle with the British would they be safe from the sort of aerial pounding the RAF had delivered at Alam Halfa.

In front of the armor sat the Italian and German infantry, mixed in among each other so that each Italian battalion was sited next to a German battalion. Between them and the British lines lay 500,000 antitank and antipersonnel mines sown in minefields whose intricate shape earned the description *honeycombed.* The main mine belts ran north-south, with a few outposts in the eastern section, while most of the infantry and antitank guns lay in and behind the western field, which was between 2,000 and 3,000 yards in depth and located 1,000 to 2,000 yards west of the first belt.[46] Rommel hoped to mire any British penetration in these defenses long enough that his mobile reserves could be brought into action to prevent a breakthrough.

The Axis powers' inability to wrest control of Malta from Britain meant the cards were stacked against Rommel from the start. The Eighth Army's strength stood at 195,000 men and 1,029 medium tanks, versus figures of 104,000 (including only 50,000 German) and 496 respectively for *Panzerarmee Afrika.* The Allies enjoyed similar advantages in antitank guns (1,451, versus

800, including only 88 of the 88s) and artillery pieces (908 versus 500).[47] Of equal importance to the outcome of the forthcoming battle was the new spirit within the Eighth Army.

THE COMING OF MONTGOMERY

During the first week of August, British Prime Minister Winston Churchill and his military advisers arrived in Egypt on a fact-finding tour. What they found, particularly the troops' lack of morale and low confidence in the theater's senior military leadership, convinced them a new approach was needed in the Western Desert and that the present high command in Cairo was not up to the task of providing it. Within a week, Auchinleck and Ritchie had been relieved of their posts. In their stead London posted General Sir Harold Alexander as commander in chief, Near East, and Lieutenant General Bernard Law Montgomery as Eighth Army commander.

For the Eighth Army, Montgomery was the right man in the right place at the right time. Like Rommel, he mixed easily in the company of his troops and was as at home in the field as he was in his headquarters. During his first weeks in command, he toured his component units, chatting with the soldiers and imparting his infectious self-confidence. He was also ideally suited to handle the tactical challenges of the El Alamein position. An infantryman by training, he had been badly wounded early in World War I and had spent the rest of the conflict as a staff officer. He was fascinated by the organizational element in warfare and was able to plan an operation so comprehensively that he could usually foresee the outcome of the battle before it had begun.[48]

The situation at El Alamein was thus tailor-made for Montgomery, as it presented him with the opportunity to plan a set-piece battle with many of the attritional qualities more closely associated with those of World War I than World War II. For once, infantry and artillery, traditional British strengths, would be equally as important as armor. Montgomery's meticulous attack might lack the dash of Rommel's improvisations, but it overcame the British penchant to use tanks without adequate support from other arms.

One of Montgomery's first steps was to do away with the Jock columns—small mixed units that combined antiaircraft, field artillery, motorized infantry, and antitank guns—and other similar "private armies" that had sprung up throughout the Allied forces; this was a matter of searching for the proper scale of formations, not a retreat from combining arms. From now on, divisions would fight as divisions, with all appropriate support from higher headquarters. Furthermore, he let it be known, there was to be no more questioning of orders from subordinate commanders.

As Montgomery planned in detail, his troops trained intensively in the desert for the offensive he was designing. His task was made easier because the Qattara Depression marked an impenetrable southern boundary to the El Alamein lines, meaning it was one of the few places in the Western Desert where neither commander could expect to mount or receive a sweeping armored thrust around his southernmost units into his rear. Montgomery wanted to make his breakthrough in the northern sector of the line and planned it for late October. To achieve surprise, the Eighth Army went to great lengths to give the Germans the impression the attack would come in the southern sector, with a starting date of late November. To this end, large numbers of dummy tanks were moved south and phony radio traffic was broadcast suggesting the deployment of British armored formations in that area.

Montgomery was well aware of the limitations upon maneuver that Rommel's perilous logistics situation had imposed upon him. He also knew that destruction of the German armor was the key to victory. Instead of sending his armor headlong into the Axis positions in search of *Afrika Korps*, he planned to wage a classical battle of attrition, wearing down, or "crumbling," as he called it, the Axis infantry formations with artillery, air, and infantry attacks before bringing his armor to bear at the places a breakthrough was most likely and where the German armor would most likely be forced to rush.

Montgomery had at his disposal XIII Corps and XXX Corps, but he wished to also create a British equivalent to the tank-heavy *Afrika Korps*, and so X Corps, previously an infantry formation, was redesigned as a Corps de Chasse, with three armor divisions and one infantry division.[49] To equip this force, a new American tank was delivered to Egypt: the Sherman, which boasted a turret-mounted, long-barreled 75 mm gun capable of firing high explosive shells to take out enemy gun positions while standing out of reach of the German guns themselves. President Roosevelt had sent 300 Shermans to Egypt when the British position looked desperate, stripping them from American units to do so.

OPERATION LIGHTFOOT: THE TURNING POINT

On September 23, a very ill Rommel left North Africa on sick leave. He was still away a month to the day later, when, as a full moon rose in the desert sky, the largest artillery barrage the world had ever seen heralded the start of Montgomery's Operation Lightfoot, the Battle of El Alamein.

For a few hours, the battle seemed to be going more or less according to Montgomery's plan. XIII Corps' divisionary attack in the southern sector penetrated the first mine belt and fixed the 21st Panzer and Ariete Divisions in the south. Farther north, XXX Corps' four assault divisions made good headway at first, overrunning the German outposts on the eastern mine belt, but as they penetrated deeper into the minefield, they became mired in the Devil's Gardens of booby traps and antipersonnel mines. Mine-clearing tanks with flails mounted to their bows broke down repeatedly, and lanes for the armor had to be cleared laboriously by hand, further slowing the advance.

By dawn on the morning of October 24, XXX Corps' infantry brigades were still between 1,000 and 2,000 yards from their objectives, as huge traffic jams developed behind them. Montgomery decided to continue the attack's tactical break-in before switching to the crumbling operation. The term *break-in* was taken from the successful but limited British attacks on the

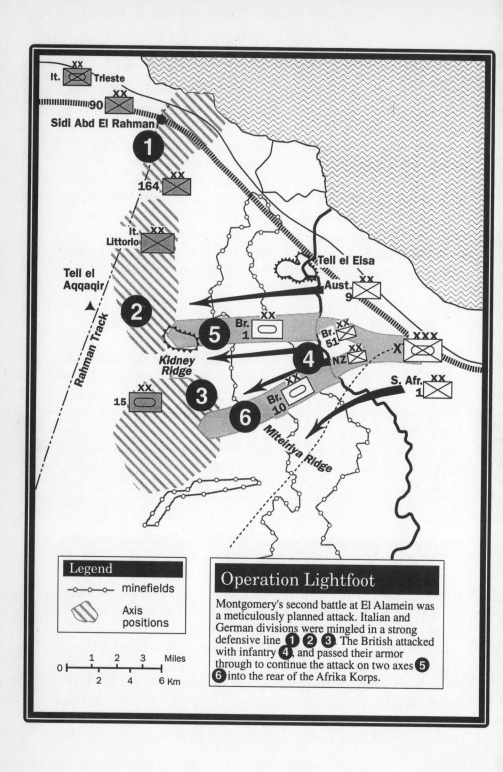

It. XX Trieste

XX 90

Sidi Abd El Rahman

1

164 XX

It. XX Littorio

Tell el Aqqaqir

2

Tell el Eisa

Aust. XX 9

5 Br. XX 1

Br. XX 51

4 NZ XX

X XXX

Kidney Ridge

3

15 XX

Br. XX 10

6

S. Afr. XX 1

Miteiriya Ridge

Rahman Track

Operation Lightfoot

Montgomery's second battle at El Alamein was a meticulously planned attack. Italian and German divisions were mingled in a strong defensive line **1** **2** **3**. The British attacked with infantry **4**, and passed their armor through to continue the attack on two axes **5** **6** into the rear of the Afrika Korps.

German trench lines in 1918. A break-in did not drive as deeply into the enemy rear, and thus was easier to execute and support logistically than the breakthroughs favored by the Germans. A new element had been added to the equation as the RAF kept up its pounding of Axis lines, flying over 1,000 sorties that day alone.[50] Rommel's replacement, General Georg Stumme, was killed on this day when he was thrown from his car during an Australian attack and suffered a heart attack. *Afrika Korps* Commander Major General Ritter von Thoma assumed temporary command of the panzer army, but Rommel was already on his way back to the desert, roused from his sickbed by a call from Hitler.

When Rommel arrived at the front, he found his defenses holding up well to the British assaults. On the afternoon of October 24, X Corps' 1st Armored Division had made another attempt to break out of the minefields through the northernmost of the two corridors along which Montgomery hoped to send his armor. By the end of the day, the division's 2d Armoured Brigade had fought itself to within 1,000 yards of its objective, a low hump of desert called Kidney Ridge, for the loss of 31 Shermans. Later that night, Major General Alec Gatehouse's 10th Armoured Division found itself in a similarly uncomfortable situation trying to open up a southern corridor to the central section of Miteiriya Ridge, with German bombs and artillery raining down upon it as its sappers inched their way forward through the dense minefields.

When the division's brigade commanders suggested the attack was so far behind schedule it should be called off, Gatehouse and X Corps commander Lieutenant General H. Lumsden met with Montgomery to discuss the situation. Both argued that the battle should be halted to avoid further waste of men and matériel, but Montgomery would have none of it, asserting that the British armor must fight its way out, no matter what losses it took. One writer called this "probably the psychological turning point not only of the Battle of El Alamein, but of the North African Campaign as well."[51]

The 10th Armoured Division eventually succeeded in opening some narrow paths in the minefields through which it passed its two armored brigades, but at dawn neither was more than 1,000 yards west of Miteiriya, and rather than expose themselves on the forward edge of the ridge to the fire of the 88s, they both withdrew to the eastern side again, Montgomery's obstinancy notwithstanding.

The Eighth Army commander now gave up his attempts to push his armored formations out in front of his infantry prior to the start of his crumbling operations. With the battle stalled along the Miteiriya Ridge, he decided to switch his focus and concentrate instead on the northernmost sector of the front, where the infantry of the 9th Australian Division, under Major General Sir Leslie Morshead, were making better headway. Montgomery permitted Morshead to go ahead with plans to advance northward toward Point 29, the crucial feature in the coastal sector of the battle, while the 10th Armoured and 51st Highland Divisions would continue their attacks around Kidney Ridge.[52]

ROMMEL GAMBLES; MONTGOMERY TRUMPS

By dawn on October 26, motorized Australian infantry, supported by artillery and tanks, had seized the lightly defended Point 29 position, but the hapless 10th Armoured Division was making little progress in a muddled operation farther south. Rommel, back in command, was concerned at the loss of Point 29, because it placed his coastal defenses in jeopardy. He therefore decided to concentrate enough armor to launch a counterattack against the British by moving 21st Panzer northward from its defensive positions in the southern sector of the Axis lines, even though he knew he did not have enough fuel to allow the division to return if events warranted it.[53] Meanwhile, he restrengthened his coastal sector by bringing the 90th Light and Trieste Divisions forward from El Daba.[54]

The next day, Rommel made a final throw of the dice, hurling the 15th and 21st Panzer Divisions against the British salient at Kidney Ridge. In the past, Rommel had reversed perilous situations in which he was outnumbered by launching ferocious combined arms attacks against the outmaneuvered British, but this was not to be one of those occasions. Despite the concentrated fire of Stuka dive-bombers and every Axis artillery and antiaircraft gun in the northern sector, the British stood firm and directed a withering fire in return at the German armor as it began to move forward. In the face of murderous fire from dug-in British tanks and antitank guns, the panzers were forced to withdraw. Meanwhile, in the north, an attempt by 90th Light to retake Point 29 was beaten off by RAF bombers and British artillery fire.[55]

Rommel now knew that any chance of outright victory had deserted him, but he still hoped to achieve a stalemate and thus maintain his El Alamein position. On October 28, he decided to concentrate almost all German units on the front in the northern sector, where the British were clearly making their main effort, and succeeded in holding off three British attacks, albeit at the cost of many panzers. Despite the extraordinarily slow progress the Eighth Army was making on the map, Montgomery's strategy of attrition was succeeding. His tanks and antitank guns were destroying panzers for which Rommel had no replacements, and while British losses in equipment were significant, they were made up from the Eighth Army's seemingly bottomless reserves.

Montgomery decided the time was now ripe to end what he termed the "dog fight" phase of the battle and launch the breakout into the Axis rear. This operation, which he named Supercharge, was originally intended to strike the Axis lines near the Coast Road. However, when intelligence reports indicated this was the area of greatest German strength, he moved the axis of attack farther south, so that it would now follow a line parallel to and slightly north of the 1st Armoured Division's original northern corridor.[56]

The plan called for the 2d New Zealand Division plus two additional infantry brigades and the 23d Armoured Brigade to create a 4,000-yard-wide breach in the Axis lines through which the infantry would advance 5,000 yards before passing the 9th Armoured Brigade through. The Ninth Armoured would then advance a further 2,000 yards to cut the Rahman track before X

Corps' armor smashed through to wreak havoc in the Axis rear areas.[57]

Montgomery launched Supercharge on the night of November 1, having delayed a day to allow the New Zealanders to assemble behind the jumping-off point. As with Lightfoot, the operation was preceded by intensive RAF bombing and a well-planned artillery barrage, and at first, all went smoothly, the infantry brigades moving forward more quickly than during the previous operation because the ground was less heavily mined. However, things broke down when the 9th Armoured Brigade tried to make its way through in almost zero visibility. When the brigade finally emerged on the other side of the breach the next morning, it came under intense fire from most of the *Afrika Korps'* remaining 88s, knocking out seventy of its ninety-four tanks.[58]

Behind the 9th Armoured Brigade, the 1st Armoured Division also had problems cutting through the traffic jams that clogged the gaps through the mine belts, but eventually it, too, broke through and prepared itself for the climactic struggle ahead. Fortunately for the British, Rommel had misjudged their intentions and concluded the main attack would come from the Australian sector, and he had ordered Thoma to counter it with all available panzers. This error was corrected, but it delayed Thoma's arrival at the breach until 11 A.M. He then made a vain attempt to halt and drive back the British assault, which he repeated with similar lack of success three hours later. In both cases the British used artillery, antitank guns, and armor in hull defilade positions, all supported by RAF bombing, to stop the German counterattack in its tracks, knocking out seventy German and forty-seven Italian tanks in the process.[59]

Panzerarmee Afrika was now holding out by sheer force of will. The *Afrika Korps* had only thirty-five working tanks left, and the army's supply situation, tenuous at the best of times, was now desperate.[60] During the course of the fighting on November 2, the army fired off 450 tons of ammunition, Rommel reported, while only 190 tons arrived in the theater, aboard three destroyers in Tobruk harbor.[61]

Rommel knew the game was up; if he wanted to save what remained of his superbly trained army, he would have to withdraw, and soon. His tired troops, who had served him so well during the previous year and nine months, were still holding off X Corps' armor, but the 51st Highland Division had opened a crack in the Axis lines, attacking southwest to displace the Trieste Motorized Division from the Skinflint area. Rommel planned a speedy getaway, with all armor and motorized units holding the British offensive off until as many dismounted infantry as possible had been withdrawn toward Fuka, about forty miles west of El Alamein. The mobile forces would then also retreat in stages to a line drawn south from Fuka.[62]

This plan was already under way when a signal from Hitler arrived at 1:30 P.M. on November 3, ordering Rommel "to stand fast and throw every gun and every man into the battle."[63] The absurdity of the order shocked Rommel and his staff, but they felt they had no alternative but to obey. Reluctantly, units already withdrawing in good order were told to turn around and form up again in defensive positions west of the Rahman track. This action, however, had little effect other than to consign thousands of Axis infantrymen to captivity. A little over a day after Hitler's order arrived, Rommel decided that saving what he could of his army was more important than blind loyalty to his *führer*, and gave the order to withdraw. The Battle of El Alamein was over.

A TIDAL STRUGGLE

Still, the British triumph was far from complete. At the conclusion of the battle, Montgomery had planned to exploit success to the utmost by catching the retreating panzer army and destroying it in detail, but it was not to be. Rommel's now-tiny force—the major German formations numbered less than 5,000 men and ten tanks[64]—effected its withdrawal with consummate professionalism, while the exhausted British could not find the energy to finish off the job. Their failure to do so guaranteed that the allies had not seen the last of Field Marshal Erwin Rommel yet.

Montgomery's victory at El Alamein severely weakened Axis strength in North Africa. Months of fighting were still to follow, including the blooding of the U.S. Army at Kasserine Pass, but it was clear that no amount of German tactical prowess could offset the growing Allied strength in the theater. The *Wehrmacht* logistics system, not truly tested in France, had not proved sufficient to supply even the resourceful Desert Fox. Armored warfare rewarded men of genius, but that genius could only be measured by the performance of machines—machines that needed to be fueled, given ammunition, repaired, and replaced when they were broken or destroyed. Even as the *Afrika Korps* struggled to stave off the crushing weight of British matériel and Montgomery's clinical application of it, Adolf Hitler threw his flawed war machine into a far greater task.

Losing the Battle of El Alamein was a bitter pill for Rommel, but did not compare to the agony he felt as he saw Hitler respond with an unstinted flow of men and matériel to the Allied invasion of North Africa in Operation Torch. Almost all of these would be killed or captured when the Germans were at last forced out of Africa on May 12, 1943, with the fall of Tunisia. Some 250,000 well-equipped Germans and Italians surrendered. If they had been provided to Rommel—as they could have been—when he was at the gates of Egypt, the war would have taken a different turn.

CHAPTER THREE

OSTFRONT, 1941–1944

Barbarossa, Zitadelle, Bagration

THE TANK BATTLES of the World War II Eastern Front were the epic armor clashes of the war—indeed, of all history. The stage was unimaginably vast: the theater of war fanned out north and east from Poland thousands of miles to the empty, unending steppes of central Russia and Leningrad, Moscow, and Stalingrad, the graveyard of the German Sixth Army. The fighting was bitterly savage: the confrontation between National Socialism and Soviet Communism consumed millions of human beings, many of whom died not heroically in battle but from acts of unspeakable cruelty. In the early years, the German generals were titans, but in time, all were humbled by their tasks: the geniuses of the invasion of France—Guderian, Manstein, Balck—all were eventually broken by the challenges of command on the *Ostfront*, as the Germans called the Eastern Front. All their tactical acumen was, in the end, not a match for the relentless pressure they faced at the hard hands of Marshal Georgi Zhukov.

Alas, the very immensity of the struggle frustrates any attempt to tell the story completely short of epic length, and an accurate picture of the Soviet side of the hill may be lost to history; perhaps, as Soviet archives are opened to Western scholars and writers or Russian historians lose their Soviet shackles, this may change. From the German side, the war in the East wears down the historian and the memoirist even as it wore down the generals.

Still, the Eastern war can be divided into three very rough periods. From fall 1941 until the siege of Stalingrad in 1942, the Germans were victorious, capturing huge Soviet armies and driving deep into the Russian heartland while the Soviets struggled to adapt to a new form of warfare and searched for a corps of competent commanders. From Stalingrad to the Battle of Kursk in July 1943, the two sides fought roughly as equals, the Soviets painfully mastering the craft of mobile warfare and the Germans countering with hard blows of their own. After Kursk, it was the Soviets in the ascendant, and by late 1944, it was the Soviet tank armies who were gulping territory hundreds of kilometers at a bite and dismembering German army groups. In the process, the Soviets developed a unique doctrine of armored warfare and equipped massive armies to animate it. This unique concept of warfare remained the driving spirit behind Soviet military power for fifty years of Cold War, a philosophy challenged—but not yet disproven—only by the advent of modern information technologies.

The story of the Eastern Front must be painted in broad, bold strokes, then, to reflect the nature of the fighting. Three campaigns encapsulate the shifting tides of the fighting: Operation *Barbarossa*, as Hitler dubbed the initial invasion of Soviet Russia; Operation *Zitadelle*, the German code-name for the battle of Kursk in 1943, which culminated in the epic tank battle at Prokhorovka, the largest clash of armor in history; and the Soviet Operation *Bagration*, establishing the Red Army of 1944 as the masters of deep operations and resulting in the collapse of the German Army Group Center and the capture of perhaps 300,000 soldiers.

OPERATION BARBAROSSA

The war on the *Ostfront* began on June 22, 1941, with Operation *Barbarossa*. However, planning for an attack to the east had been in the works since the surrender of France in the summer of 1940. On July 29, a conference convened in Bad Reichenhall under the direction of Colonel General Albert Jodl, the chief of staff of all the German armed forces, called *Oberkommando der Wehrmacht*, or OKW for short; Jodl set in motion the process of converting Hitler's desire to destroy Soviet Russia into a military operation. Over the fall months, the plan began to take shape, primarily under the direction of the *Oberkommando des Herres*, or OKH, the German army high command, and its chief of staff Colonel General Franz Halder. OKH was the direct descendant of the great Prussian and German general staff tradition. Its doctrine of fighting great battles of encirclement, or *kesselschlachten*, frustrated in France, would shape the course of *Barbarossa*.

By early December 1940, Halder had completed a draft plan that would form the basis for Hitler's "Directive Number 21," the document that would set the strategic objectives of the *Barbarossa* campaign. Issued December 18, the directive charged the Wehrmacht to be prepared "to defeat Soviet Russia in one rapid campaign." As Russia, like Germany, had long been a great land power in the central Eurasian landmass, the burden of the campaign was to be borne by the German army. Napoleon before him had relied on the mass of his infantry to overwhelm Tsarist Russia, but Hitler called upon his tanks to slay the Soviet Union: "The mass of the [Soviet] army stationed in Western Russia is to be destroyed in bold operations involving deep penetrations by armored spearheads, and the withdrawal of elements capable of combat into the extensive Russian land spaces is to be prevented."[1]

In tackling the Soviets, Hitler was taking on an opponent in every way as ruthless as himself. Soviet leader Josef Stalin did not shrink from shedding blood to attain political goals which, driven by his own lust for unchallenged power and the ideology of the communist state, were in every way as extreme as the führer's. In military terms, too, Stalin seemed to match the German dictator's power.

Although in many ways similar in size (the *Wehrmacht* invasion force consisted of 3.05 million troops, 3,350 tanks and 2,770 aircraft; the defenders of the Worker's and Peasants' Red Army fielded 2.9 million men, up to 5,500 medium and heavy tanks, and at least 1,540 aircraft[2]) and in political standing (both armies were in service to brutal dictators for whom the dictates of party and personal loyalty superseded all other concerns) the tactical and operational character of the Nazi and Soviet armed forces could hardly have differed more. Despite the primacy of Hitler and National Socialism in many aspects of German life, the tactical and operational principles of the German general staff provided the form of leadership for the *Wehrmacht*. By contrast, the lingering traditions of the Tsarist army and the attempt to revive military professionalism after the revolution had been all but eradicated by Stalin's purges of the late 1930s. The elimination of Marshal Mikhail N. Tukhachevsky, especially, and his replacement by soldiers steeped in the tactical and operational concepts of the Russian civil war established the standards by which the Red Army conducted itself in the field in 1941; not until later in the war were the Soviets able to produce an officer corps at all comfortable with mobile warfare.

By contrast, the German generals boasted the master of that métier. A substantial body of panzer commanders—Guderian, Hoth, Reinhardt, Höpner, and Schmitt—now had experience at corps and, in Kleist's case, even at the level of army, or *Panzergruppe*, in the nomenclature of the German army at the time. Perhaps most important of all, the Germans had experience at sustaining these large formations as well as fighting them.

In preparation for *Barbarossa*, the Germans made a number of modifications to these battle-tested formations. The success of the panzer divisions led Hitler to demand more such formations, but German industry could not meet the need. The result was that the number of divisions was doubled, but the number of new tanks increased only slightly, even including captured tanks. As Alan Clark observed:

> In the result there was some compensation in [the panzer divisions'] increased firepower [from tanks fitted with more powerful main guns] and the gradual substitution of the heavier [Panzer] III for the [Panzer] II, but the Panzer divisions were never to recover the numerical strength and mobility with which they had begun the battle of France. Hitler had also directed that the number of motorized [infantry] divisions be doubled, but without making any provision for an increase in the production of the vehicle industry. The result was that many of the new formations had to equip themselves with captured or requisitioned trucks, which were to prove unreliable and difficult to service under severe conditions.[3]

The regular infantry divisions were worse off, especially in terms of transport. R. H. S. Stolfi notes that the Germans purchased

15,000 Polish light wagons and horses "suited to the unpaved tracks posing as roads in Russia and hir[ed] 15,000 Poles to energize the primitive, but effective, eastern-style transportation system."[4] However, these were not used above the division and corps level.

These modest adjustments to German fighting organizations reflected the Germans' appreciation of the Red Army. In October 1940, the Foreign Armies East branch of the intelligence staff of the German army high command produced a report, based on the observations of the German military attaché in Moscow, that the Soviet army would be a serious opponent in defense, but limited in the conduct of large-scale mobile operations.[5] "It was estimated that the Red Army would still be inferior in effectiveness to the German Army, even if it had numerical superiority of two or three to one, but a warning was added that the Red Army's best allies were time and space, the lack of roads, and the bad weather."[6] The Germans, partly because of the relatively close ties between the two armies between the wars, understood that most of the brightest leaders of the Soviet army had perished in the purges, and they rated few Red commanders highly.[7] The German army also had a generally poor view of the tactical skill of the individual Red Army soldier but did appreciate his ability to endure hardship.

These military assessments provided the background to German planning for Operation *Barbarossa* when initial work began in the summer of 1940. Similar to the planning for the invasion of France, German planning for Barbarossa followed a long and winding road. From July 22 to 29, 1940, Halder came to the conclusion that "an attack launched from assembly areas in East Prussia and northern Poland toward Moscow would offer the best chance of success."[8] The goal was to destroy the Soviet armies defending Moscow, seize the city, then compel the other Soviet forces, especially those in the Ukraine, to face attacks from an unexpected direction. The military aim of the campaign was, Halder asserted,

> To defeat the Russian Army or at least to occupy as much Russian soil as is necessary to protect Berlin and the Silesian industrial

97

area from air attack. It is desired to establish our own positions so far to the east that our own air force can destroy the most important areas of Russia.[9]

Halder turned to Brigadier General Erich Marcks, chief of staff of the 18th Army, to flesh out this general concept but keep to a narrow corridor in a race to prevent the Soviet armies from trading space for time. Still, the overall scope of conquest was staggering:

[Marcks's] aim was to defeat the Red Army and seize the territory west of a line North Dvina [River], Middle Volga [River] and lower Don [River], that is to say, [the cities of] Archangel, Gorki and Rostov [or past Leningrad in the north and well past Moscow in the center] in order to safeguard German soil from Soviet bombing.[10]

A second factor, both for Halder and Marcks, in determining the primacy of a thrust toward Moscow, was geography. The Pripet Marshes, a vast bog about 150 miles wide and 300 miles deep, lay just within the borders of Belorussia to the south and east of the German-Soviet frontier at Brest-Litovsk in Poland. Few roads traversed the marshes, which also were heavily forested in parts; it was poor tank country. The cities of Minsk, Orsha, and Smolensk lay on the direct axis to Moscow, with the region from Orsha to Moscow known as the Orsha land bridge; to the north was the watershed for the rivers flowing to the Baltic Sea, to the south was the watershed to the Black Sea.

The Orsha landbridge was the gateway to Moscow and it formed the gap between the two major water obstacles, the West Dvina and the Dnieper [Rivers]. Before the Germans could arrive at this landbridge they had to cross heavily wooded forest belts, fifty miles or more in depth, by way of roads. These forest roads would have the effect of funneling movement and stringing out formations in great depth. Moscow lay about 700 miles from the frontier.[11]

Marcks's plan was to attack through this land bridge toward Moscow, with a supporting attack against the Baltic states toward

Leningrad and a third thrust through the Ukraine toward Kiev and the Dnieper River. However, his plan was not the only candidate. Against Halder's original wishes, the OKH operations division produced a plan that put the main thrust south of the Pripet Marshes and then into the Ukraine. Following a corrupted version of a plan originally conceived by Tukhachevsky, the Soviets had placed the weight of their forces in the south;[12] one feature common to all the German plans was that the primary objective was to destroy Soviet forces rather than seize terrain. Also, Jodl got into the act by suggesting not a two-pronged but a three-pronged attack, with two axes north of the marshes and one south. The legacy of Jodl's draft was crucial: the pace of the central attack toward Moscow should be keyed to progress through the Baltics; this Hitler seized upon when he insisted upon seizing Leningrad. Marcks's basic concept resurfaced in a plan drawn up by Colonel General Friedrich Paulus, then the chief of the army high command operations section, although the importance of the southern attack through the Ukraine now superseded that of the Baltics. Paulus's survey also

> dealt with the well-known but little understood problems of time and distance in the Soviet Union, the indifferent leadership of the Red Army, the difficulty in assessing the fighting value of the Red Army soldier, and the lack of unity among the many races which form[ed] the Soviet peoples. For the first time, too, the question of the Soviet preponderance of manpower was raised.[13]

In late November and early December 1940, the German high command conducted a series of map exercises to understand the ramifications of some of these problems; the size of the theater was creating worries, especially the reverse funnel that saw the potential front widen from 1,300 miles at the current border up to 2,500 miles by the time the intended advances were achieved. Albert Seaton's summary of the discussion of logistical problems is worth quoting at length:

> Other problems were ventilated, including the difficulties of maintaining a force of three million men and half a million horses in a

vast country where there were few roads and where the railway could not be used for through running since the track was wider than that used in Germany and Central Europe. The Commander-in-Chief, Replacement Army, [Colonel General Friedrich] Fromm, had already emphasized that there were only sufficient reinforcements available, just under half a million, to replace the wastage for a summer campaign. There was too an acute shortage of motor vehicles, although it was hoped that this might be made good by purchase from the French civilian output. The vehicle fuel position was very tight indeed, there being no more than three months' reserves of petrol and one month's diesel in Germany. Tires were a problem because of the lack of pure and synthetic rubber, so that consideration was given to equipping lighter vehicles with steel-shod wheels. German armor production at the beginning of 1941 was less than 250 tanks and armored assault guns a month. German industry was still capable of enormous expansion but its basis at this time lacked depth and it was dependent on imported raw materials from the USSR and elsewhere.[14]

These war games formed the background of the army's first briefing to Hitler on December 5. The issues that arose also formed the basis of a divergence of opinion between Hitler and his generals that would eventually lead to strategic paralysis: the immensities of the Soviet Union reconfirmed the generals in their opinion that the first need was to destroy the Red Army before undertaking other strategic objectives. However, they were undone by Hitler's hankering after economic objectives, the desire to protect the fatherland from air attack, the racial goals of National Socialism, and the imprecise goals stated originally by Halder. For example, *Führer* Directive Number 21 listed under its general intentions for *Barbarossa* the goal of forming a barrier against Asiatic Russia on the general line Archangel-Volga.[15]

The attack itself was to be carried out by three army groups, with the *schwerpunkt*, or main effort, with Field Marshall Fedor von Bock's Army Group Center, which was aimed at Moscow. Army Group Center boasted fifty divisions in all, with four army-level commands of two infantry armies and two *Panzergruppen;* the mobile forces included nine panzer divisions and six motorized infantry divisions. Bock's initial thrust would be a two-pronged attack to encircle the Bialystok salient with his mobile units while the infantry armies would reduce the encirclements; Operation Barbarossa saw the realization of the Germans' dreams of *kesselschlachten*, or cauldron battles, which would refine the hammer-and-anvil tactics of the invasion of France to those of pure mobility. The panzers would be operating truly independently, with the hope of catching the Red Army before it could retreat to the Russian hinterlands.

Army Groups North and South would conduct secondary attacks, in the north from East Prussia through the Baltics toward Leningrad, in the south from southern Poland and Rumania into the Ukraine. Field Marhsall Ritter von Leeb's Army Group North would consist of twenty-six divisions with one panzer group of two corps totaling three Panzer and three motorized divisions. Army Group South, commanded by Field Marshall Gerd von Rundstedt, with forty-one German divisions and fourteen Rumanian divisions, fielded five panzer and three motorized infantry divisions.[16] The OKH reserve, including two panzer and two motorized divisions, totaled twenty-eight divisions altogether.[17]

The German generals, despite earlier worries about a two-front war, now were nearly unanimous in believing their forces adequate to Hitler's demands. According to Halder's diary, in May 1941, the Germans estimated the Red Army could throw up 121 rifle divisions and twenty-one cavalry divisions. About Soviet armor they were more vague, but believed that the Red Army had about five tank divisions and thirty-three mechanized brigades in the west. Intelligence estimated a further twenty-five divisions were deployed against the Finnish and Turkish borders and perhaps as many as thirty divisions might be in the Far East guarding against a Japanese attack. The total Red Air Force strength was believed to be over 4,000 first-line aircraft and the Soviet tank strength 10,000. Aircraft and tanks were thought to be qualitatively inferior to those of the Germans. The German planners thought they could win in a campaign of six to seventeen weeks.[18]

However, the Germans' official estimates of the Soviet armed forces were based more on what they believed were the dictates of common sense rather than hard intelligence. Quoting from the official *Handbook on the Armed Forces of the USSR*, Seaton observed that the estimates were "arrived at by rough-and-ready, rule-of-thumb methods based on population strength and estimated industrial potential."[19] Not surprisingly, this doubtful methodology produced a number of inaccurate conclusions.

THE SOVIET ARMY

The purges and executions of the late 1930s, the poor performance of the Soviet Army in the Winter War with Finland, and the dominant figure of Josef Stalin made the Red Army a much less capable force man-for-man than the *Wehrmacht*. Still, despite its disorganization and leadership at the top, the Red Army was a large force and its leaders were inclined to use it liberally. Stalin and his generals viewed their soldiers' lives cheaply, as indeed many of the soldiers themselves did. As for the generals, Stalin preferred political reliability and loyalty as virtues far transcending tactical cleverness or operational astuteness; indeed, these attributes were taken as suspicious in themselves. Stalin had found it necessary to eliminate Tukhachevsky, in part because his military ideas consituted a political challenge. Although the Soviets retained a strong interest in armor after Tukhachevsky's demise, they had repressed the sophisticated doctrines and concepts advanced by Tukhachevsky and his reform-minded colleagues. The Red Army stuck by its revolutionary principles.

The Soviets were ill prepared to fight a defensive war; one principle both Stalin and Tukhachevsky shared was a devotion to offensive action. This was in part due to the Russian experience of World War I and the Soviet experience of the Civil War, but the result was that military thinking about defenses had gotten short shrift; the 1936 field regulations devoted only about 20 of its 300 pages to defense, describing it as "a temporary phenomenon designed to economize force, gain time, hold critical areas or disrupt an advancing enemy, pending a resumption of the all-important offense."[20]

The army's tactical organization was simpler than the Germans', and if that made for inflexibility, it also made for interchangeability. In 1941, Soviet tanks were not centralized in divisions, but rather each infantry division had an organic tank battalion of about thirty tanks or armored cars.[21] The three- or four-battalion tank brigades equipped with main battle tanks lacked any organic infantry, but lighter tanks were organized into mechanized brigades with a balance of tank battalions and truck-borne infantry.[22] Overall, the Soviets had lots of tanks, but in a variety of models, many of which were obsolete; the outstanding Soviet tanks of World War II, the medium T-34 and heavy KV1, were in production by mid-1941, but fewer than 1,000 T-34s and 500 KV1s were fielded, and, because of Soviet organizational principles, were distributed piecemeal throughout the army.[23] Maintenance also was not very good: as of June 15, 1941, just a week away from the German invasion, 29 percent of tanks needed heavy repairs, another 44 percent needed or were undergoing less serious repair, and only 27 percent were fully operational.[24] The Soviet air force reflected a similar picture.

Unfortunately, the Soviet forces were disposed to repel an invasion of the Ukraine rather than one pointed toward Moscow. This misreading of German intentions was due primarily to Stalin's belief that the Germans would not attack and that he could acquire territories in the Balkans if Germany became bogged down in the Mediterranean or in an invasion of Great Britain. When presented with comprehensive evidence of the German plan based on British intercepts of German coded message traffic under the famous Ultra program, "the Russian leader thought that it was a plant, sharing the view of Voroshilov that 'We have the time to play the role of gravedigger to the capitalist world—and give it the finishing blow.'"[25]

The Soviet forces were divided into four army groups, or *fronts* in Soviet parlance. The Southwestern Front, headquartered at

Kiev in the Ukraine and under the command of Colonel General M. P. Kirponos, was the strongest formation, with four infantry armies and six mechanized corps. In the center, opposite German Army Group Center, stood the Soviet Western Front, headquartered at Minsk and under Colonel General Dmitri Pavlov. He, too, commanded four armies [Soviet formations were of irregular strength] and six mechanized corps. The forces in the north were divided into two smaller fronts, the Northern Front, under Lieutenant General M. M. Popov at Leningrad, and Colonel General F. I. Kuznetsov's Northwestern Front at Riga in Latvia. Popov's forces were three infantry armies and one mechanized corps; Kuznetsov also commanded three armies and one mechanized corps.[26] Finally, within their fronts, the Soviet forces were deployed forward to cover territory acquired by Stalin in Poland and the Balkans and away from the incomplete but substantial fortifications of the Stalin line.

The Stalin line represented a further dilution of the sparse defensive strength of the Red Army. Soviet doctrine developed in the 1930s called for a two-echelon defense within rifle divisions, with two regiments forward and one regiment as a shock group to counterattack; overall, divisions were to cover eight to twelve kilometers of front and be arrayed five to eight kilometers deep. A modification in 1940 reduced division frontage to six to ten kilometers and increased the number of antitank guns in each unit. Unfortunately, the Red Army divisions facing Operation *Barbarossa* were only at about 60 percent of formal strength and were forced to deploy in single-echelon formations with a depth of just three to five kilometers in order to cover the huge defensive zones laid out by Stalin. The result, as described by David Glantz, was a defense riddled with holes and unable to maneuver:

> Division defenses were subdivided into battalion defensive regions and company strongpoints that were often noncontiguous and not linked together by interlocking fire. Few of the gaps were covered by fire. In the almost complete absence of antitank defense, engineer obstacles, or trenches, enemy forces could and did penetrate through those gaps into the depth of the defense, thus disrupting

the command and control of the division as a whole and its parent rifle corps or army . . . .[A]wkward use of tanks further inhibited the integrity of the defense. Tank regiments and battalions were supposed to hold separate positions or lines, provide direct fire support for infantry, and conduct counterattacks against penetrating enemy units. In practice, however, Soviet commanders subdivided tank regiments and battalions into small groups and counterattacked from march formation without proper reconnaissance or use of maneuver.[27]

Thus, though German and Soviet forces were roughly equal in size and armament, the *Wehrmacht* enjoyed huge tactical and operational advantages in the *Barbarossa* invasion. Indeed, the Soviet organizations and dispositions, reinforced by Stalin's dictum to fight far forward, allowed the Germans to conduct the campaign precisely according to their wishes: to engage and encircle the Red Army as near the frontier as possible, to place their main effort in the center aiming toward Moscow, and to win a decisive victory in a rapid offensive. By nearly all tactical and operational measures, the Germans placed their strength against relative Soviet weakness.

INITIAL SUCCESS

German chances for decisive victory rested primarily on the fortunes of Bock's Army Group Center and especially his two panzer group commanders, Heinz Guderian and Hermann Hoth. Bock's army group was spearheaded by the two panzer groups, one in the north of his sector and one in the south. These achieved remarkable successes from the very outset. After just a week of fighting, Guderian and Hoth linked up to form the Bialystok pocket, and about one week later again had nearly completed the encirclement of large Soviet forces west of Minsk. In these two massive cauldron battles, Army Group Center took more than 330,000 prisoners, destroyed nearly 3,200 tanks, more than 1,800 artillery pieces, and 344 aircraft, although a good bit

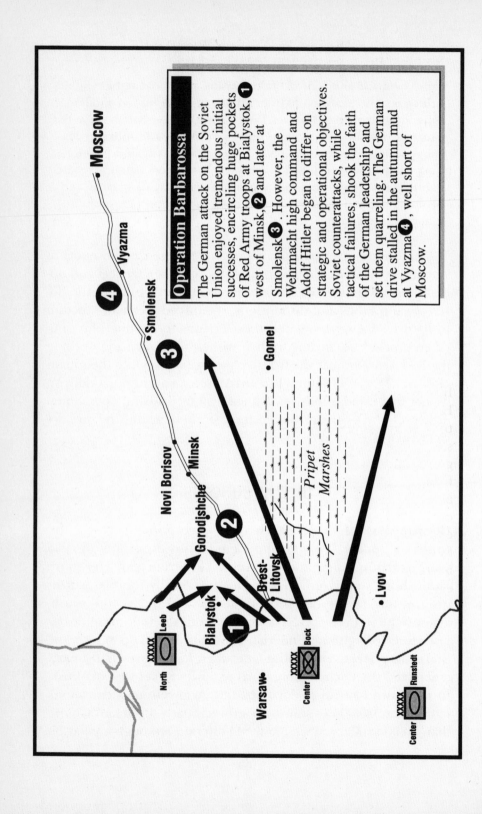

Operation Barbarossa

The German attack on the Soviet Union enjoyed tremendous initial successes, encircling huge pockets of Red Army troops at Bialystok, ❶ west of Minsk, ❷ and later at Smolensk ❸. However, the Wehrmacht high command and Adolf Hitler began to differ on strategic and operational objectives. Soviet counterattacks, while tactical failures, shook the faith of the German leadership and set them quarreling. The German drive stalled in the autumn mud at Vyazma ❹, well short of Moscow.

Moscow

Vyazma ❹

Smolensk ❸

Gomel

Novi Borisov

Minsk

Gorodishche ❷

Brest-Litovsk

Bialystok ❶

Pripet Marshes

Lvov

Warsaw

North
XXXXX
Leeb

Center
XXXXX
Bock

Center
XXXX
Runstedt

of the Soviet air force had been destroyed on the ground by the *Luftwaffe* in the first strikes of the campaign.[28]

However, before *Barbarossa*, Bock had projected that the first great encirclement of Soviet forces would not be complete until the panzers penetrated as far as Smolensk, twice as deep into Russia as Minsk. Even with the massive Bialystok and Minsk pockets sealed but not yet completely reduced by the following infantry formations, Bock stuck fast to his original concept: he wanted to push on toward Moscow.[29]

Bock conceived a victorious drive through Smolensk into the Moscow-Gorki space and decisively extracted the bulk of his mobile troops from the encirclement [where, in fact, they were doing much of the fighting as the infantry formations could not keep up] and retained operational freedom for the Panzer groups to drive on to Moscow. . . . He presented Germany on [July 3] with the immediate collapse of the Soviet Union.[30]

It was an opportunity that Germany—especially Hitler and Halder—were not yet prepared to accept, and that the Red Army tried to deny them: the Soviets hastily organized a counteroffensive of four armies. The Soviet attacks were weak; short on tanks, guns, and air support, the counteroffensive was primarily carried forward by infantry. It was also diffused; the armies attacked abreast, over fronts of thirty to fifty kilometers, and none of the divisions breached the German tactical defenses. Smolensk was encircled. On July 16, the 7th Panzer Division arrived at Jarcevo, fifty kilometers east of the city. Army Group Center was forced to halt east of Smolensk until almost the end of August. It was necessary to secure lines of communication by reducing the pockets. More important was Hitler's obsession with taking Leningrad, which pivoted Army Group Center in that direction and then on an excursion into the Ukraine.

Here, the *Wehrmacht* reached a turning point in the 1941 campaign, and perhaps the war. One of the great unanswered questions of World War II is whether the panzer formations retained sufficient strength to carry the attack of Army Group Center past Moscow.[31] For the most part, they were in good shape: German manpower losses as of August 2 were 179,000 of a force of three million, well below their anticipated loss rates.[32] The panzer groups, though they had borne the brunt of the fighting and maneuvering, were at about 65 percent of strength at the time of the decision to halt the attack toward Moscow. A key issue was the ability to project logistics power deep into the Soviet Union, a country with a primitive road network and differently gauged railroads. However, German railway engineer units had an impressive record of constructing rail lines at approximately twenty kilometers per day.[33] By the end of July, they were able to push a line into Smolensk.

However, more than the strength of the troops would determine the extent of the German conquests. The closing of the Smolensk pocket marked a natural pause in the *Barbarossa* offensive; whatever prospects it had for further success now would be irrevocably lost due to the indecisiveness of the German high command and especially Hitler. Even the bold Guderian became consumed by local threats, wishing to turn his Second *Panzerarmee* to the southwest, toward Roslavl, to secure his right flank. In postwar memoirs, all the generals have sought to escape the blame for the blunders that followed, seeking to pin the blame on the *führer*, but what seems most likely is that all involved were intimidated by the enormity of the risk and the task they had undertaken with *Barbarossa* and the sheer immensity of the Red Army and its resources; for every formation surrounded and eliminated, it seemed a new one would spring forth.

The crisis began July 27, when Bock summoned the senior leadership of Army Group Center to a conference at his headquarters at Novy Borisov. This was no commander's huddle; Berlin wished to reassert its control over the *Barbarossa* campaign. The situation maps showed huge Russian formations that had been bypassed. Were these still threats? The generals were not sure, but to Hitler, they certainly were threats. The *führer* particularly wanted to destroy the Soviet Fifth Army, centered on the town of Gomel but bulging to the south and west back into the Pripet Marshes.

While the Germans were stretching their troops and doctrine to their limits, the Soviets were struggling to respond. Stalin's reaction to the initial defeats was to charge the Western Front commanders with negligence and purge them; Front Commander General Dmitri Pavlov and his chief of staff, as well as Fourth Army Commander General Aleksandr Korobkov, were executed. This interpretation neatly overlooked the fact that the purges of the late 1930s had replaced innovative combat leaders with politically reliable cronies. More important, it glossed over the systemic failures of the Red Army to come to grips with the *blitzkrieg;* indeed, it exacerbated them. Nevertheless, sheer necessity forced field commanders and their staffs to develop ad hoc methods for discovering the keys to this new form of warfare and ways to train troops in accordance with its principles. For example, the deputy commander for tank forces in the Western Front conducted his own analysis of armor operations in early September, concluding that the Soviets' losses resulted from inadequate reconnaisssance of the Germans and the terrain and poor coordination between arms, dispersal of armor, and the slowness of infantry at securing the small, local advantages that might come from tank attacks.[34]

In their attempts to halt the German drive at Smolensk, the Soviets had taken the first steps toward recreating the ability to operate large armored forces. These were painful and wasteful efforts, launched from sheer desperation. On July 6, Colonel General Semen K. Timoshenko, commander of the Soviet Central Front, committed his V and VII Mechanized Corps in a piecemeal fashion against Hoth's drive to the north of the city; his tank forces were shredded in a few days. The Soviet general staff's attempts to create reserves for a serious counteroffensive once the Germans had been halted, they hoped, at the Dnieper River, were in a shambles: the reserves were needed immediately at the front and the Germans would not be stopped. Still, the closing of the Smolensk pocket strained the Germans at least momentarily.

To relieve the stranded forces in the pocket—which, because of its great size, necessarily was punctuated with holes in the lines—Timoshenko committed two full armies, including four tank brigades, all equipped with the brand-new T-34 tank. The T-34 was perhaps the finest medium tank produced during the war, with the possible exception of the German Panzer Mark V. But beyond its design qualities—including its low-slung silhouette, its reliable automotive system, adequate armor, and 76 mm main gun, later replaced by a more powerful 85 mm gun—the best quality of the T-34 was that the Soviets could produce it in huge numbers. This more than offset its drawbacks, like the cramped two-man turret. The T-34 was a simple design that could be built by relatively unskilled workers, and as the Soviet industrial economy was disrupted by the German invasion, this simplicity of design was a vital dimension.

Though Timoshenko's counterattack failed to open the Smolensk pocket for long, a number of divisions did escape. More importantly, it was the continuing scale of the Soviet counterattacks that shook the Germans' faith and set them to quarreling. For example, Guderian had long chafed at the restrictions placed upon him by Fourth Army commander Field Marhsall Walter von Kluge, even though he needed Kluge's infantry to follow up the charges of his panzers. Guderian was constantly dreaming up schemes to push his operational freedom to the limits. By the time of the July 27 commanders' conference, Guderian and Kluge could no longer work together; in his memoirs, Guderian wrote, "The relationship between the commander of the Fourth Army and myself had . . . become strained to an undesireable degree."[35] To solve the problem, Bock transferred a number of infantry divisions to what now became *Armeegruppe Guderian* and approved the attack toward Roslavl, which at least could be argued to support the Gomel plan.

THE HALT BEFORE MOSCOW AND ITS CONSEQUENCES

Even before Guderian could close or reduce the Roslavl pocket, the depth of Hitler's misgivings about the direction of the campaign emerged in the person of Colonel Rudolf Schmundt, who had flown out from *führer* headquarters to bestow the panzer general with the Oak Leaves to his Knight's Cross medal. Hitler was wavering over the course of *Barbarossa;* he had not decided to continue the thrust toward Moscow. Rather, Hoth's Panzer Group 3 was to be sent north to the Baltics to outflank Leningrad, while Guderian was dispatched to the Ukraine. Then, on September 5, Hitler reversed course again, recalling not only Hoth and Guderian, but Höpner's Panzer Group 4 plus additional infantry and air armies for a climactic drive on Moscow before the fall rains came. However, the opportunity was missed; Guderian's forces had yet to completely reach the Ukraine, let alone fulfill their tasks there. Although they were quite effective in the south, encircling another huge pocket at Kiev, the panzers could not return in time and fell just short of Moscow. Bock had taken Smolensk, not 200 miles from the Soviet capital, just twenty-three days after the start of *Barbarossa.* Whether taking Moscow or the region just east of the city would have driven the Soviets out of the war is a matter of conjecture. Whatever chances the German *blitzkrieg* had presented, the *führer* had refused.

In the spring of 1942, Zhukov drove the Germans back from Moscow in a desperate counterattack that gave the Soviets some breathing space around the capital, but left them too weak to stop the Germans when, at Hitler's direction, they again turned east through the Ukraine and out into the great steppes of the Eurasian landmass toward the Volga River and Stalingrad. Throughout the summer and fall, the panzers again enjoyed huge successes, driving, in the late autumn and early winter, to the gates of Stalingrad itself. This was a prize Hitler coveted.

By the winter of 1942, the Soviets had suffered eighteen months of agonizing operational defeats and were holding on by their fingernails: the revolutionary principles of the Red Army had not been sufficient to withstand the onslaught of the panzers. The Soviets paid an extremely heavy price for the purges of the late 1930s, in view of their inability to coordinate combined arms tactics among armor, infantry, and artillery, let alone airpower; an even greater confusion at operational echelons of command; and combat leaders who clearly were not up to the rigors of mobile warfare. At the same time, the Red Army had earned a considerable degree of combat experience. The general staff had recognized the problems almost from the outset of the war and had created an organization to collect and distill the combat lessons learned on tactical techniques, operational concepts, and organizational ideas. The famous Stalingrad counteroffensive begun in November marked the first time these lessons would be applied to the battlefield, and that marked the first great maturation of the Red Army in the use of armor: the Soviet tank army was an innovative achievement, combining armor and infantry to create and exploit operational opportunities.

The attack began on November 19, striking German Army Group B at its weakest point, the Rumanian Third Army, to the north of the city. Attacking also from the south, Russian forces eventually encircled the German defenders, capturing Sixth Army commander Field Marshall Friedrich Paulus and more than 100,000 troops. Despite the clear victory at Stalingrad, the Soviets were aware of their shortcomings. Most worrisome had been the need to employ the tank and mechanized corps to complete the breakthroughs, sapping their strength, embroiling them in local actions, and limiting their utility as exploitation forces. The result, according to one Soviet study, was that the mobile formations were exhausted prematurely: "All this shows that the preparation, organization, and technique of committing mobile units into breaches and the exploitation of successes have not been studied sufficiently either by units of combined arms or by the tank commanders."[36] This was not merely a typical communist critique of commanders but a realization that mobile warfare placed a great strain on leaders and staffs and that Soviet planning had been inadequate.

SPRING 1943: THE CREATION OF THE KURSK SALIENT

Still, with its success at Stalingrad, the Red Army had achieved a new maturity in modern armored combat. Its tactical prowess still was far below that of the Germans, but its ability to cover its weaknesses with superior planning and risk-taking at the operational level, combined with the ebbing of German strength and the difficulties posed by defeats in the Mediterranean and the possibility of an Allied offensive in the West, put the Red Army on more even terms with the *Ostheer*, or Eastern Army. Now, for perhaps the first time since 1941, the Soviets had opportunities for strategic offensives. The Axis front remained lightly held, and Germany's allies were less than fully committed to Hitler's goals in the East.

The opportunities and potential rewards seemed greatest in the south, where the Germans' Army Group Don had been thrown back to the city of Rostov, and in the Caucusus, where Field Marshall Kleist's Army Group A had been driven back to the north coast of the Black Sea. On January 15, 1943, even before the final chapters of the Stalingrad saga were written, the Soviets took the attack again, striking again at Army Group B, with its Italian, Hungarian, and Rumanian formations, on a broad front and driving them back hundreds of kilometers and opening a huge gap between it and Field Marshal Erich von Manstein's Army Group Don. Manstein had predicted this Soviet attack, and by the end of the first week in February, General Nikolai Vatutin's South-West Front had crossed the River Donets and threatened to cut off the city of Kharkov, the fourth largest in the Soviet Union; in desperation, the Germans broke up the forlorn Army Group B and assigned a number of SS panzer units, under *Oberstgruppenführer* Paul Hausser, to Manstein to prepare a counterattack.

However, Manstein preferred to let the Red Army offensive run out of steam and to pry some additional needed mobile forces from Hitler and OKH before striking back. Indeed, he was sure he had too much ground to cover and too few forces to hold the entire Donets basin. Under normal circumstances, he could never have hoped to convince the *führer* to fight the campaign his way, but the loss of the Sixth Army at Stalingrad had chastened Hitler; Manstein would be given a large measure of operational freedom. Recalling the four-hour conference of February 6, 1943, during which he laid his plans before the *führer,* Manstein wrote:

At the time I had the impression that he was deeply affected by [the Stalingrad] tragedy, not just because it amounted to a blatant failure of his own leadership, but also because he was deeply depressed in a purely personal sense by the fate of the soldiers who, out of faith in him, had fought to the last with such courage and devotion to duty.[37]

Still, despite granting Manstein's wish for operational freedom, Hitler was unhappy about the prospect of yielding ground; to Manstein, Hitler's experience of World War I had forever frozen his understanding of military operations. The *führer* expected the Soviet offensive to collapse of its own weight without further sacrifice of territory, and he expected that Hausser's I SS Corps would provide sufficient reinforcement. Indeed, just ten days after the conference, Hitler flew to Manstein's new headquarters at Zaporozhye to call a halt to the retreat and order that Kharkov, which had fallen the previous day, be retaken. Manstein rode out the *führer's* fury even as he rode out that of the Red Army. At yet another conference on February 18, Manstein pleaded for patience, but as the Soviets also had broken through the German lines along the Mius River, from which Manstein had withdrawn the First and Fourth Panzer Armies in preparation for his counterattack, Manstein's game was a close-run thing.

The Soviets had overreached themselves, however, thinking the Germans thoroughly beaten, and had misread the ability of their own armored forces to sustain themselves hundreds of kilometers from their lines of departure; Soviet logistics were not up to the task. On February 20, Manstein counterattacked into the overextended Soviet positions. The First and Fourth Panzer Armies slashed into the Red Army from the south, while an army detachment—a combined-arms organization of tanks and infantry, a battle group on a large scale—under General Werner Kempf drove down from the north and Hausser's I SS Corps struck at Kharkov. The German field marshal had gauged his attack nearly perfectly, and the Soviets were driven back to the east bank of the Donets as far north as Belgorod; farther than that was out of reach for Manstein's mobile forces, and Army Group B no longer existed to plug the last bubble in the German lines. This salient was centered on the city of Kursk and bulged between Manstein's forces—now to be called Army Group South—and Kluge's Army Group Center to the north.

To prevent Manstein from pursuing his offensive farther into the Kursk salient, Stalin in mid-March again dispatched Zhukov to the front, in hopes that he would repeat the magic of Stalingrad. Zhukov moved rapidly to restore the deteriorating situation, firing General Filip Golikov—though his forces were performing better than were Vatutin's—and moving forces from the general reserve. On March 18, the Germans retook Belgorod, but the Soviet Twenty-first Army held a good position just outside the town and it was backed up by the First Tank Army in front of Oboyan to the north. Both sides needed rest; the Germans were strung out from their counteroffensive, and the Soviets, though they had established a patchwork line of defenses, were too disorganized and too weak to attack.

Both sides' tank arms were undergoing major changes. After the experiences of early 1943, the Soviets again engaged in ruthless self-criticism. On the matériel front, the Red Army was growing stronger at a very fast pace; with simple weapons and simple organizations, the Soviet army was able to field massive combat formations quite quickly. The T-34 and KV-1 remained serviceable basic designs; 2,000 tanks were rolling off the assembly lines east of the Urals each month.

On the German side, *the Panzerwaffe* was going through a kind of midlife crisis. The venerable Panzer IV was outclassed by the T-34 in every way save for those few Panzer IVs that were equipped with the new 75 mm main gun. The industrial effort to create new designs suffered both from Hitler's fascination with the technology of warfare and the jealousy of the *Wehrmacht*'s gunners, who constantly diverted tank chassis to self-propelled artillery.

To respond to the challenge of the T-34, the Germans had advanced three designs: a new medium tank, the *Panzerkampfwagen* V Panther; the heavy Panzer VI Tiger; and a light reconnaissance tank called the Leopard, a model that never came into mass production. Two competing prototypes of the medium and heavy tanks were built, slowing the development process, and through the course of 1942, design changes, primarily in armor, further slowed the pace of fielding the new tanks. The interim solutions—equipping not only the Panzer IV but also the remaining Panzer IIIs and Czech tanks with a 75 mm gun extended the service life of the original German tank fleet, but it also created an unending spare parts and logistics nightmare.

As the Germans' technological edge disappeared, so did their organizational strength. The tank strength of the panzer division had been diluted, balanced by additional infantry, but by the end of 1942, the self-propelled guns began to reach the field in increasing numbers, not replacing wheeled artillery formations but replacing the third tank battalion, further weakening the offensive capabilities of the panzer divisions. These self-propelled guns also were under the division artillery chain of command, complicating the ability to create the ad hoc battle groups that were truly the panzer divisions' strength.[38] The panzer troops' morale reflected the bureaucratic bumbling and the loss of its record of invincibility.

To repair the dilapidated state of the *Panzertruppe*, Hitler rehabilitated Colonel General Heinz Guderian, in disgrace since the defeat of Army Group Center before Moscow in 1941. In view of the bad blood between Guderian and his *führer*, the tank general insisted on certain terms before he would accept a position as Inspector-General of Armored Troops. As Guderian explained to Colonel Rudolph Schmundt, Hitler's adjutant:

> I must therefore insist that I be subordinated neither to the Chief of the Army General Staff nor to the Commander of the Training Army but directly to Hitler. Furthermore, I must be in a position to influence the development of our armored equipment both with the Army Ordnance office and with the Armaments Ministry, for otherwise the re-establishment of the combat effectiveness of this arm of the Service would be impossible. Finally, I must be able to exert the same influence over the organization and training of tank units in the Waffen-SS and the Luftwaffe as in the Army.[39]

Guderian's request for complete control reflected not only his ego but the low state into which the panzer arm had fallen. The efforts to reequip the German tank formations was proceeding haltingly, and unity of effort was impossible, given the rivalries with the other branches of the army, the Waffen-SS (the Nazi Party's private army, complete with its own ranks, special uniforms, and chain of command), and the *Luftwaffe*. Eight days after his meeting with Hitler, Guderian assumed his duties as inspector of German tank troops, but already his mandate was diluted; bureaucratic maneuvering—changing the term *assault guns* to *heavy assault guns*—deprived him of control of almost all self-propelled guns. However, Guderian, along with Albert Speer, the new armaments minister, was able to restore a sense of purpose to German armor efforts.

After visits to the front, Guderian quickly became convinced that the bulk of 1943 should be spent restoring the strength of the *Panzerwaffe*. It certainly needed help; after Stalingrad, German total tank strength on the *Ostfront* had sunk to 495, an average of 27 tanks for each of the eighteen panzer divisions.[40] Guderian argued that the Germans did not possess sufficient strength for a strategic offensive as they had in 1941 and 1942.

However, the panzer general did not appreciate how Hitler's strategic position depended upon his mystique of victory, now tarnished by Stalingrad and the defeats in North Africa. His Balkan allies, particularly the Rumanians, were wavering, as were the Italians, facing an impending invasion in Sicily. Turkey sat on the fence, listening both to importunities from Germany, her World War I ally, and Britain. Also, there were good military reasons to attack: the German war machine required prisoners of war to serve as slave labor. The pressures to resume the strategic offensive, even on a less ambitious scale than previously, were overwhelming. Manstein, the genius of 1940 and the savior of the German cause after Stalingrad, tried to split the difference, recommending a repeat performance of his backhand approach of that spring, luring the Soviets to attack and then cutting them off at the limit of their logistics, but since Manstein's plan would involve the sacrifice of the lower Donets River basin, which Hitler feared would sour negotiations with the Turks and weaken Rumanian resolve, it was rejected.

IRRESISTIBLE KURSK

After the spring *rasputitsa,* as the Russians called the seasonal thaw that made the dirt roads all but impassable, even to tracked vehicles, the Germans, who had been scouring the situation maps in search of a suitable location for an offensive, were drawn to the Soviet salient centered on the town of Kursk, which jutted miles into the German front between Manstein's Army Group South and Kluge's Army Group Center. After an early April conference of senior commanders, the *Oberkommando des Herres* chief of staff, Colonel General Kurt Zeitzler, sent Hitler a plan that sent two large panzer forces converging against Kursk. From the north would come Colonel General Walther Model's Ninth Army, reinforced with tanks, while, from the south, Fourth Panzer Army, under Colonel General Hermann Hoth, would drive up in a pincer movement. The plan was code-named *Zitadelle,* Operation Citadel. Hitler approved the plan almost immediately, issuing Operations Order Number 6 on April 15, 1943. Its beginning revealed how heavy a bet it would be for the Nazi regime, even allowing for Hitler's heightened rhetoric:

> I have decided to undertake as the first priority offensive of this year the Citadel offensive, as soon as the weather permits. This offensive is of decisive importance. It must be carried out quickly and shatteringly. It must give us the initiative for the spring and summer of this year. Therefore all preparations are to be carried through with the greatest care and energy. The best formations, the best armies, the best leaders, great stocks of ammunition are to be placed at the decisive points. Every officer and every man must be indoctrinated with the decisive significance of this offensive. The victory of Kursk must be a signal to the world.[41]

At last, on June 18, Hitler approved the final version of Operation *Zitadelle.* Army Groups Center and South would strike on axes converging on Kursk, destroy the Soviet forces in the bulge and regain the strategic initiative. The heavy blows would involve the new Tiger and Panther tanks and the Ferdinand assault gun. This was to be, as Glantz observed, the fifth installment of the *blitzkrieg,* "a demonstration that, since September 1939, had

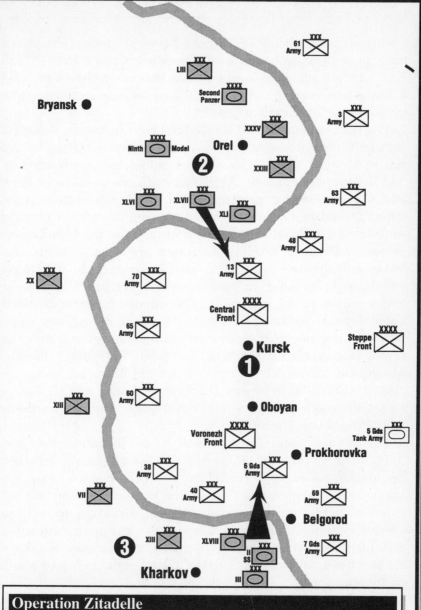

Operation Zitadelle

The German plan for Operation Zitadelle involved a two-prong attack on the town of Kursk. **❶** From the north, **❷** the panzers of Walter Model's Ninth Army would strike, while from the south **❸** the blow would come from Eric Manstein.

Note: Soviet army formations correspond most closely to corps in other armies.

occurred in late spring or summer. Every previous operation of such strategic scale had reaped immediate victory, [and] . . . all had achieved remarkable operational success in their early and intermediate stages. . . . Who could possibly have imagined stopping *blitzkrieg* in its early stages?"[42]

The German plan called for simultaneous thrusts by two giant panzer forces along narrow corridors toward Kursk. In the north, Model's Ninth Army's attack would be spearheaded by XLVII Panzer Corps, with XLVI Panzer Corps on its right flank and XLI Army Corps, consisting of two infantry divisions plus the 18th Panzer Division, on the left. Following this assault echelon would be the 4th and 12th Panzer Divisions and the 10th Panzergrenadier Division. Leading the attack would be battalion task forces with the new heavy Tigers and Ferdinands, blasting their way through the Soviet defenses to open a corridor for the light and medium tanks to exploit. The northern pincer boasted about 1,200 tanks and self-propelled guns, slammed into an attack corridor no more than thirty kilometers wide. From the south, Hoth's 4th Panzer Army and Army Detachment Kempf would launch attacks from the area around Belgorod. Forces included XLVIII Panzer Corps, II SS Panzer Corps, and III Panzer Corps; the southern pincer was even stronger than the northern one, with about 1,500 tanks.

The ripeness of the Kursk salient was not lost on Zhukov and the Soviet general staff. On April 8, the Soviet general delivered his appraisal of likely German actions for the coming campaign season. He predicted that "in the first stage, the enemy will apparently attempt to mass maximum force, including up to 13 to 15 tank divisions, with a great amount of air support, and strike with his [forces from Army Group Center] to bypass Kursk on the northeast, and with his [Army Group South] to bypass Kursk on the southeast."[43]

Zhukov and his chief of staff, Marshall Aleksandr M. Vasilevsky, preferred to strengthen their defenses, absorb the coming German attack, and then launch a counterattack on other fronts. However, Stalin was drawn to a preemptive attack as outlined by Vatutin; the German strategic offensives of 1941 and 1942 had all yielded significant victories. His senior generals, however, doubted whether their forces could be readied in time to get their blow in first. In discussions on April 12, Stalin provisionally accepted Zhukov's recommendations. The Soviets began to dig deep lines of defenses replete with tank traps, strong points, and mobile counterattack groups with armor. Zhukov had in mind a larger and meticulously planned version of the defense of Moscow in 1941 to stop the panzers.

Hitler dithered in preparations. The new panzers and assault guns, the technology in which he put such stock, were slow to reach the field. He first set the attack date in mid-June; by late April, Manstein's scouts had begun to report the extent of Soviet defenses. In June, Hitler deferred the plan another three weeks to allow for more new tank production.

With the delay, Manstein, Model, and Kluge began to worry, feeling their window of opportunity closing as the Russians prepared their defenses. On June 16, Guderian joined the chorus of negative voices, reporting that the new Panzer V Panther was having mechanical troubles and he did not wish to commit it yet in the East. The same day, the German joint high command recommended that *Zitadelle* be canceled. Still, Hitler wavered, calling meetings and moving from headquarters to headquarters. On July 1, a final review was held at Zeitzler's headquarters. The die was now cast: the attack would commence July 5.

Breaking through a fixed, dense layer of defenses with no obvious weak point and little maneuvering room was a new problem for the Germans; their past practice, in France in 1940 and in Russia in 1941 and 1942, had been to run to daylight. Now, thanks to the armies of workers that had made Zhukov's defensive scheme a reality over the spring months, there was no daylight, no open country. In the north, Model took a page from the book of British General Sir Bernard Law Montgomery and his tactics at El Alamein, using his infantry, supported by a heavy artillery barrage, to pry open cracks through which he could introduce his armor. To the south, Manstein, with experienced subordinates like Kempf and Hoth, tried a different set of tactics, concentrating his armor in a narrow wedge and thus hoping for both speed and firepower.

On July 4, Manstein began probing attacks along the southern

face of the Kursk salient, with his armor near the stem of the pro-
trusion and infantry farther to the west. His goal was to take the
heights commanding the German lines west of Belgorod.
Zhukov was near the front along the north face, at the headquarters of Central Front commander Kliment Rokossovsky;
Vasilevsky was in the south with Vatutin at the Voronezh Front
command post. This set a pattern for subsequent large-scale
Russian operations, including the great offensives that were to
come. Thanks to Ultra intercepts relayed from the West, the Soviets knew to the hour when the German preliminary artillery
strikes were to occur, and planned a preemptive barrage of their
own for 4:30 A.M. on July 5. The German attacks were thrown off
schedule from the start.

In the north, Model's Ninth Army began its attacks at 5:30
A.M., with tanks and *panzergrenadiers,* but this was a diversion from
the main thrust, which kicked off two hours later with a longer
artillery preparation and finally with the new Tiger tanks and
Ferdinand self-propelled guns followed by several hundred
Panzer IVs and infantry. Knowing where the attacks were likely to
come, the Soviets had laid fresh minefields during the day July 4,
and now Model's tanks, unsupported by infantry, found themselves ensnared in the mines; a total of about 100 tanks and self-
propelled guns would be lost or disabled the first day.
Nevertheless, the Germans drove slowly but steadily ahead, pushing the Soviet 15th and 81st Infantry divisions out of their first
defensive lines. Near the end of the day, the Tiger spearheads became separated from the following medium tanks and infantry,
stranded between the Russian lines with no protective support.

The following day, Model renewed his attacks, but still could
not fight his way clear of the thick Soviet frontline defensive
belts. When it appeared that a breakthrough had appeared in
the area of the Soviet 15th Infantry Division, Model launched
three panzer divisions into the breach, but by the evening of July
6, he had only penetrated to a depth of 10 kilometers, at a cost
of 25,000 casualties and a loss of about 200 tanks.[44] Rokossovsky
countered with three of his own tank corps, but they, too, found
themselves mired in their own minefields. Both the German attack and the Soviet counterattack bogged down, but the conse-

quences were much worse for the Germans. Model, making no headway, threw in his last reserves of armor on July 8, hurling the 4th Panzer Division plus the remnants of the 2d and 20th Panzer Divisons at the village of Teploye at the western flank of his line. Rokossovsky, grasping the Germans' desperate straits, had packed the village with two infantry divisions, a divison of artillery, two brigades of tanks, and one of assault guns, but still the Germans drove the Soviets back to the heights south of town, where a lone antitank brigade held the line. Three times Colonel V. N. Rukosuyev's 3d Antitank Brigade, supported by tanks, was driven off the crest by the 33d *Panzergrenadier* Regiment and the 3d and 35th Panzer Regiments; three times they reclaimed the lost ground. Model's last strong chance to break through had been stopped.

Still, the Ninth Army commander did what he could to reorganize his remaining units to keep the pressure up, but with fading strength on July 10 and 11. As Robin Cross summed the situation:

> Ninth Army's spearheads were now stuck fast before Rokossovsky's last major lines of defense, which they had been unable to breach by frontal assault. The downhill ride to Kursk lay agonizingly beyond the reach of Model's armor. . . . On the first day of the offensive, Ninth Army had advanced five miles. In the following seven days, it managed only another six, and now its force was spent.[45]

In the south, Manstein fared better, though not as well as hoped. If the opening phases of the Kursk battle had seen deliberate German attacks against prepared Soviet defenses, its climax came in a massive, swirling meeting engagement on July 12, as Hausser's II SS Panzer Corps advanced toward the town of Prokhorovka.

The Soviets quickly had realized the crisis in the south. By July 6, Vatutin had reported to Stalin, dramatizing the scale of the German attacks and requesting reinforcements. Although the Stavka wished to conserve as much strength as possible for the coming counteroffensive, the Soviet plan rested on a successful defense of the Kursk salient. Red Army Chief of Staff Vasilevsky, in consulta-

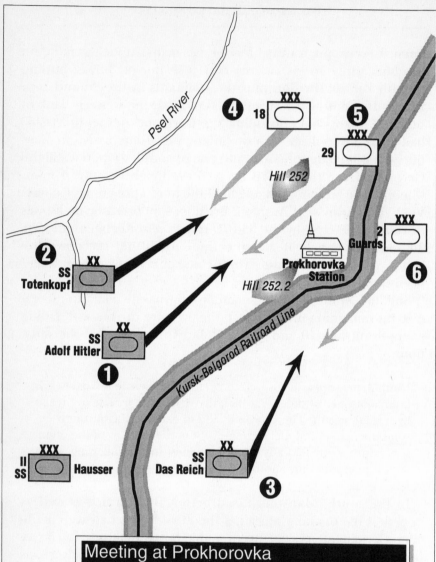

Meeting at Prokhorovka

The climax of the Battle of Kursk came July 11 near Prokhorovka, with the German II SS Panzer Corps meeting the tanks of the Soviet Fifth Guards Army head on.

The fight began ❶ at 4:30 a.m. with the Adolf Hitler SS Panzer division attacking toward Hill 252.2. Following ❷ was the Totenkopf SS Panzer division, with the Das Reich SS Panzer Division ❸ echeloned to the right rear. The Soviets countered with the 18th ❹ and 29th ❺ tank corps in the Prokhorovka corridor and 29th Tank Corps ❻ to the south. The battle marked the Soviets' growing tank prowess.

tion with Zhukov, proposed a number of moves, including stripping the 5th Guards Tank Army from General I. S. Konev's Steppe Front, placing it under Stavka control, and advancing it to Stary Oskol, where it could quickly reinforce Vatutin's threatened Voronezh Front. Zhukov's intent was to knife into Fourth Panzer Army's flanks as it made for Oboyan.

Konev initially objected, wishing to keep his command intact for a larger-scale attack, but the general staff overruled Konev. He, in turn, notified Colonel General Pavel Rotmistrov, the Fifth Guards Army commander, that he must rapidly move his forces over 200 miles of open roads and then be prepared to attack immediately. By 1:30 A.M. the following day, Rotmistrov was on the march, with fighter escorts covering him during daylight hours, driving his troops from his headquarters in the front elements. He later wrote:

> It grew hot as early as [8:00 A.M.] and clouds of dust billowed up. By midday the dust rose in thick clouds, settling in a solid layer on roadside bushes, grain fields, tanks and trucks. The dark red disc of the sun was hardly visible through the grey shroud of dust. Tanks, self-propelled guns and tractors, armored personnel carriers and trucks were advancing in an unending flow. The faces of the soldiers were darkened with dust and exhaust fumes. It was intolerably hot. Soldiers were tortured by thirst and their shirts, wet with sweat, stuck to their bodies. Drivers found the going particularly hard. The crew members tried in every way to make it easier for them by taking their place at the controls every now and then and letting them rest during brief halts. The hardships had to be endured as time was running short.[46]

Rotmistrov's three tank corps were to concentrate in a narrow corridor between the Psel River and the Belgorod-Kursk rail line.

However, the rainy weather of the first week of the *Zitadelle* offensive continued, swelling the rivers and bogging down wheeled vehicles. The rains again came July 10, when German air scouts discovered that the river near Oboyan was hopelessly flooded. The prospect of a hard slog through marshy ground to an opposed river crossing covered by a town and high ground overlooking the flooded plain of the approach was not a happy one for Manstein and his staff, but having paid so dearly to break through the Soviet front lines, and with Model's attacks in the north petering out—and also the news of the Allied landing in Sicily—the Germans sought an alternative to make a final effort to break through to Kursk and salvage the offensive.

With XLVIII Panzer Corps stalled along the road axis to Kursk, Fourth Panzer Army commander Hoth decided to swing II SS Panzer Corps to the east to flank the Soviet defenses; there was open country to the northeast of Prokhorovka. By shooting through the corridor between the Psel and the rail embankment, the Germans hoped to break through to the Soviet rear. It was a less direct route to Kursk but one that might even allow for a larger encirclement; the panzer divisions of Army Detachment Kempf were at last beginning to make some progress to the east and south and could support the attack by II SS Panzer Corps, and XXIV Panzer Corps was being moved up from the region near the River Don to further strengthen Manstein's Army Group South.

The race to Prokhorovka, by two huge and powerful tank formations, was on. Even as the 5th Guards Tank Army was speeding from its positions in reserve, Hausser's scouts began to probe the frontline defenses to the northeast. He sent his three divisions abreast or in a flat wedge formation, with the *Leibstandarte* Adolf Hitler SS Panzer Division in the lead and in the center, flanked by the *Totenkopf* "Death's Head" SS Panzer Division on the left and the Das Reich SS Panzer Division on the right.

The German thrust began in earnest on July 11 with the SS Adolf Hitler Division attacking through the Prokhorovka corridor at 4:30 A.M. with the intent to seize the higher ground, called Hill 252.2, just to the west of the Prokhorovka rail station. Its initial efforts were successful, overrunning the Soviets' front lines and repulsing a tank counterattack with heavy losses. Although the advance of July 11 amounted to just a few miles, Hausser sensed his opportunity for a breakthrough and planned to send the SS *Totenkopf* Division through the corridor as well to reinforce the SS *Leibstandarte* Adolf Hitler attack; the SS Das Reich remained echeloned to the south and rear, across the railroad embankment, to guard against Soviet counterattacks and hold open the corridor for following forces that would swing northward toward Kursk.

The German attack of July 11 had preempted the preparations for the Fifth Guards Tank Army's planned attack, stripping the Soviets of their artillery and intended line of departure. Still, the situation was critical and would not permit the Soviets to draft elaborate and detailed orders, nor could they avoid a fight. As future Soviet Premier Nikita Krushchev, then Front Commander Vatutin's political officer, framed the situation, "The next two days will be terrible. Either we hold or the Germans will take Kursk."[47] Although the clash in the Prokhorovka corridor would be, on its face, just the kind of meeting engagement that favored the Germans' tactical prowess, several factors worked to the Soviet advantage. Perhaps the greatest was the limited maneuvering room: the battlefield was sharply marked by the Pysol River, running southwest to northeast, and the rainy weather made the marshy ground a firm left-hand boundary for the Germans. Similarly, the railroad, paralleling the river near Prokhorovka, marked a similar boundary to the right, as did the town itself. Though the corridor was cut with a few gullies where the ground fell away to the river, its four- to five-mile width was mostly flat and would be packed tightly with armor. There simply would not be room for large maneuvers. The Soviet attack order called for the Fifth Guards Tank Army to advance in the corridor with the 18th Tank Corps to the right and the 29th Tank Corps to the left; each would have a two-mile front with a density of about seventy combat vehicles per mile.[48] Outside the corridor, on the flank defined by the rail embankment, the 2d Guards Tank Corps would conduct a supporting attack. Rotmistrov had a further tank corps and an additional mechanized corps in reserve.

Another advantage was the relatively high state of maintenance of the 5th Guards Tank Army vehicles. Though they had been on the road for 200 miles, their march did not compare with the week's combat suffered by the Germans. As a result, Rotmistrov attacked with about 850 pieces of armor, mostly T-34s but also including T-70 light tanks and SU-85 self-propelled guns, while Hausser could muster only around 300 of the 470 tanks, including about 100 Panzer VI Tigers, with which he had begun the Zitadelle offensive.[49] The loss of the bulk of its artillery on July 11 also forced Rotmistrov to shorten his preparatory bombardment and to advance his time of attack in order to gain some element of surprise.

After dawn aerial skirmishes, the two tank armadas "approached each other in combat formation like lines of jousting knights," as Frederick Turner put it:

> Two approximately equal forces of armor were on a collision course, each advancing in a tremendous dust cloud [the fertile topsoil of the Ukraine dried out rapidly despite the continuous rains]. The sun in the east behind the Soviet tanks helped illuminate the leading German tanks and blinded the German gunners. As the armored waves thundered toward each other ... the [Soviet] 18th Tank Corps was approaching the Totenkopf Division head-on in the north and the 29th Tank Corps moved toward the Adolf Hitler Division in the south near the rail embankment. Never, in the 27 years since the introduction of the first tanks in combat in September 1916, had there been a clash of armor on such a massive scale.[50]

The Soviets also were on slightly higher ground, and the faster T-34s rapidly began to close the gap on the better-armored panzers, equipped with larger guns and high-velocity tank-killing rounds; any hit by a Tiger or one of the Ferdinand self-propelled guns would destroy a T-34 or even a KV-1. These new vehicles, the pride of Hitler's arms industry, halted and used their superior range and their crews' superior gunnery to take out a number of Soviet tanks with an initial volley, but the Soviet tankers pressed their attack; if they could get in among the more ponderous heavy panzers, they could use their agility to get flank and rear shots and to break up the cohesion of the German formations and disrupt command and control.

As the two phalanxes butted together, tank engaged tank, one looming out of the suffocating dust; the bitter, greasy, black smoke; the grunting tank engines and the whine of gear boxes, the flames of wounded tanks and the roar of exploding ammunition for an instant to fire point-blank on its enemy—or perhaps even a friend; in the wild melee, confusion reigned. He who fired first survived; there was little time to distinguish friend from foe. The fighting was savage, even by standards of the Russian front: surviving tank crews were machine-gunned as they fled their burning vehicles or they were strafed from the air or they were simply run over; ammunition was at a premium. The *Leibstandarte* Adolf Hitler requested ammunition resupply from II SS Panzer Corps at 11 A.M., reporting some 100 Soviet tanks destroyed; a second, feverish call came a half hour later. At 2 P.M., SS Totenkopf requested ammunition urgently.[51]

In the morning, the two sides' formations intermingled and the Germans were driven back from the ground they had won the previous day. The melee expanded across the front and to a depth of several miles as unit cohesion and command disintegrated on both sides. These initial battles were nearly pure tank fights between small bands—they could hardly be called units—of tanks; dismounted infantry could not keep up with the wheeling tanks and the panzers and T-34s were too closely joined to permit artillery fire support or air cover. Planes and artillery took to pounding each other or their opponents' rear areas to disrupt resupply and attempts to command the battle.

Around noon, the rains came again, permitting the Russians to infiltrate infantry through the gullies and small farms along the river. Rotmistrov committed his second echelon, but made only small, local progress as the Germans repulsed these efforts with counterattacks. Hausser, too, threw in his reserves and won back some ground in the south, but the Totenkopf Division was stalled in the north and the chaotic situation was beyond Hausser's ability to control. The Prokhorovka corridor was a kaleidescope of burning vehicles and confusion: contradictory reports swamped Hausser's headquarters; the panzer commander barked at his division commanders to give accurate and timely situation reports.

Tactically and operationally, Prokhorovka ended in a standoff; the great meeting engagement saw the two sides butt heads, but neither gave way. Losses were severe for both, too: Hausser lost 350 to 400 tanks, including more than two-thirds of the Panzer VI Tigers, while those that survived were in poor condition to continue any attacks, although initial orders were to renew the offensive; units were disorganized and widely scattered. The German frontline trace at sunset was only slightly farther east than at dawn, and only in the south; the route to Kursk was as long as before. Hausser reported to Manstein that any further attacks were beyond the reach of the II SS Panzer Corps. Soviet losses were somewhat lower, perhaps 350 tanks, and the survivors outnumbered the Germans substantially, but Rotmistrov's formations were as useless for further operations as were Hausser's. The formal mission of the 5th Guards Tank Army, to penetrate farther into the right of the German advance—to sweep into the flank of XLVIII Panzer Corps—could not be achieved.

At the strategic level, Operation *Zitadelle* had failed, as Hitler recognized on July 13 when he called a halt to the offensive and relieved Hausser. The effects of the German defeat went well beyond the tank graveyard at Prokhorovka and the Kursk salient. The Red Army and its generals were now a match for the best the Germans could offer. The German advantages of 1941 and 1942 were all but washed away; not even the subtle leadership of Manstein or the energy of Guderian could do more than prolong the struggle. At the end of the day, the victory of Kursk was a signal to the world, just as Hitler had foretold. However, the victory was Stalin's, not Hitler's, and the signal was of the Red Army's new ascendancy over the *Wehrmacht*. The strategic initiative on the *Ostfront* had changed hands.

Soviet counteroffensives now fell upon the Germans in increasing strength and along fronts where the Nazis could not match Soviet strength. The first came into Model's flank and through a salient in the lines of Army Group Center. Within a month, the Soviets, coordinating the actions of three fronts, had driven through the Second Panzer Army and past Orel, and within six weeks they had penetrated to a depth of up to 160 kilometers. The second came against Manstein's Army Group South, again with three fronts attacking toward Kharkov and threatening to cut off the German forces facing the Caucusus and in the Crimea. Manstein had some success with local counterattacks, but even his genius could not stave off the growing Soviet strength, confidence, and expertise at large-scale armored operations. The third blow again fell in the south, driving the Germans from the eastern Ukraine. By fall, Manstein's lines extended in a southeasterly direction from Kiev to Zaporozhye and then due south; by the end of the year, these, too, were lost. In the spring, Zhukov delivered the final blow to Manstein and to Kleist's Army Group A in the Crimea. The Soviet marshal's attention shifted again to the north.

OPERATION BAGRATION

Since the immediate counterattacks after the failure of *Zitadelle,* German Army Group Center's front had been relatively quiet, the scene of half a dozen secondary Soviet attacks against which the Germans had held, but the Russian victories in the Ukraine had driven the German armies to within fifty miles of the line of departure for Operation *Barbarossa* in 1941. It also had completely uncovered Field Marshal Ernst Busch's southern flank, leaving him with a crescent-shaped front stretching 1,100 kilometers through Belorussia and eastern Poland from Brest-Litovsk in the south, along the southern rim of the Pripet Marshes, and arcing northward to Vitebsk, where his lines tied into Army Group North. The marshes offered Busch some protection along the southern face of his front, but they also could screen a Russian force as it moved along the edge of the marshes to attack Busch's rear at Kovel, where his lines merged with those of German Army Group North Ukraine to his south.

Busch, replacing Kluge, still commanded a large force, perhaps 500,000 men in total, but it had very little mobility or firepower, with just two panzer divisions and thirty-eight infantry divisions, arranged in three infantry armies, and General Hans Reinhardt's Third Panzer Army. The infantry were supported sparsely by artillery and hardly at all by the *Luftwaffe;* the regional air command, *Luftflotte* six, had but forty fighters. For perhaps the first time in the entire war, the Red Army would enjoy the benefits of unchallenged air superiority, and the Germans would learn how hard it was to operate when constantly strafed and bombarded. Perhaps the greatest drawbacks hampering Busch was Hitler's concern about the impending invasion in the West and his unwillingness to moderate his demands or tactics in the East. Army Group Center would not be reinforced, but would be ordered to stand fast.

In preparation for the summer 1944 campaigning season, the Soviets had reshuffled their organization and senior commanders. By late spring, the new lineup was set, and in May, Zhukov, Vasilevsky, and the general staff operations chief, General A. I. Antonov, began work on an ambitious operation they called *Bagration*, targeted at Army Group Center. The plan was to envelop the Germans in about seven weeks and to a depth of 250 kilometers. By May 20, a draft was prepared for Stalin, and the various front commanders were called to Moscow for briefings. For the rest of the month, these commanders and their staffs hammered out the details of the attack, with Zhukov and Vasilevsky again going forward to command groups of fronts early in June; planning continued, with air commanders brought in to synchronize air support, and it climaxed with a central war game.[52]

The planned offensive was truly a massive undertaking. The Soviets anticipated attacking in six fairly widely dispersed corridors; the German system of armored, mobile tactical reserves would be overwhelmed not only by the weight of the Soviet thrusts but by their relative simultaneity and their dispersion. The Soviets massed troops and firepower in support of the operation: 124 divisions, totaling 1.2 million troops; 5,200 tanks and self-propelled guns; and 6,000 aircraft. Artillery strength was estimated at 31,000 guns and mortars, concentrated at more than 200 barrels per kilometer on the attack fronts.[53] In addition, the Soviets prepared logistically for deep operations: each front had been alloted 12,000 three-ton trucks. As Albert Seaton summed up the Soviet preparations:

> The Soviet preponderance over the Germans in tanks was reckoned at ten to one and in aircraft seven to one, but in fact it was much more than this. Five lines of ammunition, twenty refills of vehicle fuel and thirty days' rations were brought up within reach

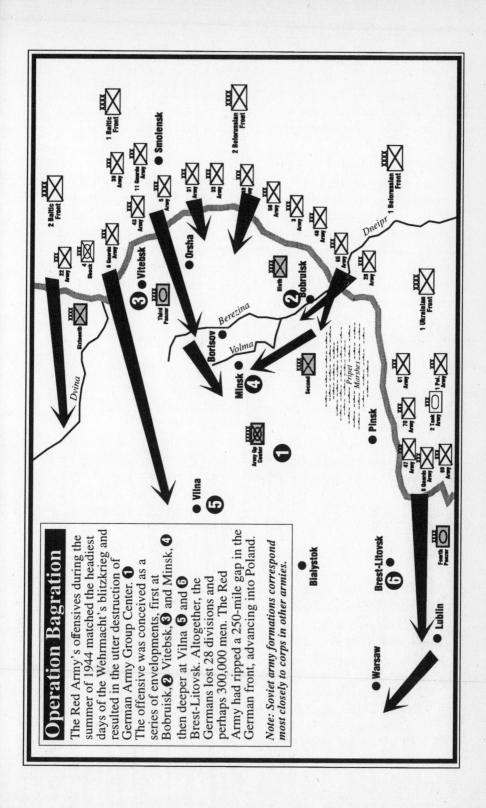

Operation Bagration

The Red Army's offensives during the summer of 1944 matched the headiest days of the Wehrmacht's blitzkrieg and resulted in the utter destruction of German Army Group Center. ❶ The offensive was conceived as a series of envelopments, first at Bobruisk, ❷ Vitebsk, ❸ and Minsk, ❹ then deeper at Vilna ❺ and Brest-Litovsk. Altogether, the Germans lost 28 divisions and perhaps 300,000 men. The Red Army had ripped a 250-mile gap in the German front, advancing into Poland.

Note: Soviet army formations correspond most closely to corps in other armies.

of formations. Energetic and aggressive ground reconnaissance began all along the line from Pskov to the Carpathians by fighting patrols or by company and battalion probing attacks.[54]

These preparations represented the distilled wisdom of three years' hard learning at the hands of German tank geniuses like Guderian and Manstein. The Red Army was now ready to sit their schoolmasters' examination. They were guided by a redrafted thesis of armored warfare, *Combat Regulations for Tank and Mechanized Troops of the Red Army, Part II,* a thorough updating of the 1942 manuals that had guided the Soviets through the seesaw battles of 1943. The new regulations covered all possible matters regarding the tactical employment of armored forces in battalion, regiment, and brigade operations, and would serve as a recipe for the attacks to come in Operation *Bagration.*

The manual not only returned to many of the principles that had been elaborated by Tukhachevsky, the prewar tank visionary, but incorporated the practical lessons learned in combat. Perhaps most importantly, the manual listed as one of its four fundamentals of tank tactics the "Coordination of Tanks with Other Branches of Arms."[55] According to the manual, "modern combat is conducted with the united strength of all weapons; therefore, their coordination is a prerequisite for success in battle."[56] It went on to cover the roles of infantry, artillery, air support, engineers, and chemical troops in working with armored formations in all manner of situations; extensive sections were devoted to command and troop control, reconnaissance, and supply, and to march organization and security. It was a cookbook approach to tank operations, but it was fundamentally sound.

For example, one hard-won aspect of the Red Army's maturity was its acceptance of the inevitability of meeting engagements, those fluid battles which, throughout the war, the Germans had sought and hoped to master through tactical flexibility and superior leadership. If the Soviets did not seek the chaos and complexity of meeting engagements, they were now at least prepared to accept them as the price for success and especially success in the deep operations they desired. "As a rule," stated the manual, "a meeting engagement of tank and mechanized troops occurs in the depth of the enemy positions when exploiting a success or when counterattacking against an attacking enemy. The approach march against the enemy and the ensuing combat occurs many times with one or two open flanks."[57] Here was a measure of uncertainty that Red Army officers had previously been loath to accept. Yet, after successes in encounters such as at Prokhorovka, the Soviet tankers gained confidence, seeing the tank's unique advantages being magnified in meeting engagements: "By swift maneuver and sudden appearance in front of an enemy they seize an advantageous position. . . ."[58]

Operation *Bagration*, then, as well as being great in scope, would differ in quality from previous Soviet offensives. The Germans would be caught unprepared for this new kind of enemy. However, at Army Group Center, Busch was anticipating an attack; despite intense Soviet security measures, the Germans were able to discover that the Red Army was shifting forces from the Ukraine to Belorussia and was bringing the local formations up to full strength. As Seaton observed, "There was a feeling of tenseness in both commanders and troops on the German side which had never been experienced before, and from about 10 June onwards Busch expressed his anxiety to the Army High Command (OKH)."[59] Still, Hitler's sense of political and economic considerations, as always, trumped any expressions of operational necessity or facts of military intelligence. He remained focused primarily on the West, but in the East his concerns were for the Balkans in the south and the Finns in the north. What little attention he was able to give Busch's area of operation was counterproductive: he ordered that Army Group Center detach six divisions to garrison the fortresses of Bobruisk, Mogilev, Orsha, and Vitebsk. Busch's armies were now a tethered calf awaiting the slaughter. *Führer* Order Number 11 had sealed their fate; it read:

> The "Fortified Areas" will fulfill the function of fortresses in former historical times. They will ensure that the enemy does not oc-

cupy these areas of decisive operational importance. They will allow themselves to be surrounded, thereby holding down the largest possible number of enemy forces, and establishing conditions favorable for successful counterattacks. . . . Each "Fortified Area Commandant" should be a specially selected, hardened soldier, preferably of general's rank. . . . Only the commander-in-chief of an army group in person may, with my approval, relieve [the commandant] of his duties, and perhaps order the surrender of a fortified area.[60]

Operation *Bagration* was to open on June 22, timed to the anniversary of the German invasion three years earlier, but before the tanks rolled, partisans in the German rear areas sabotaged rail lines and communications cables; in the week leading to the attack, Soviet artillery raids ranged German artillery and command centers and air attacks also targeted the German lines of communication. The ground offensive opened with probing attacks as prescribed in the new Soviet operations manual. The initial attacks were to be carried out with infantry and artillery; only after the gaps in the frontline defenses were found or created would the main mobile groups be committed. Where defenses were thin, the infantry continued their advance. Where resistance was determined, as around the "fortresses," artillery was brought up in great concentrations to soften up the strong points.

Reinhardt's Third Panzer Army held the northern position in Busch's line, near the city of Vitebsk, with LIII Corps in the immediate area around the city and IX Corps to the north and VI Corps to the south. Dubbing his formations around Vitebsk a "panzer army" was a cruel joke, for his troops were almost all infantry with the exception of a tank destroyer battalion and an assault-gun brigade; neither was suited for mobile warfare. Almost from the start of the offensive, Reinhardt was in trouble. Near the town of Obol, the 25th Infantry Division took the brunt of the initial Russian attacks, and despite desperate actions, an eight-kilometer gap was ripped in the German front on the first day. By the second day, gaps in the German line were fifty kilometers wide to the north of Vitebsk; the Soviet penetration reached a depth of more than fifteen kilometers. To the south of the city, the gap in the German line was nearly as great. VI Corps had been overrun by the Russian infantry and the following Fifth Guards Tank Army, which was now about to break free, in the German rear. While VI and IX Corps were shattered, LIII Corps had escaped the inital attacks unscathed, but now were all but cut off from their neighbors to the north and south. The Soviet mobile formations began turning their pincers inward to encircle Vitebsk.

Even as the battle between the two armies was building, the German high command began their usual round of infighting. First to realize the danger to LIII Corps, Reinhardt ordered it to withdraw on the evening of June 23. Returning from leave to his headquarters at Minsk as the Soviet attacks began, Busch immediately contravened Reinhardt's order, nor would he allow Reinhardt to detail units from Vitebsk to try to stabilize the front in the IX and VI Corps areas. However, Busch was merely complying with Hitler's orders and would not move without agreement from the army high command. The following day, the German Army chief of staff, Colonel General Kurt Zeitzler, arrived in Minsk to discuss matters with Busch. Busch asked for permission to withdraw, and it was Zeitzler's turn to refuse, although he fudged matters by allowing the three divisions of LIII Corps to withdraw to the outskirts of Vitebsk. He could do no more and returned to the *führer's* headquarters at the Obersalzberg near Berchtesgaden in Bavaria.[61] While the German generals talked, the Soviets completed the encirclement.

That afternoon, Zeitzler telephoned Reinhardt directly to ask if the withdrawal of LIII Corps were absolutely necessary. Reinhardt replied that the corps was cut off and the Soviets tightening the noose; what was at issue now was not withdrawal but a breakout and the orders must be issued immediately. Zeitzler explained that the *führer* was reluctant to sacrifice the equipment around Vitebsk, to which Reinhardt answered that there was also the matter of five divisions' worth of troops. The luckless Zeitzler again went to put the issue to Hitler, while Reinhardt held the line. Ten minutes later, he returned with the message that "the *führer* has decided that Vitebsk is to be held."[62] Just as Reinhardt hung up, a message reached the Third Panzer Army from LIII Corps confirming that Vitebsk was surrounded and that several divisions no longer were functioning formations. Again Busch requested permission to withdraw from Vitebsk, but this time the reply was that a counterattack should be undertaken to open the road to LIII Corps. Two hours later, at 6:30 P.M., another message came that LIII Corps was to break out but that a single division should be nominated to hold Vitebsk; despite the illogic of the *führer's* order—a single division could hardly be expected to hold what a corps could not, making its sacrifice entirely pointless—Reinhardt passed the message to Vitebsk, nominating the 206th Infantry Division as the sacrificial lamb.

In any event, the Germans had waited too long to withdraw from Vitebsk. The next day, as the enfeebled LIII Corps tried to break out of its encirclement, it could not easily disengage from the Soviet Thirty-ninth Army, which surrounded the city; the German perimeter began to collapse. The inevitable end came on June 26 and 27 as the breakout attempt became hopeless. The weakened infantry divisions lacked mobility and firepower, making their progress agonizingly slow. At 9 A.M. on June 27, a final radio message came from LIII Corps reporting that the breakout attempt had progressed fifteen kilometers to the south and west of Vitebsk, but that ammunition shortages and unrelenting Soviet air attacks were limiting further headway. It was every man for himself as the Germans lost any large-unit cohesion and formed ad hoc battle groups—little more than desperate men attempting to infiltrate to the safety of their own lines, such as they might be found—to avoid capture or fighting the Soviets. A corporal of the 505th Engineer Battalion described what the failed breakout was like for the average soldier:

> The first Russian aircraft appeared with the dawn and soon the first bombs were falling. Then more aircraft came. The Russian Air Force appeared on a scale never before experienced during the war. Bombs hailed down on the bridge, but fortunately most

of them landed in the water. . . . Vast numbers of troops with their equipment were backed up before the bridge waiting to cross. . . . Late in the morning the Russians attacked with tanks. They were beaten off and were unable to break into the bridgehead. But from then on the T-34s stayed within sight of the bridge and kept it under direct fire. On top of it all it was a clear day with its roasting summer heat. . . . That evening the bridgehead was still holding but the bridge itself had become impassable for motor- and horse-drawn vehicles. Under the enemy fire the bridge was being swept away from the [engineers] piece by piece. Dead men and horses floated among the beams and posts, while wounded clung to pieces of wood. . . .

Save yourself if you can was the new watchword. The Russians were said to have crossed the Düna somewhere else and were already ahead of us. . . . We drove several more kilometers and spotted more Russians, about two battalions or more, ahead of us and to the sides. Their tanks swarmed out of the evening horizon everywhere, including to the west of us.

There was an outburst of rifle fire and our machine was hit. We left the motorcycle where it was, having no time to destroy it, and ran off on foot. Like rabbits before the hunt we raced across the field as bullets chirped all around us. There were many other soldiers with us. The enemy fire so intensified that one could not hear the individual shots above the whistling; there was just a rising and falling buzzing and whirring. When it became too bad I threw myself to the ground. There were plenty of others on the ground, but many of them did not get up again. . . .

We escaped the enemy fire in the twilight, and the damned aircraft, too, left us in peace. Everyone was feeling the effects of hunger and terrible thirst, and the many stuck and abandoned vehicles were scoured for food and drink.

We assembled in a wood. Orders passed among the cluster of troops who had got this far. Numbers of units were called out. In this way I made contact with my company, or at least what was left of it. There were barely 10 men from the battalion's other two companies. The battalion staff no longer existed. . . .

A general came with several officers and informed us that we were surrounded. The Russians had crossed the Düna northwest of us while we were still holding the bridge. They also came from the southeast over the land bridge between the Düna and Dnieper

[Rivers]. The word was that at dawn we would attack in order to force a breakout to the west. Every soldier was to fight as an infantryman, no matter what branch of the service he belonged to. . . .

Before midnight the Russians began to lay harassing fire from artillery and Stalin Organs on the wood. It was impossible to sleep. I sought cover behind tree trunks, but had to constantly change positions, listening for the howling of incoming shells before leaping behind the nearest thick tree or into a depression in the ground. Wounded screamed. They faced the worst fate of all. Anyone who could not walk had to be left behind. . . .

As it became light we left the cover of the wood and worked our way forward, creeping and crawling. On a rise we could see the heaps of dirt belonging to a Russian position. Those at the front leapt to their feet and charged the position with loud shouts. . . . Enemy fire began to whip toward us. . . . The first assault wave fell, the second hesitated and went to ground. The surprise attack had failed. . . . Another charge, again murderous fire, more losses. . . . No one made it to the top of the rise. All of those still alive pressed themselves into the ground and tried to find cover. Finally the enemy fire was so heavy that it drowned the cries of the wounded. . . .

I lay among the dead, living and wounded under the blazing sun, not moving and almost without sensory perception. I no longer felt thirst or the heat. To stand up meant certain death. I lay there until afternoon, when the firing and bursting shells began to abate. The Russians probably realized that they were not going to be attacked again, because they had eliminated most of us. Finally the firing stopped.

A little later I saw several soldiers to my right get up without being fired upon. Then I stood up, too feeble and shaky to still be afraid of surrendering. . . .[63]

In the fighting around Vitebsk, the Germans lost 35,000 men, including 10,000 taken prisoner. By June 27, Reinhardt's Third Panzer Army ceased to exist. Elsewhere along the Army Group Center Front, the story was much the same. Busch's ability to command his forces was shattered almost from the start, as the Soviets interfered with long-range radio communications and the Red Air Force's command of the skies made movement by air or ground extremely hazardous. The Germans, who so relied upon the agility of their command and staffs to maximize the tactical acumen of their small units, were reduced to fighting in an uncoordinated and isolated way.

To the south of Vitebsk, the Red Army's pincer movements thrust through the German lines toward Busch's headquarters at Minsk. After three days of heavy fighting, the Russian first-echelon formations had broken through the frontline defenses of the German Fourth Army, ripping a 100-kilometer gap between it and Reinhardt's Third Panzer Army. A similar gap was created to the south of the Fourth Army, where its lines tied in with the Ninth Army, near the city of Bobruisk. As the battle became fluid, the Soviets committed their mobile groups to exploit the openings. On June 28, the Fifth Guards Tank Army, still commanded by Rotmistrov, the hero of Kursk, began a rapid advance through open country down the Minsk road, while to the south, IX Tank Corps allowed the Red Army to encircle Bobruisk and most of the German Ninth Army by June 27.

The previous day, Busch had traveled to Hitler's headquarters to try to impress upon the *führer* how serious the situation was; the German high command, eyes fixed upon the Normandy landings in the West, was slow to realize the danger to Army Group Center and the new capabilities of the Red Army for deep operations. Hitler's first reponse was to draw a they-shall-not-pass line generally along the Berezina River, which roughly followed the arc of the original German front lines and lay to the east of Minsk, but by June 28, it was apparent that the Soviet penetration had gone beyond the river.

In desperation, Hitler turned to Model, the defensive genius of the *Ostfront* and now a field marshal, relieving the hapless Busch. Model was then in command of Army Group North Ukraine, a post he was to retain even as he assumed control of Army Group Center. Model's actions were too little—he transferred a number of units from the Ukraine to Army Group Center, only to lose them by so doing—and too late. The collapse of

Army Group Center was now purely a function of the Soviets' ability to sustain their offensive.

This was a great surprise to the Germans, Model included. An estimated 100,000 men were lost in the encirclement and destruction of the Fourth and Ninth Armies, the Soviets leaving the reduction of the pockets to infantry while the tanks rolled on westward. Within two days of taking command, Model had to admit that the Soviet objectives ranged far deeper than he had realized; his efforts were now turned to saving the extreme right and left wings of the army group's position: a rump of Reinhardt's Third Panzer Army remained north of Vitebsk, while the Second Army was untouched west and south of the Pripet Marshes. However, the Germans had yet to appreciate the full measure of Soviet intentions, for further thrusts were just beginning to break upon them in the north, through the Baltics and near Kovel, at the border of Belorussia and the Ukraine; there was a still deeper set of envelopments that Zhukov and Vasilevsky had in mind. Albert Seaton summarized the effects of Operation *Bagration* succinctly:

> About 28 divisions of Army Group Center had been lost as fighting formations, and the total casualties were put as high as 300,000 men. A gigantic, 250-mile breach gaped in the German line and, as the route to the Baltic States and East Prussia seemed to be open, border guards and training regiments from East Prussia, even the *Führer's* own guard battalion, were rushed eastwards towards the great battle area to fill the gap. For Germany the defeat was of dimensions as great as Stalingrad.[64]

The Red Army was now master of the art of large-scale blitzkrieg warfare. Though it never achieved the tactical flair and panache of the *Wehrmacht*, it had a massive and perhaps deeper wisdom than its German counterpart, one especially suited to the vast open spaces and sweeping, swirling tank clashes of the Eastern Front. The Germans could not match the Soviets in the scale, not only of their forces and operations, but in their thinking; perhaps dazzled by their own tactical genius, the Germans eventually became blinded to Soviet operational designs until it

J.F.C. Fuller, visionary of the British Royal Tank Corps and principal architect of the British victory at Cambrai—the first great tank battle

British Mark V tanks advancing at the Battle of Amiens in 1918. The Mark V was the successor to the Mark IV models that had so shocked the Germans at Cambrai the previous year.

Gen. Heinz Guderian, the father of *blitzkrieg*, seen here watching Allied prisoners march past after his panzers had advanced 220 miles in seven days to reach the French ports

The Panzer IV, the mainstay of the German armored fleet during the early years of World War II

The other defining element of *blitzkrieg,* the JU-87 Stuka dive bomber, releasing its bombs. As he swooped down, the Stuka pilot would sound a wailing siren, further terrifying his enemies below.

Erwin Rommel, legendary commander of the Afrika Korps. A tactical genius who could never be counted out, Rommel instinctively understood the advantages of the armored offensive in desert warfare.

Bernard Law Montgomery, Rommel's British nemesis in North Africa. A cautious and conservative commander, Montgomery stiffened the Eighth Army's spine and dealt the Germans a critical blow at El Alamein.

An Afrika Korps "Flak 88" crew engages Eighth Army armor at Mersa El Brega in April 1941. Originally designed as an antiaircraft weapon, the "Flak 88" was also the most deadly antitank gun of World War II.

A British Grant tank passes a destroyed Axis vehicle in the desert. The Grant's two main guns enabled it to engage both enemy armor and soft targets, but it suffered from an awkward design.

Photogenic but unreliable, the British Crusader tank broke down at the rate of one every ten miles when traveling in column.

A Panzer Mark III races through the desert. Frequent upgrades made this early German tank a threat to Allied armor throughout World War II.

Field Marshal Erich von Manstein, perhaps the greatest German commander of the Eastern front, whose operational genius was nevertheless unable to stem the Red tide

A German King Tiger unit faces east toward the steppes on which the Soviets shattered Hitler's dreams of an empire built by *blitzkrieg*.

Field Marshal Georgi Zhukov, the savior of the Soviet Union who drove the *Wehrmacht* from the gates of Moscow all the way back to Berlin

A column of Tiger Is at Kursk, where the tide of the war in Europe turned irrevocably against the Germans

A column of T-34s, part of Timoshenko's Army of the Don, bears down on the rear of the German columns sweeping toward Stalingrad in early 1942. The T-34 was arguably the best medium tank of the war and the single most important weapon in the Soviet arsenal.

SS *Obersturmführer* Michael Wittmann, the most celebrated tank commander in history, almost single-handedly dealt a crippling blow to the British 7th Armoured Division at Villers-Bocage.

The leading Allied commanders in Normandy: Patton, Bradley and Montgomery *(left to right)*. A greater contrast than that between the swashbuckling Patton and the conservative Montgomery is hard to imagine.

British infantry follow a Churchill tank through the dense undergrowth of the Norman *bocage*.

An M5 Stuart tank with a "Rhino" hedgecutter attached crashes through a Normandy hedgerow. Made for German beach defenses, the Rhino allowed American tanks to finally break out of the *bocage*.

Not all the Normandy fighting was conducted in the hedgerows. Here British infantry supported by a Churchill advance through a wheatfield during Operation Goodwood.

The juxtaposition of this Sherman with a destroyed Panzer V Panther in the Ardennes highlights the American tank's rudimentary appearance compared with the sleeker German model.

SS *Obersturmbannführer* Joachim Peiper *(left)* with SS *Standartenführer* Fritz Witt in Kharkov, March 1943. Peiper's battle group came closest to punching through the Allied lines in December 1944 during the Battle of the Bulge, murdering dozens of civilians and Allied prisoners in the process.

Loaded with German paratroops, a *Kampfgruppe Peiper* King Tiger (Tiger II) advances through the Ardennes on December 18, 1944. At almost 70 tons, the King Tiger was the heaviest tank of World War II, but was underpowered and mechanically unreliable.

Israel Tal, who used modern technology and old-fashioned discipline to mold the Israeli Armored Corps into a fearsome fighting machine

Two British-made Israeli Centurion tanks fight their way forward during the battle for the Gaza Strip in 1967. "There will be only the assault and the advance," Major General Israel Tal told his troops before attacking into Gaza, and their success set the stage for their country's lightning victory in the Six Day War.

An Israeli M-51 "Supersherman," boasting a medium-velocity French 105mm gun on a modified Sherman hull

An Israeli Centurion charging to intercept Egyptian T-62s on October 6, 1973. The tank commander is standing aloft in his turret, an Israeli custom that has cost many commanders their lives.

Israeli M48 Pattons attack Rafa Junction in 1967. "There will be no halt and no retreat," Tal ordered his troops before the assault.

Exuberant Egyptian troops crossing the Suez Canal atop a T-55 tank, October 6, 1973

An Egyptian T-54 tank fighting alongside infantry in the Yom Kippur war. The soldier on the right shoulders an RPG-7 antitank rocket launcher, while the infantryman on the left carries an AK-47 assault rifle.

An Israeli M60 pauses during a Sinai tank battle in the Yom Kippur war.

An American M1A1 Abrams fires its 120mm main gun in a night exercise in Saudi Arabia prior to Operation Desert Storm. The Abrams' thermal-vision nightsight, depleted uranium armor, and advanced fire-control equipment made it more than a match for its Soviet-made counterpart, the T-72.

The other half of the U.S. armor force in the Gulf, the Bradley fighting vehicle. Firing depleted uranium rounds, its 25mm main gun was credited with putting a number of Iraqi tanks out of action.

was too late to reply. Certainly, the Soviets put great faith in their peculiar, scientific, and measured approach to mechanized warfare, for though the norms and units of fire evolved, the Soviet Army clung tightly to these basic concepts for fifty years of Cold War.

CHAPTER FOUR

FRANCE, 1944

Breakout from Normandy

ON JUNE 6, 1944, Allied troops returned to Western Europe in Operation Overlord. The eleven divisions that stormed the beaches of Normandy presented Adolf Hitler with every German leader's worst nightmare: a two-front war. Overlord, the largest and most ambitious amphibious operation in history, was, despite the years of preparation, a tremendous risk. Only the Germans' inability to accurately predict where the invasion would come, combined with Allied air supremacy and Hitler's failure to authorize the immediate deployment of reserve panzer divisions to crush the Allied beachheads, prevented the *Wehrmacht* from hurling the Allies back into the sea at the first attempt. This was only the opening blow in what promised to be a bloody and bitter series of campaigns if the Nazis were to be finally defeated. Breaking out from the D-Day perimeter through the Normandy hedgerows would be a painful, step-by-step slog where the advantages of armor would be negated until, at last, George Patton's Third Army shook itself free into open country.

CAUGHT IN THE WEB OF THE BOCAGE

After the invasion, the next step toward Berlin required rushing as many troops and as much matériel as possible to Normandy; amphibious operations were fragile undertakings, especially during the first days. By June 30, the Allies had managed to land

875,000 troops on the beaches and advance in some cases up to fifteen miles inland. Nevertheless, things were not going entirely their way. General Sir Bernard Law Montgomery, commander of the British 21st Army Group and the most senior Allied commander on the ground in Normandy, had planned to be much farther from the beaches by this stage, but fierce German resistance, organized by his old enemy, Field Marshal Erwin Rommel, had delayed his progress.

To Montgomery's dismay—for his ego had grown even faster than his reputation—the American units on the other, western flank of the Allied front were having better luck. There, Major General J. Lawton "Lightning Joe" Collins led the troops of his U.S. VII Corps in a three-day attack across the Cotentin peninsula. The operation culminated on June 17, when U.S. troops reached Barneville on the western Cotentin coast, trapping three German divisions on the northern end of the peninsula around Cherbourg, which was about to be transformed by Hitler into yet another of his fortress cities. These divisions were destroyed by the end of the month as VII Corps turned and drove north toward Cherbourg. Meanwhile, to the southeast, the remainder of Lieutenant General Omar Bradley's First Army was struggling to expand the bridgehead southward toward the key German stronghold of Saint-Lô.

Pushing inland from the Normandy beaches was almost exclusively infantry work: the field-by-field, farm-by-farm rooting out of an entrenched enemy. The First Army troop roster reflected this reality: by June 15, First Army had expanded to include four corps: V, VII, VIII, and XIX, with but one armored division to complement its eight infantry and two airborne divisions, which, once on the ground, were walking infantry. The German troops opposing them also lacked armored punch and mobility: the German Seventh Army boasted six infantry, one parachute, one air landing, and one static division.[1] These units were of mixed quality. Static divisions were the least effective of the German organizations in Normandy. Many of the nominally German troops manning the static divisions were not German at all, but were drawn from the countries overrun by the Germans in Eastern Europe. These Serbs, Russians, and Poles had little heart for a fight

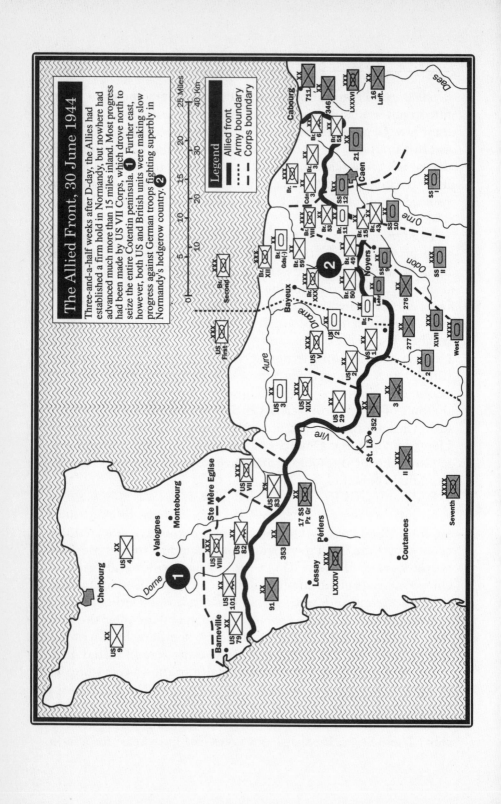

The Allied Front, 30 June 1944

Three-and-a-half weeks after D-day, the Allies had established a firm hold in Normandy, but nowhere had advanced much more than 15 miles inland. Most progress had been made by US VII Corps, which drove north to seize the entire Cotentin peninsula. ❶ Further east, however, both US and British units were making slow progress against German troops fighting superbly in Normandy's hedgerow country. ❷

Legend

▬▬▬ Allied front
········· Army boundary
‒ ‒ ‒ Corps boundary

0   5   10   15   20   25 Miles

0   10   20   30   40 Km

to the death against the Allies and often surrendered after putting up only token opposition. However, there were also several crack German outfits opposing the V, VII, and XIX Corps, and these put up dogged resistance that slowed the American advance to a crawl. Here the Germany army would continue to demonstrate that, soldier for soldier, it was still the finest army in the world.

The unique topography of the Norman countryside, *bocage*, or box country, consisted of small fields surrounded by tall hedgerows, the roots of which were firmly embedded in solid earthen walls up to three feet thick and twelve feet high.[2] Without question, box country was infantry country. Certainly, the Allies had underestimated the extent to which such terrain would inhibit their ability to advance. The *bocage* was ideally suited for the sort of defensive struggle being waged by the Germans. For weeks after the invasion, Allied mechanized forces could take advantage of their mobility only by driving along the narrow roadways that joined the farms and villages of Normandy. These routes, hemmed in by the hedgerows and overhung with tree boughs, were perfect for ambushes, and many an Allied tank commander fell victim to a German sniper's bullet as he popped his head out of the turret to get his bearings. The hedgerows also provided excellent cover for antitank guns, including the ferocious German 88 mm guns and bazookas; the network of small farms acted as a giant net to contain the Allied attacks. Meanwhile, the leafy branches gave German vehicles and defenses some cover from the Allied air forces, which enjoyed almost complete air superiority over Normandy from the start of the invasion.

The experienced German troops used these natural advantages to offset the Allies' superior numbers. Among the fiercest opponents encountered by the Americans during that first week on the continent were the paratroops of the 6th Parachute Regiment, no longer jumping from airplanes, but elite troops nonetheless. Led by Colonel H. Freiherr von der Heydte, a veteran of the German airborne landing on Crete in May 1941, the regiment bitterly defended the town of Carentan, which marked the hinge between VII and V Corps, and was also on the road to Saint-Lô.[3] When they finally relinquished their hold over the town on June 12 and the sheer weight of American numbers made further resistance in the streets of Carentan pointless, the paratroops merely withdrew to a line just to the south, there to delay any further American advance. In the next five days, the U.S. forces succeeded in pushing the Germans only a few miles farther south of Carentan, and the area remained the most vulnerable point of the Allied line, only about six miles from the sea. Farther east, the front bulged southward where XIX and V Corps were pushing toward Saint-Lô. However, by June 18, this attack, spearheaded by the 29th Infantry Division, had also bogged down five miles short of the town, which sat astride the junction of all roads leading south and east, and was therefore a vital Allied objective.

THE PANZERS COMMITTED PIECEMEAL

In a thirty-five-mile front of dense bocage between Saint-Lô and the coastal town of Ouistreham, the vast bulk of the armored firepower available to each side was brought to bear. The Second British Army, under Lieutenant General Sir Miles Dempsey, with two armored divisions supported by one airborne and five infantry divisions, was locked in a fierce struggle with German Panzer Group West under General Geyr von Schweppenburg, who commanded one static and four armored divisions. This clash was the key to the Allied plan for breaking out of the eastern flank of their enclave. The plan centered on the town of Caen, the regional capital of about 50,000 inhabitants located ten miles from the shore. Like Saint-Lô to the west, Caen was a strategic crossroads and chokepoint that controlled access to the heartland of France. Rather optimistically, Montgomery had hoped to capture Caen on D-Day itself, assigning the mission to the British 3d Infantry and 6th Airborne Divisions.

Advancing south from the beachhead, the British divisions' progress was rudely interrupted by the unexpected intervention of the 21st Panzer Division; Allied intelligence had placed this German armor unit, part of Rommel's Army Group B reserve, farther from the coast. From Caen, 21st Panzer, equipped mostly with matériel captured from the French in 1940, was immediately thrown into the line with the hope of preventing the British 3d Infantry Division from linking up with the Canadian forces to its right. The 21st Panzer Division was commanded by Major General Edgar Feuchtinger, an artilleryman by trade, with no experience of combat or tanks. Colonel Hans von Luck, a veteran panzer officer who commanded a battle group under Feuchtinger, believed the latter's position resulted from Hitler's knowledge of his strong Nazi party loyalty.

Despite the advantage of surprise, 21st Panzer's patrols failed to reach the coast by nightfall.[4] Luck recalled that his

> reconnaissance battalion went straight into the attack from its march and, supported by a Panzer company, penetrated to Escoville against their surprised opponents. Then all hell broke loose. The heaviest naval guns, up to 380 mm in calibre, artillery and fighter-bombers plastered us without pause. Radio contacts were lost, wounded came back and the men of the reconnaissance battalion were forced to take cover.[5]

This aborted effort constituted the only German armor counterattack on D-Day and pointed up the difficulty the Germans had in getting tanks forward to defend against the Allied invasion. The other two armor divisions under Rommel's direct control were too far away to influence the battle; 116th Panzer was beyond the Seine, and 2d Panzer was beyond the Somme. Another three armor divisions, including the formidable Panzer *Lehr* and 12th SS Panzer, were also in reserve in Normandy, but 12th SS Panzer was stationed the other side of Lisieux, 40 miles east of the fighting, while Panzer *Lehr* was closer to Chartres, 100 miles to the southeast of the battle raging north of Caen.

The senior German commanders who wanted to hurl these crack outfits at the Allies before Dempsey's troops had time to establish themselves on the shore had another probelm. The divisions came under the control of *Oberkommando der Wehrmacht*, or OKW, the armed forces high command, which in reality meant they could only be released from reserve on the orders of Hitler himself; the *führer,* somehow still arrogant after eighteen months of unremitting defeat, insisted on controlling tactical battles from his headquarters. In a chain of events regarded by some historians as one of the turning points of the Normandy campaign, Hitler, as was his custom, slept late on the morning of D-Day, and then delayed approving Supreme Commander West Field Marshall Gerd von Rundstedt's request to counterattack with the two divisions until 4 P.M., too late for them to reach the front that afternoon.[6]

Rommel had insisted in the months prior to D-Day that the Germans' best chance of repelling an Allied invasion lay in positioning the panzers close to the shore, where they could respond immediately to an invasion and prevent the Allies from gaining a foothold on the Continent. His proposed solution was that the six panzer divisions in Schweppenburg's Panzer Group West, which prior to the invasion functioned as the Germans' armor reserve pool in France, be placed under his direct command. Rundstedt, Rommel's notional superior in the complicated German chain of command, disagreed. Rundstedt, a very correct and dignified officer dubbed "The Last Prussian" by his biographer,[7] leaned toward a more orthodox defensive strategy, preferring to mass his armor well to the rear, ready to counterattack in force once the Allies' landing places and angles of attack had been revealed.

The problem with Rundstedt's strategy, as Rommel knew well from his days being bombed and strafed by the Royal Air Force in the Western Desert, was that it failed to take the Allies' overwhelming aerial superiority into account. Moving through the constricted terrain of the bocage, even intermittent air attacks would have snarled the panzers' advance and deployment, and Rommel knew that those German units not already stationed close to the beaches would not be able to move to the invasion site without taking unacceptable losses from the air. The upshot of this quarrel was that Rommel was given three of the panzer divisions, 2d, 21st, and 116th Panzer. Control of the other three tank divisions in Panzer Group West would remain with OKW in Berlin.[8] As Rommel had predicted, once unleashed by Hitler, Panzer *Lehr* and 12th SS Panzer spent much of June 6 and 7 hiding in ditches and hedgerows from incessant Allied air raids.

When these two divisions finally reached the front, however, their impact was immediate. 12th SS Panzer, manned by the fanatical teenagers of the Hitler Youth, went into action on June 7 northwest of Caen, on the left flank of 21st Panzer. It, too, failed to break through to the sea, but the blooding it gave the Canadian 3d Infantry Division that day and night effectively quashed Montgomery's hope of taking Caen by assault. On June 9, Panzer *Lehr*, formed from the panzer corps' demonstration units and considered the *Wehrmacht's* best armor division, arrived to extend the line of tanks at Tilly to the west of 12th SS Panzer. The three panzer divisions thus formed an apparently impenetrable shield against which Dempsey's sluggish attack was blunting its spearhead.

SHOWDOWN AT VILLERS-BOCAGE

Montgomery decided that further headlong assaults on Caen itself would only bring needless casualties. As the Germans lengthened their line, so Montgomery shifted his attempts to pierce the German line to the west. The area between the 2d British Army and the 1st U.S. Army appeared to be weakly defended by the Germans. The objective of the thrust was the hilltop town of Villers-Bocage and the nearby heights of Point 213, fifteen miles southwest of Caen. The ensuing battle would pit some of the most experienced tank warriors in either army against each other and resulted in perhaps the most famous small unit engagement in the history of armored warfare.

Montgomery chose as his spearhead for the attack the Desert Rats of the 7th Armoured Division, who had served him so well in North Africa. This premier British tank division boasted four armored regiments, totaling almost 300 tanks.[9] On the night of June 12, the division's forward brigade, 22d Armoured, made its camp six miles from Villers-Bocage, which sat astride and dominated the entire road network of the surrounding area.

The Germans were aware of the strategic importance of the town, which lay in Panzer *Lehr's* area of operations. Even this elite division's two tank and four infantry battalions were overstretched trying to cover every inch of their ten-mile front.[10]

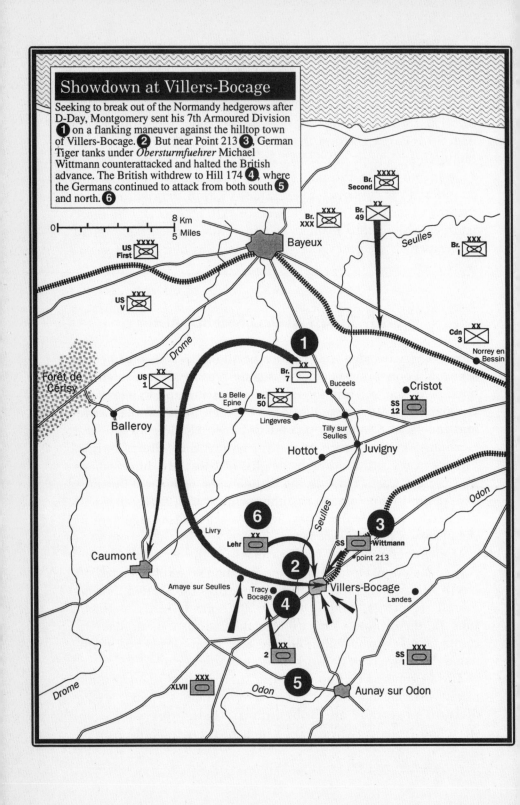

Showdown at Villers-Bocage

Seeking to break out of the Normandy hedgerows after D-Day, Montgomery sent his 7th Armoured Division **1** on a flanking maneuver against the hilltop town of Villers-Bocage. **2** But near Point 213 **3**, German Tiger tanks under *Obersturmfuehrer* Michael Wittmann counterattacked and halted the British advance. The British withdrew to Hill 174 **4**, where the Germans continued to attack from both south **5** and north. **6**

0   8 Km

0   5 Miles

Br. Second

Br. XXX

Br. 49

Br. I

Seulles

US First

US V

Cdn 3

Norrey en Bessin

Drome

Forêt de Cerisy

US 1

La Belle Epine

Br. 7

Buceels

Cristot

SS 12

Br. 50

Lingevres

Tilly sur Seulles

Balleroy

Hottot

Juvigny

Bayeux

Odon

Seulles

6

Lehr

Livry

SS Wittmann

point 213

3

Caumont

Amaye sur Seulles

Tracy Bocage

2

Villers-Bocage

Landes

4

2

SS I

XLVII

Drome

Odon

5

Aunay sur Odon

When 22d Armoured's leading elements pressed forward at first light on June 13, they entered Villers-Bocage at about 8 A.M. to find the town virtually undefended. After the hard slogging of the previous week, the Desert Rats were pleasantly surprised at the ease with which they were able to secure this vital communications hub. Their exhilaration was not to last long, however; the Germans had mastered the art of the rapid counterattack on the Eastern Front. Even as the townspeople came out to welcome their British liberators, German armored cars could be seen in the distance, carefully observing British movements and relaying the information to higher headquarters.[11]

One of the German officers receiving this intelligence was *Obersturmführer* Michael Wittmann, commander of No. 2 Company, 501st SS Heavy Tank Battalion.[12] The 501st was part of I Panzer SS Corps' armor reserve. Since June 7 they had been moving from Beauvais, on the other side of the Seine, to shore up the gap in the German line at Villers-Bocage. By moving at night, they had managed to evade the scrutiny of Allied intelligence and the menace of Allied aircraft, and now two companies, armed with lethal Tigers, were maneuvering beyond Villers-Bocage.

In full view of the Germans, A Squadron of the 22d Armoured Brigade's 4th City of London Yeomanry Regiment marched toward Point 213 in their Cromwell tanks. They advanced despite the misgivings of their regimental commander, Lieutenant Colonel Lord Arthur Cranley, who had been denied permission by Brigadier Robert "Looney" Hinde, 22d Armoured's commander, to conduct further reconnaissance in the area before committing his troops. While the lead elements of A Squadron took up positions on Point 213, along with infantry from A Company 1st Battalion, The Rifle Brigade, the main body of the British column, consisting of twenty-five tanks and half-tracks from both units, halted several hundred yards away, on the main road out of the town.[13] As Wittmann gazed through his field glasses from an observation point in the wooded hills a few hundred yards north of the road, he saw British troops hanging around their vehicles with no apparent concern over the risk of ambush.

"They're acting as if they've won the war already," said his amazed gunner, Corporal Balthasar "Bobby" Woll.

"We're going to prove them wrong," replied his commander.[14]

Wittman, a highly decorated officer, was no braggart. He was already revered for his exploits on the Eastern Front, where he had personally accounted for the destruction of 119 Russian armored vehicles.[15] Now he was about to make his presence felt on the Western Front, against the Allies' most experienced unit.

Realizing that the British column was extremely vulnerable, Wittmann decided to attack on his own, without waiting for his other tanks—four Tigers and a Mark IV Special—to support him. His first round, from eighty meters, destroyed the Cromwell at the head of the British column.[16] Because the road was lined with the thick, high hedgerows typical of the *bocage*, this one shot stopped the rest of the armored vehicles in their tracks. They couldn't get around the smoking lead tank, and, as confusion and panic set in, retreating proved equally impossible. Wittmann, knowing his tank's armor was impervious to the Cromwells' 75 mm main guns, then proceeded to motor the length of the British column, shooting up one vehicle after another. When the 8th Hussars, the divisional reconnaissance regiment, tried to come to their comrades' aid, they were engaged by Wittmann's four other Tigers and repulsed after taking losses.[17]

Having destroyed all but one of the British vehicles on the road, Wittmann pulled onto the highway and finished off the final Cromwell in his path by ramming it with his own vehicle, which weighed more than double the British tank.

In less than five minutes, Wittmann had single-handedly eliminated the Desert Rats' leading column. He now turned his attention to the British forces remaining in the town center, where the dismounted crews of the four Cromwells in the regiment's headquarters group were caught similarly unawares. Wittmann immediately knocked out three of the four tanks. The fourth, commanded by Captain Pat Dyas, only escaped destruction by reversing into the garden of a nearby house. Unfortunately for Dyas, his swift evasive action had left his gunner behind, and he was forced to watch in frustration as Wittmann drove past, his head out of the turret, presenting Dyas with what would have been a perfect flank shot.[18]

Wittmann's Tiger then clanked its way farther down the town's main street toward a road junction at the western edge of Villers-Bocage, which was held by the Sherman Fireflies of the 4th City of London Yeomanry's B Squadron. About 200 yards from the junction, Wittmann was engaged by the Firefly commanded by Sergeant Stan Lockwood. The Firefly crew pumped four seventeen-pounder rounds at the Tiger, and at least one hit, but it caused only superficial damage. Wittmann returned fire, uncharacteristically missing the British tank with his first round, which nevertheless temporarily disabled the Firefly by bringing down a wall of the nearest house on top of it.[19]

Realizing the British hold on the junction was too strong for even his seemingly superhuman crew to dislodge, Wittmann took advantage of Lockwood's discomfiture and reversed away. Returning back up the main street, he encountered Dyas's Cromwell, which he quickly knocked out, killing one crewman instantly and machine-gunning another to death as he tried to flee. Dyas, although wounded, escaped with the help of a French girl to B Squadron's lines. There he radioed the news of A Squadron's demise to Cranley, who was still in his Scout car on the high ground near Point 213. Cranley replied that while he knew the situation was desperate, there was little he could do as his own position at that moment under attack by Tigers.[20]

These were the Tigers and the Mark IV Special of Wittmann's company, plus perhaps three other tanks and supporting infantry.[21] The German force made short work of the surrounded British troops, all but one of whom were killed or, as was the case with the unfortunate Cranley, taken prisoner. Wittmann's Tiger company was then joined by that of *Hauptsturmführer* W. Mobius, and together with infantry support, they renewed the attack on Villers-Bocage.

This time, however, the British were prepared. The 7th Armoured Division's antitank regiment had taken up positions in and around the town, and its six-pounder guns extracted a heavy toll from the German armor. Wittmann's Tiger was an early victim, when a six-pounder shot off one of his tracks, and he and his crew had to bail out and escape on foot. Two other Tigers and the Mark IV Special were also knocked out, but their crews likewise escaped, as most of the British infantry had been lost earlier in the day, and so were not available to mop them up.[22]

The British hold on Villers-Bocage was now extremely tenuous. Not only had the 22d Armoured Brigade been severely mauled at the hands of Wittmann's Tigers, but the spearhead of the 7th Armoured Division now found itself in a salient pressed between Panzer *Lehr* to its north and the 2d Panzer Division to its south. The latter division's arrival in the Villers-Bocage area came as a total surprise to the Allies. Aerial observation had failed to detect its movement from Amiens across the Seine, probably because it moved only at night.[23] The 7th Armoured Division commander, Major General Bobby Erskine, therefore ordered the 22d Armoured commander, Hinde, to withdraw B Squadron from the town itself and consolidate his forces around Tracey-Bocage and Hill 174, two miles west of Villers-Bocage.

What the British tankers needed to help preserve and exploit their gains was some supporting infantry, but the XXX Corps commander, Lieutenant General G. C. Bucknall, was reluctant to detach any of his infantry reserves to help the armored brigade out. Rather, he pinned his hopes on a conventional attack by the 50th Division south against Panzer *Lehr* positions around the village of Hottot, west of Tilly. The attack against the dug-in Germans petered out on the evening of June 13, and with 2d Panzer's strength and confidence growing by the day, the chance for an Allied breakthrough at Villers-Bocage had passed. Bucknall ordered Erskine to withdraw, but before 7th Armoured could get under way, 2d Panzer attacked, only to be stopped by highly effective fire from U.S. artillery units supporting the U.S. 1st Infantry Division at Caumont. Despite this rebuff, the German threat was still considered too great to leave 7th Armoured in its exposed positions, and it pulled back on the night of June 14, ceding to the Germans both the territory and the battle of Villers-Bocage. *Obersturmführer* Michael Wittman had been pleasantly surprised to find the shooting as good on the Western Front as it had been on the Eastern.

EPSOM AND CHARNWOOD

The British failure at Villers-Bocage meant the front remained static for the next several weeks. Five days after 7th Armoured's withdrawal, Allied strategy was dealt a further blow when a furious gale blew up over the English Channel. The Great Storm lasted four days and severely damaged the two complex artificial harbors the Allies had built to land supplies along the Normandy coastline. The amount of men and matériel the Allies could bring ashore dropped by two-thirds and did not pick up until the end of the month.[24] Timing is everything; had General Eisenhower decided not to proceed with the invasion on June 6, the Allied armies' next attempt would have been under way when the great storm struck. The bad weather also kept all aircraft in Normandy grounded, but the Germans were unable to capitalize on this rare opportunity to move unmolested by Allied fighter-bombers.

The OKW, following the invasion on a large-scale map at a headquarters hundreds of miles from the action, was increasingly out of touch with the situation on the ground in the theater. It ordered an attack by six panzer divisions on the boundary between the U.S. and British armies, with a follow-on drive to Bayeux. Unfortunately for the Germans, of the six divisions OKW named in the order, three were still en route to the theater and two were holding the line around Caen,[25] leaving the frustrated Germans watching the opportunity for counterattack go begging.

The grounding of the Allied aircraft did allow the German reinforcing divisions to make faster progress toward the front, however. Alerted to their impending arrival by Allied intelligence, Montgomery was concerned to ensure that the initiative did not slip from his grasp. This meant abandoning tentative plans to push VIII Corps southeast of Caen, as such an offensive would have required him to wait at least a week while the corps completed its arrival in the theater and would, in addition, have been hampered by a lack of maneuvering room between Caen and the sea east of the River Orne. A delay that long would also have risked running headlong into the fresh panzer divisions forming up on the easternmost part of the front. Montgomery scrapped the plan in favor of a simpler one in which VIII Corps would punch south toward the River Odon from positions southwest of Caen.

The plan, code-named Operation Epsom, catered to Montgomery's specialty: the set-piece battle. It had as its primary objectives the seizure of positions on the Odon and then the Orne Rivers (the two rivers converge just south of Caen). By attacking south then southeast, Montgomery hoped to thus isolate Caen and cut off its defenders, while menacing the Germans' eastern flank. VIII Corps was to provide the main punch, with I Corps holding the eastern flank and XXX Corps supporting on the west. VIII Corps consisted of three divisions, 15th Scottish, 43d Wessex, and 11th Armoured, with additional firepower provided by the 4th Armoured Brigade and an extra tank battalion, for a total of about 60,000 troops and over 600 tanks.[26] The VIII Corps commander was Lieutenant General Richard O'Connor, the hero of the Western Desert who had escaped from an Italian POW camp in late 1943 and now stood ready to conduct his first battle since Beda Fomm in 1941.

Arrayed against the British were the cream of the German panzer divisions on the Western Front, most of which were drawn from the *Waffen SS*. Of these, the 1st SS Panzer *Leibstandarte* Adolf Hitler Division and the two-division-strong II SS Panzer Corps had just arrived in the region to reinforce their colleagues in the 12th SS Panzer (Hitler Jugend), 2d SS Panzer, 21st Panzer, and Panzer *Lehr* Divisions. These tired but highly motivated troops had spent the past three weeks digging in along the banks of the Odon, and they were determined to extract the highest price possible in men and machines for any ground won at their expense.

A preliminary supporting attack by XXX Corps 49th Division on June 25 managed to rip a jagged hole three miles wide and one mile deep in Panzer *Lehr*'s positions about twelve miles west of the city, but stiff resistance prevented the capture of Rauray. Epsom began in earnest the next morning, with the battlefield enshrouded in thick fog, as the Scottish infantry of the 15th Division marched toward the Hitler Jugend positions behind a fearsome barrage from the 700 guns of the combined artilleries of I,

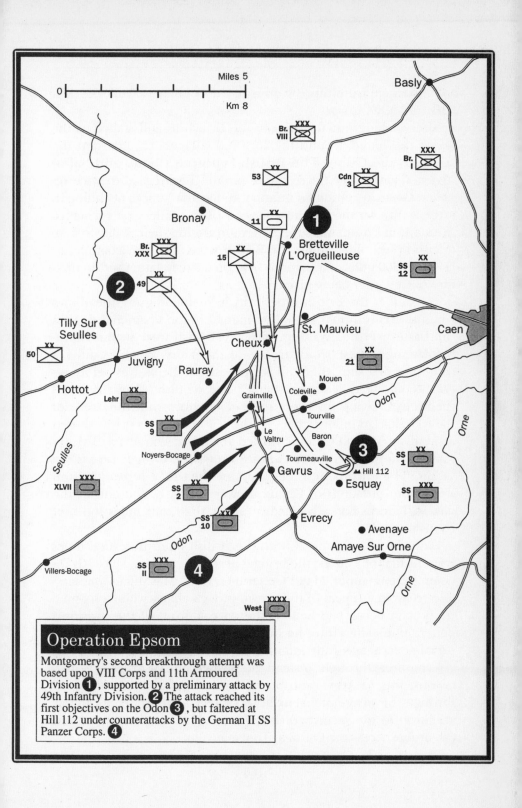

Operation Epsom

Montgomery's second breakthrough attempt was based upon VIII Corps and 11th Armoured Division ❶, supported by a preliminary attack by 49th Infantry Division. ❷ The attack reached its first objectives on the Odon ❸, but faltered at Hill 112 under counterattacks by the German II SS Panzer Corps. ❹ some barrage from the 700 guns of the combined artilleries of I, VIII, and XXX Corps.

After making initial progress, the British assault stalled as the *bocage* thickened around the fortified villages that guarded the route to the Odon. The British captured Cheux and Saint-Mauvieu only after fierce hand-to-hand fighting, and twice repelled German combined infantry and armor attacks by calling in artillery fire on the counterattacks. British artillery performance throughout Epsom was superb, demonstrating their ability to conduct set-piece operations; the British were able, for example, to bring all 300 guns of a corps to bear on a single target within minutes of the order being given.[27]

To counter the British superiority in men and guns, the *Waffen SS* units drew on their know-how gained in the savage fighting on the Eastern Front. Waiting until the British were within point-blank range, these shock troops of the Third Reich would kill with their first shot, then quickly reposition themselves before artillery could be called in on them.[28] The Scottish regiments found themselves paying for every mile of territory with hundreds of their khaki-clad infantrymen. As the 15th Division's drive faltered around midday, O'Connor hurled the 11th Armoured Division forward in an attempt to capture intact the bridges across the Odon. The entrenched teenagers of the *Hitler Jugend* division held them off south of Cheux, however, and by the end of the day, VIII Corps had advanced no more than four miles south of its starting line.[29]

Dawn broke on June 26 with the British line still several miles from its first objectives: the bridges across the Odon. The 15th Division's commander, Major General G. H. A. MacMillan, was anxious to avoid a repeat of the previous day's chaos, when a six-mile traffic jam developed behind the narrow front of the division's penetration. Therefore, he decided to quit relying on the traditional spearhead—four infantry battalions marching in line—to effect a breakthrough. Instead, he pushed one of his reserve battalions, the 2d Argyll and Sutherland Highlanders, southward through the village of Cheux at top speed, with orders not to pay attention to the security of its flanks.[30] The battalion's goal was the bridge across the Odon at Tourmauville.

A brief fight with a pair of German tanks two miles from the river left one smoking and the other in retreat, and from there a quick sprint through the cornfields, braving the fire of three machine guns, took them over the bridge.[31]

Dempsey followed up the next day with the 11th Armoured Division, pouring them into the bridgehead on the south bank of the Odon, but when wireless intercepts warned him of the impending arrival of the II SS Panzer Corps, comprising the 9th and 10th SS Panzer Divisions, he decided to strengthen the bridgehead before pushing on to the Orne. The German commanders, meanwhile, were once again caught off guard. Von Rundstedt and Rommel were both en route to brief Hitler at Berchtesgaden, and so command temporarily devolved onto the Seventh Army commander, Colonel General Friedrich Dollmann.

The nervous Dollmann ordered II SS Panzer Corps commander *Oberstgruppenführer* Paul Hausser to launch an immediate counterattack. On June 29, the British captured Hill 112, which dominated the surrounding area, and Hausser's request that he be given a little more time to plan such a major operation was rebuffed. Later that day, the 9th and 10th SS Panzer Divisions were launched at Cheux from the west, supported by elements of Panzer *Lehr*, 2d SS Panzer, and 1st SS Panzer Divisions.

The attack was beaten back well by the 15th Division, with supporting fire from corps artillery and naval guns in the Channel, plus significant aerial support. The division had been alerted to the Germans' move by the capture of an SS officer carrying documents detailing the attack. In despair at this latest setback, Dollmann killed himself. This was the pivotal moment of the Epsom battle, now going the Allies' way. They had gained the high ground of Hill 112, had a sizeable bridgehead south of the Odon, and had firmly rebuffed a determined counterattack. Once again the senior British command misread the situation.

Unaware of the 15th Division's success and believing the Germans to be still preparing their main attack, Dempsey ordered the 11th Armoured withdrawn from the south bank of the Odon. His reasoning was that the division was too exposed below the river, with not enough depth to beat off the expected panzer thrust. The withdrawal of 11th Armoured left the infantry around

Hill 112 at the mercy of the German armor, and on June 30, the position reverted to German control. Later that day, as vicious fighting raged around the hill, Montgomery called off the operation, realizing that there was no hope left of making a decisive breakthrough, and that casualties, which totaled over 4,000 for VIII Corps, were already unacceptably high.

The dwindling manpower resources of the British military meant Dempsey's Second British Army was now reduced to a strategy of besieging Caen. In this way, Montgomery hoped to draw the German armor toward Caen, where Rommel would have to use it to plug gaps in the German line, rather than mount a decisive counterattack. Then, with the panzer divisions tied down on the eastern flank fighting the weaker of the two Allied armies, Montgomery hoped to launch the breakout with the stronger First U.S. Army.

Some historians have challenged Montgomery's claim that this was always his intent, charging him with shaping his version of the facts to suit the results of his less-than-successful offensives on the eastern flank. In addition, Carlo D'Este argues in *Decision in Normandy*, while Montgomery's Caen strategy kept the panzer divisions off balance, forced to react to Allied attacks rather than mass for a counterattack, these divisions were never intended for use against the Americans anyway. The Germans positioned them around Caen in the hope of using them in an offensive aimed at Bayeux.[32]

Whatever Montgomery's original motives, there is little doubt that the Americans had not yet felt the full weight of the German armor in Normandy. Bradley now had fourteen divisions in Normandy, opposed by only six German divisions, three of which were cobbled together from the remains of others ground up in the D-Day battle. The pressure was now building on the U.S. commanders in the west to use their advantage to good effect.

Meanwhile, the German chain of command was again thrown into temporary disarray after Dollmann's suicide on June 28. He was replaced in command of the Seventh Army by Hausser. Rommel and Rundstedt were at Hitler's East Prussian headquarters in Rastenburg, where their explanations of the futility of Hitler's strategy of fighting for every inch of land fell on deaf ears. When they returned to France, Schweppenburg, with the support of Rommel and Hausser, submitted a report to Rundstedt that stressed the need to sacrifice some territory in order to conduct a flexible defense. In particular, Schweppenburg argued that the Germans must abandon Caen and establish a new defensive line out of range of the Allied naval guns.[33]

On July 1, Rundstedt spoke with Field Marshal Wilhelm Keitel, chief of OKW, and warned him of the perilous state of affairs on the Western Front. When Keitel asked him what the Germans should do, Rundstedt's recorded response—"Make peace, you fools!"—earned him a mention in the history books, but also cost him his job. Enraged by the report and Rundstedt's tactless advice, Hitler ordered his dismissal the next day. Schweppenburg followed several days later. Rundstedt's replacement was Field Marshal Gunther von Kluge and General Heinrich Eberbach took over for Schweppenburg at Panzer Group West. The changes did little to correct the Germans' immediate problem, however, which was Hitler's refusal to sanction any tactical withdrawal to give his forces more freedom of maneuver.

Following Montgomery's orders, on July 3rd, Bradley began wheeling the VII, VIII, and XIX U.S. Corps, pivoting on Caumont, with the goal of facing east on the Caumont-Vire line. He pushed VIII Corps southeast down the western coast of the Cotentin, with VII and XIX Corps joining in over the next several days. After advancing less than 2,000 yards a day in the dense *bocage*, the offensive ran out of steam by July 11.[34] One of the factors that slowed and eventually halted the advance was the unexpected appearance of two panzer divisions, Panzer *Lehr* and 2d SS Panzer, that had eased themselves away from the face-off around Caen to harass and attack the First Army. Bradley's force was now opposed by seventy infantry battalions and 250 tanks.[35] With the exception of Montgomery himself, there was now a growing sense of unease among the senior Allied commanders, who feared the Normandy campaign was bogging down in a stalemate.

Under steadily increasing pressure and in the full realization that in order to successfully pivot the Americans and sweep east he would have to hold the Caen-Falaise plain, Montgomery had no option but to launch another assault on Caen. Operation Charnwood opened the night of July 7 with an Allied carpet-bombing of the German positions. About 460 Halifax and Lancaster four-engined bombers dropped 2,300 tons of bombs on Caen's northern suburbs. The bombs were equipped with time fuses, set to detonate among the city's *Hitler Jugend* defenders as the Allied ground offensive got under way before first light the next morning.[36] This highly unusual use of strategic bombers in direct support of a ground attack had little real impact on the conduct of the battle, as few German gun positions, vehicles, or troops were found in the target area.[37]

Nevertheless, on the morning of July 9, British and Canadian infantry advanced into Caen, which by now was little more than a vast expanse of smoking ruins. The remnants of the *Hitler Jugend* division fought for every inch of ground, led by their charismatic commander, Major General Kurt Meyer, who at one stage was seen striding down a rubble-strewn street carrying a *Panzerfaust* antitank rocket launcher. Hitler's refusal to allow even tactical retreats by his commanders cost Meyer's division dearly. It lost all but forty of its tanks, including twenty panzers on July 8, and many antitank guns in the defense. After two days of bitter house-to-house fighting, the division fell back across the Orne on July 9, with a battalion of infantry left.[38] When, in cautious pursuit, the Allies reached the northern bank of the Orne, they found the Germans had blown every bridge across the river and organized even stronger defenses on the south bank.

The tactical advantage gained by the British in Charnwood was also minimal. The Germans still controlled the commanding heights of Bourguebus Ridge four miles southeast of the city, as well as the Colombelles steelworks in the town's eastern suburbs. Observation posts in the steel plant's tall smokestacks afforded the Germans an excellent view of all Allied movement toward their lines.

OPERATION GOODWOOD

While Montgomery pondered his next move, Rommel and Eberbach prepared an elaborate defense in depth for the area south of the Orne. On the front line they placed their dwindling infantry forces, supported by panzers. Behind these lay a dozen of the *bocage*'s archetypal villages, natural hubs of an interlocking defensive network that the Germans had strongly fortified. The German artillery, including about 300 guns and 272 *Nebelwerfer* rocket launchers, was situated on Bourguebus Ridge. Five miles farther back sat the armored reserve of forty-five Panthers and eighty medium tanks in another belt of fortified villages.[39]

Rommel was to be robbed of the chance to command the defense of these positions. On July 17, luck finally ran out for this armored warrior who led from the front with verve and daring. Returning from the front to Army Group B headquarters at La Roche–Guyon, Rommel's staff car was attacked by two RAF Spitfires. The open-topped vehicle crashed into a tree, and Rommel sustained severe head injuries. Too seriously hurt to continue in command, he returned to Germany, where he was on convalescent leave when implicated in the July 20 assassination attempt against Hitler, and forced to take his own life.

With help from his two army commanders, Bradley and Dempsey, Rommel's North African nemesis, Montgomery, finally arrived at the strategic decision that was to loosen and then release the Germans' grip on Normandy. On July 11, Bradley suggested an offensive south through Saint-Lô and then westward to take control of the Brittany coast before driving east into the heart of France. In order to keep the German armor bottled up in the Caen region, Dempsey proposed a further British assault on the German forces there. As he envisioned it, this operation would rely on the Allied preponderance in armor and airpower to blast a way through the German defenses.

A misunderstanding between the Allied commanders about Goodwood's ultimate objectives was to have serious ramifications later, and it would make the operation the most controversial episode of the Allied campaign in Europe. The genesis of the controversy was Dempsey's original operational order, dated July

13. This stated that on July 18, VIII British Corps, in which all three British armored divisions were to be grouped, was to cross the Orne "and establish an armoured division in each of the following areas: Bretteville Sur Laize—Vimont—Argences—Falaise."[40] The order was transmitted to the Supreme Headquarters Allied Expeditionary Force, or SHAEF, under American General of the Armies Dwight Eisenhower, the supreme Allied commander in Europe. Eisenhower and his staff were delighted to see this mention of Falaise, which lay about twenty miles south of Caen. Surely, they thought, with such far-reaching goals, Montgomery was abandoning his cautious approach, and this would be the operation to break through the German lines on the eastern flank of the bridgehead.

However, Montgomery, far from abandoning his methodical style of campaigning, was concerned that Dempsey and O'Connor might be about to abandon it on his behalf, so on July 15, he visited them in O'Connor's headquarters and amended his original order, handwriting a personal directive entitled "Notes on Second Army Operations." Under this new directive, the British VIII Corps's mission was restricted to pushing all three armored divisions into the Bourguebus–Vimont–Bretteville Sur Laize area, well to the north of Falaise. In fact, this much less ambitious order only mentioned Falaise in the context of armored cars, which were to attack south in the town's general direction.

No one who read the July 15 directive could have been in much doubt that Montgomery's objectives in Goodwood did not include the capture of Falaise or a decisive breakthrough on the eastern flank. Eisenhower, however, never read the directive, as it was not transmitted. A copy of a revised Second Army operational order, issued July 17, was sent to SHAEF, but failed to arrive. Thus the SHAEF commander and his staff continued in their mistaken belief that Montgomery intended to seize Falaise during Goodwood.[41]

Bradley's offensive, code-named Operation Cobra, was scheduled to kick off July 19, while Dempsey's subsidiary operation, Goodwood, was to be launched a day earlier. However, the Americans' continued difficulties around Saint-Lô meant they were unable to keep to the schedule. Under Bradley's plan, VIII

U.S. Corps, the spearhead of the newly stood-up Third U.S. Army, would drive west into Brittany while First U.S. Army attacked east toward Le Mans. Key to this undertaking, however, was the capture of Saint-Lô, the crucial hinge upon which the American forces were to pivot, but even after a determined push by XIX Corps, which drove the defenders—including Panzer *Lehr* Division—back several miles, Saint-Lô remained in German hands until July 19, too late to stick to the original Cobra plan.

Goodwood, however, got under way on time. It was preceded by a supporting offensive by XXX Corps and XII Corps designed to fix the German forces holding the territory west of Caen for which Operation Epsom had been fought. Then, as dawn broke at 5.30 A.M. on July 18, the largest air attack ever launched in support of ground forces was unleashed upon the Germans by wave after wave of RAF and USAAF bombers. The 4,500 aircraft used in the operation saturated a 6,400-meter strip of the German defenses with high-explosive bombs. British artillery and naval gunfire provided a further pummeling, throwing almost 250,000 rounds at the German positions.[42]

Watching this awe-inspiring drama of destruction played out before them were the crews of the British tanks for whose benefit the barrage was being laid on. Following a suggestion from Dempsey, Montgomery had grouped all three British armored divisions in Normandy—11th Armoured, 7th Armoured, and the Guards—in British VIII Corps. It was the British commanders' intention that these divisions would provide sufficient armored punch to sweep aside any German resistance left in the corridor pulverized by the bombers.

First, however, they had to reach that corridor. This entailed a night movement to the west bank of the Caen Canal and the Orne, which flowed parallel with each other out of the city to the northeast. At Benouville, about three miles northeast of Caen, the three divisions gathered in the darkness and prepared to cross the only six bridges left standing across the waterways. To minimize the inevitable traffic jam caused by such a bottleneck, only the lead division in the attack, 11th Armoured, was to cross the Orne prior to the start of the operation. Even this measure barely sufficed to limit congestion as the thousands of wheeled and tracked vehicles converged on the three pairs of bridges.

Each armored division had about 286 tanks, 261 scout cars, and 100 armored cars, plus over 2,000 trucks.[43] Thus the three divisions together numbered more than 8,000 vehicles. To ensure that the Germans were hit with the heaviest armored punch Second Army could throw as early as possible, Dempsey ordered O'Connor to funnel his tanks and motorized battalions across first, leaving the other divisional elements stranded on the west bank.

The first tanks to lumber across the bridges were those of the 29th Armoured Brigade, 11th Armoured's tank brigade. Once across the water, they faced an obstacle of a different kind: a minefield laid by the British 51st (Highland) Infantry Division, which had been ordered to prepare for a *German* attack up to three days before Goodwood. By the time the Goodwood plans firmed up and British commanders realized the problem, the division had only two nights to clear the minefield. Complicating the sappers' task further were the facts that the minefield had been hastily laid and poorly charted, and then it had been churned up by artillery fire. All the Highland engineers could do in the circumstances was clear seventeen lanes through the minefield, each wide enough for a tank to pass through with about ten meters to spare on either side.[44]

Despite these hurdles, the 29th Armoured Brigade was in position to launch the ground attack punctually at 7.30 A.M. As soon as the thunder of the bombing missions had ceased and the swarms of four-engined planes slipped over the horizon, a two-word order reverberated around the expectant crews of the 3d Royal Tank Regiment, 29th Armoured's leading element: "Move now." Hunched in their turrets, the crews lurched their vehicles forward, and the attack was on.

For the first four miles, they made good headway, as expected. Having watched the bombardment from a safe distance just prior to jumping off, the British tankers found it hard to imagine that any German defenders had lived through the massive air raid, let alone that some might still have the stomach for a fight. They were soon to discover how misplaced these thoughts were.

The bombing raid had indeed spread indescribable chaos and

destruction throughout the German lines. In many cases it had buried tanks or flipped them onto their turrets. For the German soldiers caught in the bombers' path, the effects were often fatal. Many of those not killed by the blasts were so shell-shocked they were unable to do anything but surrender. Some were even driven medically insane. A number actually committed suicide waiting for what seemed inevitable death.

When the bombardment stopped, however, the spine of the German Army in Normandy stiffened. Despite the horrendous tonnage of bombs that had just been dropped on them, most German soldiers in the corridor through which the British attack was to pass came out from their foxholes or from under their vehicles and began to dig out their tanks and guns from the earth covering them. Those men, many of whom had fought their way out of tough situations in North Africa or the Eastern Front, were not going to yield Normandy to the Allies without a fight.

The first British unit to understand that the operation would be no cakewalk was the 29th Armoured Brigade's second echelon, the 2d Battalion of the Fife and Forfar Yeomanry, which suddenly found itself losing one tank after another to fire from the village of Cagny, which lay to the left of the 11th Armoured Division's advance.

The fire was coming from a battery of 88 mm antiaircraft guns, augmented by an 88 mm antitank gun and a Mark IV panzer, but might not have caught the Scottish tanks at all had not Major Hans von Luck arrived in the village at that moment. Only thirty-three, Luck was already a veteran of the Polish, French, North African, and Russian campaigns, and he had just returned from three days of leave in Paris as the bombing ended. He now commanded the 21st Panzer Division battle group responsible for that area of the front and was piecing together the shattered elements of his command into a coherent defense when he happened upon the battery of 88s.

The antiaircraft guns belonged to a Luftwaffe unit, and when Luck discovered them, their barrels were still pointing skyward. Realizing the impact the 88s could have if turned on the British tanks, Luck ordered the captain in charge of them to redeploy them as antitank guns and engage the flank of the British ar-

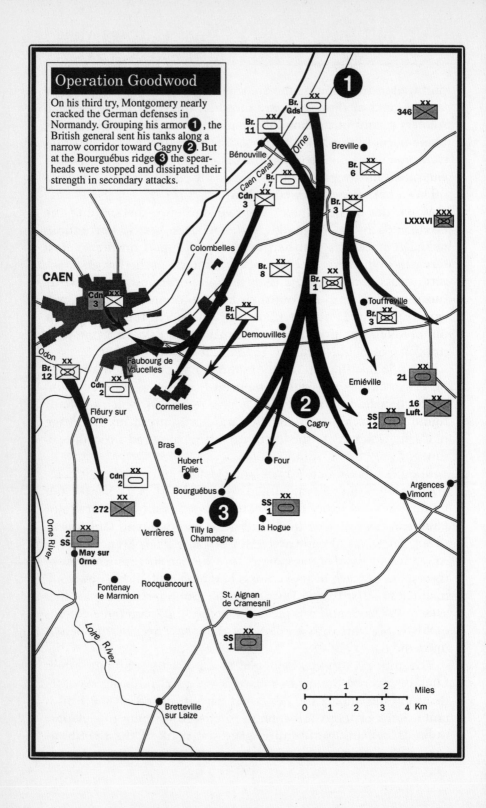

Operation Goodwood

On his third try, Montgomery nearly cracked the German defenses in Normandy. Grouping his armor **1**, the British general sent his tanks along a narrow corridor toward Cagny **2**. But at the Bourguébus ridge **3** the spearheads were stopped and dissipated their strength in secondary attacks.

CAEN

Bénouville
Caen Canal
Orne
Breville
Colombelles
Touffreville
Demouvilles
Emiéville
Faubourg de Vaucelles
Cormelles
Cagny
Fléury sur Orne
Bras
Four
Hubert Folie
Bourguébus
Argences
Vimont
Verrières
Tilly la Champagne
la Hogue
May sur Orne
Fontenay le Marmion
Rocquancourt
St. Aignan de Cramesnil
Bretteville sur Laize
Odon
Orne River
Loire River

Br. Gds
Br. 11
Br. 7
Cdn 3
Br. 8
Br. 1
Br. 51
Br. 12
Cdn 2
Cdn 3
Cdn 2
272
2 SS
SS 12
SS 1
SS 1
16 Luft.
21
Br. 6
Br. 3
Br. 3
346
LXXXVI

| 0 | | 1 | | 2 | | Miles |
| 0 | 1 | 2 | 3 | 4 | | Km |

mored advance, which was already bypassing Cagny. When the captain turned obstinate, arguing that his job was destroying planes, not tanks, Luck had had enough. In one of the more celebrated exchanges of Normandy lore, he drew his pistol, leveled it at the young officer, and told him, "Either you're a dead man or you can earn yourself a medal."[45]

The captain did as he was told, and soon had his 88s positioned in an orchard on the northern edge of the village, where they enjoyed a clear field of fire over cornfields into the passing British tanks. Within minutes, the sixteen Fife and Forfar Shermans that were masking Cagny until the Guards Armoured Division arrived were smoking hulks, their surviving crew members scrambling frantically back to the rear, their faces blackened by burns and soot. This engagement stalled the advance of the Guards Armoured Division, which was supposed to attack toward Vimont, keeping Cagny on its right. The presence of the German guns prevented the division's tanks from bypassing Cagny, but believing the village to be much more strongly held than in fact it was, the British waited until 4 P.M. to enter it. In the meantime, six Tigers of the 503d Heavy Tank Battalion had moved up from their position in Emieville and also began to engage the British armor as it headed south for the Caen-Vimont railway embankment or turned east toward the Tigers.

To the west of Cagny, the 11th Armoured's attack was sputtering to a halt in front of Bourguebus Ridge. The first serious German defenses it encountered were three batteries of antitank guns belonging to Assault Gun Battalion 200, part of Luck's battle group. The assault guns were testaments to German ingenuity. They consisted of 75 mm antitank guns affixed to French Hotchkiss tank chassis that the Germans discovered in a factory outside Paris. Now, sitting in le-Mesnil-Frementel and Grentheville, the three batteries' combined force of eighteen guns was reaping destruction in the Norman cornfields, knocking out the Shermans and Cromwells that were the pride of U.S. and British industry.

Once the assault guns had been outflanked, the British tanks found themselves at the mercy of more 88s and panzers located on Bourguebus Ridge itself, plus the German artillery sitting behind the ridge, out of range of the British guns north of the Orne, and ready to rain a barrage down into the British armor as it approached the slopes.

At noon, with the battle in the balance, two key factors weighed against the British. One was the almost total absence of supporting infantry in the front line of the attack. Under orders from O'Connor to take the villages of Cuverville and Demouville, just to the east of Caen, 11th Armoured commander Major General "Pip" Roberts reluctantly assigned the task to his 159th Infantry Brigade. The brigade spent most of the morning clearing these villages, with the result that the 29th Armoured Brigade led the charge toward Bourguebus with only one battalion of infantry to help deal with the antitank positions in its path. This was a direct result of the British Army's thinning supplies of infantry; military historians have since pointed out that Goodwood was undertaken with a tank-heavy spearhead not because this made the most sense tactically, but because the British had more tanks than infantrymen to spare.

The second factor hurting the British ability to seize the heights of Bourguebus was their poor coordination of air support. German fire had knocked out the tank of 11th Armoured's only RAF Forward Air Controller during the first two hours of battle, with the result that the division lost its ability to call in air strikes. When his attack faltered in front of the ridge, O'Connor immediately requested another large air raid to knock out the German 88s and artillery around the ridge. Just as immediately, but for reasons that are still unclear, Second Army turned him down.[46]

By noon, the initiative had passed from the British. The tanks of 11th Armoured had not advanced since 11 A.M., while Guards Armoured was taking heavy punishment on the left flank and 7th Armoured was still struggling across the bridges and through the friendly minefield. The failure to clench the British armor into a tight fist dissipated the force O'Connor had intended for the attack, without which he was unable to punch through the German defenses. Instead, the battle degenerated into the sort of armored slugging match that suited the Germans well.

Oberstgruppenführer "Sepp" Dietrich, commander of I SS Panzer Corps, moved the Panther battalion of 1st SS Panzer Division toward Bourguebus, where the British attack was now clearly aimed. The Panthers, which Dietrich had been keeping in reserve, immediately counterattacked the tanks of the 29th Armoured Brigade, milling about on the lower slopes of the ridge. More Tigers and Panthers arrived to form an armored screen around the fortified villages of Bras, Soliers, Four, and Cagny, and soon the largest tank battle of the Normandy campaign was raging on the plain below Bourguebus Ridge.

The Germans had the upper hand. Their panzers were outnumbered by British tanks, but from their positions 150 feet above the floor of the plain, they had excellent fields of fire from which to rain solid shot down on the thinly armored Shermans and Cromwells. In addition, unlike the British tankers, the panzers were ably supported by antitank guns, artillery, and infantry on the ridge and in the network of fortified hamlets at its base. O'Connor tried to launch a two-pronged assault against the ridge, but 7th Armoured's sluggishness meant that the leading elements of its armor brigade, 22d Armoured, which was to supply the left punch, did not arrive until 5 P.M., far too late to be of use to 29th Armoured. At times, the panzers were only kept at bay by rocket-firing RAF Hawker Typhoons.[47]

By the end of the day, the 11th Armoured Division had lost 126 tanks, 90 from enemy fire, while the Guards Armoured had lost 60 in its first battle. The Germans had suffered their share of knocked-out panzers, too, but here again Teutonic resourcefulness showed through. Despite working in spartan conditions, mechanics in the German tank workshops in nearby woodlands labored successfully night and day to repair tanks salvaged from the battlefield. Dietrich later told Allied interrogators that his 1st and 12th SS Panzer Divisions would not have been able to keep their armor in the battle were it not for the prodigious service of these mechanics.[48]

For the next two days, the two sides battled to a stalemate. Losses of tanks and men mounted on both sides, but the British had little to show for their sacrifice. By July 20, they had gained loose control over parts of Bourguebus Ridge, but nowhere had they advanced more than seven miles from their jumping-off point, at a cost of 400 tanks and over 5,500 men killed, wounded, and missing. Montgomery, his credibility in shreds after he had given overly optimistic reports of the battle's progress to his superiors and to the press, was forced to call off the offensive when heavy rain made further progress unlikely. Nevertheless, the Allies could more easily replace both men and matériel than could their opponents, who had been stretched to the breaking point by Goodwood. The German right flank was now very vulnerable, and in attempting to shore it up, the Germans had to commit the very panzer divisions they were soon to need thirty-five miles to the west.

OPERATION COBRA

It was now Bradley's turn to test the Germans' defenses. However, the numbers were even more in his favor than they had been in Dempsey's during Goodwood. His thirteen infantry and four armored divisions faced two armored, one mechanized, three infantry, two parachute, and one air landing divisions on the German side of the front. Moreover, the German units were being steadily whittled down so that many were divisions in name only.

With Saint-Lô having finally fallen to the U.S. XIX Corps on July 19, after two days of bitter fighting, Bradley began forming up his breakout force—VII Corps—north of the Saint-Lô–Periers road. Opposite them sat the German LXXXIV Corps west of Saint-Lô, and the II Parachute Corps to their east. Unlike Dempsey, his British counterpart, Bradley was not short of infantry, so instead of leading with his armor, he opted to attack with three infantry divisions, holding two armored and one motorized infantry division in reserve as an exploitation force.

The attack would, like Goodwood, first be preceded by a massive Allied bombing raid on a narrow front. The offensive was to begin July 24, but bad weather forced a last-minute postponement. The word did not reach about 350 of the bombers, however. Then, instead of approaching the target zone by paralling the Saint-Lô–Periers road, which formed the boundary between U.S. and German forces, as Bradley thought had been agreed upon with the air chiefs, these bombers flew perpendicularly, south over the heads of their own troops. The result was that when some of the bombers released their loads too early, the bombs fell short on the U.S. 30th Division, which lost 25 dead and 131 wounded.

Despite this tragedy, some luck stayed with the Allies. Bradley had feared the errant bombing would take away Cobra's element of surprise, but the Germans instead credited their own artillery fire with stopping the U.S. attack. The offensive was rescheduled for the next day, but when it restarted, the bombers repeated their mistake, flying over their own troops and releasing some bombs too early. This time, the results were even worse: 111 U.S. troops were killed, including Lieutenant General Lesley McNair, Chief of U.S. Ground Forces, who was visiting the front lines to observe the bombing, only to become the highest ranking Allied officer to be killed in Northwest Europe.

The disaster dismayed Bradley, and although the infantry attack launched at 11 A.M. as planned, the demoralized troops did not make the progress expected. The Germans who had caught the full force of the 1,800-plane bombing were faring much worse, however. Panzer *Lehr* was dug in along the four-mile front raked by the bombers, and the losses it suffered would have rendered most military units combat ineffective. The bombardment had knocked out all its frontline tanks and had killed, wounded, or driven mad 70 percent of its 2,200 soldiers. The 30 percent who remained fought with a grim determination. Entrenched infantry and antitank guns resisted VII Corps' push all afternoon, with help from the fewer than fifteen tanks the division was able to bring up from reserve. Behind them, German artillery that the bombing was meant to suppress came to life, laying down lethal fire in the path of the advancing Americans.

In these circumstances, VII Corps gained less than two miles on July 25, but its progress was not as labored the following day, and by July 27, corps commander Major General Collins began to realize that he was not faced with the kind of layered defenses that had soaked up Goodwood's energy, but rather a thin shell that showed all the signs of cracking. To punch through the remaining German defenses, Collins took a gamble that paid off. He committed two of his armored columns to the fight early, risking congestion at the front if the tanks could not make a clean break.

With the U.S. VIII Corps now joining the battle on VII Corps' right flank, the dogged German resistance began to wilt before the onslaught of the Shermans. American armor began to outflank the defensive positions and seize crossroads in their rear to prevent the Germans from escaping with their matériel. One reason the Americans were able to advance much more quickly than in previous Normandy offensives was their development of a tank capable of breaching the defensive strengths of the *bocage*.

Nicknamed the Rhino, it was invented by a pair of 2d Armored Division enlisted soldiers, one of whom, Sergeant Curtis Culin, was later feted as the developer of the secret weapon that won Cobra.[49] The Rhino was simply a Sherman tank with steel teeth fashioned from German beach defenses fixed to its front. With such a device attached, the tank had only to drive into a hedgerow and tear through it, earth, roots, and all, instead of going around it or, most dangerously, over it, exposing the tank's vulnerable underside to antitank fire. The invention conferred great maneuverability upon Allied armor, as it meant Allied tanks were no longer restricted to the Norman roadways but could roam at will through the *bocage*.

The breakthrough came on July 27. The previous night, Brigadier General Maurice Rose had driven his Combat Command A of the 2d Armored Division beyond the division's immediate objectives of Saint-Gilles and Canisy, and by dawn on July 27, they were in possession of the high ground to the south. This position served to guard the left flank of the divisions now pouring south through the overwhelmed German defenders. During that fateful day, as the 2d Armored Division, or Hell on Wheels, as it was—and is—known, headed south on the eastern flank of Cobra, the 3d Armored and 1st Infantry Divisions advanced down the western flank toward the vital crossroads town of Coutances.

From there they would be able to cut off German units retreating from the coast.

Two panzer divisions, 2d SS and 17th SS (the latter really a *panzergrenadier* formation), were hastily dispatched to intercept the American advance, and their furious resistance prevented 3d Armored and 1st Infantry from reaching Coutances on July 27. The arrival next day of the 4th and 6th Armored Divisions put the panzers to flight and Coutances fell into American hands. The Americans had used the time afforded by the stalemate in the *bocage* to good effect, training in the basics of infantry-armor co-operation. Now the value of those rehearsals showed through, as U.S. armor and infantry units coordinated their attacks with a far greater degree of success than the British had managed on the eastern flank of the bridgehead.

The situation was now ripe for exploitation, and Bradley decided to unleash against the Germans the Allied commander perhaps best suited to make the most of the opportunity: Lieutenant General George S. Patton, Jr.

As commander of the 2d Armored Division in Tunisia, and then as 7th Army commander in Sicily, Patton had made a name for himself as a hard-driving leader with an extraordinary talent for conducting fast-paced mobile warfare. However, he had been relieved of command in Sicily in August 1943 after two notorious incidents in which he slapped soldiers he accused of malingering.

Recognizing that talents as prodigious as those of George Patton were at a premium, his superiors quietly prepared for his return to the battlefield. They gave him command of a fictitious army group in England as part of the massive deception plan aimed at keeping German divisions bottled up in northern France expecting a second invasion in the Pas de Calais region. Eisenhower wanted him on the ground in Normandy, and he was due to take command of the Third U.S. Army on August 1. However, the unexpectedly rapid progress of the Cobra offensive prompted Bradley to give Patton temporary command of VIII Corps in the meantime, to allow him to exploit the breakthrough to maximum effect in the waning days of July.

As Allied fighter-bombers ranged unchallenged across the Normandy skies, sweeping much of the remaining German armor

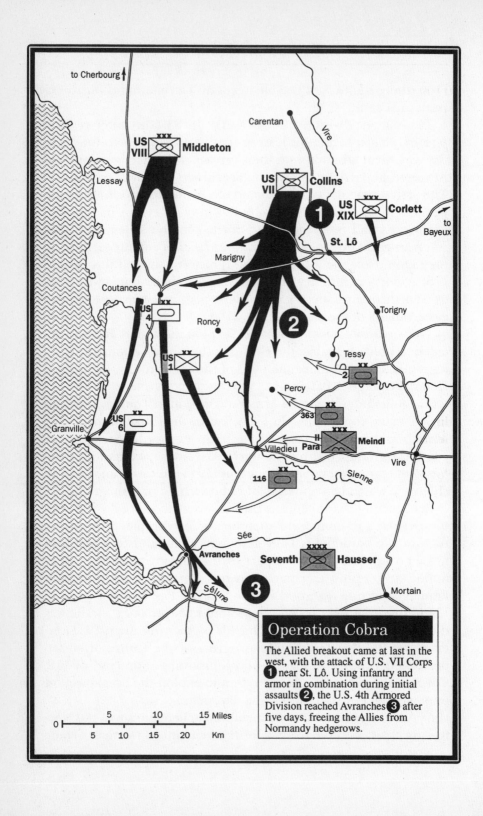

to Cherbourg ↑

Carentan

Vire

US VIII ✕✕✕ Middleton

Lessay

US VII ✕✕✕ Collins

US XIX ✕✕✕ Corlett

①

to Bayeux

St. Lô

Marigny

Coutances

Roncy

Torigny

US 4 ✕✕✕

②

Tessy

US 1 ✕✕

2

Percy

363 ✕✕

US 6 ✕✕

Granville

Villedieu Para ⫿ ✕✕✕ Meindl

Vire

116 ✕✕

Sienne

Sée

Avranches

Sélune

③

Seventh ✕✕✕✕ Hausser

Mortain

5   10   15 Miles

0

5   10   15   20   Km

Operation Cobra

The Allied breakout came at last in the west, with the attack of U.S. VII Corps ① near St. Lô. Using infantry and armor in combination during initial assaults ②, the U.S. 4th Armored Division reached Avranches ③ after five days, freeing the Allies from Normandy hedgerows.

from the roads before the advancing Americans, VIII Corps's spearhead division, 4th Armored, forged ahead. On July 30, it reached Avranches, at the base of the Cotentin and the gateway to Brittany. Five miles south of Avranches, on the road into Brittany, lies the town of Pontaubault. Although largely evacuated by the fleeing Germans, the town threatened to slow Patton's advance as it contained only one standing bridge across the river Selune.

Patton's advance quickly won him command of XV Corps as well. Knowing that it was essential that he pass his two corps over the bridge and into Brittany in rapid time, but fearful of a *Luftwaffe* attack if a huge traffic jam developed at the bottleneck, the Third Army commander threw away the rule book and improvised. He sent his senior staff officers, and in some cases his division commanders, out to the crossroads at either side of the bridge to personally direct traffic. On the Normandy side they funneled vehicles from an amalgam of units across in no particular order. On the Brittany side, the assortment was separated by marking each of several roads that led away from the bridge for a different division. Patton thus pushed seven divisions across the Selune in three days.[50]

Brittany now beckoned. Once through the Avranches-Pontaubault corridor, Patton, following Bradley's orders, directed VIII Corps to head westward onto the peninsula and secure its ports, the original Cobra objectives. As the Germans retreated before them, VIII Corps made such rapid progress that it occasionally outran its supply lines, a problem that was to hamper Patton's lightning offensives for much of the campaign in Europe. The Germans fell back on the fortified ports. There they made a stand and held out until September.

The rest of Patton's army had meanwhile turned left at Pontaubault and headed for Mortain, twenty miles to the east. From there the divisions pushed southeast against increasingly disjointed German opposition, and by August 8, the newly formed XV Corps was at Le Mans, over eighty miles from Avranches. At Le Mans, the corps turned north and two days later was at Alençon. By August 13, it had reached to within a few miles of Alençon. Patton's troops now formed a huge bulge east of Brittany, which at its northern edge represented the bottom half of a huge pincer surrounding Kluge's forces. Dempsey's British forces, slowly advancing south of Caen, formed the top half.

HITLER'S LAST GAMBLE IN NORMANDY

As Patton's drive punched deeper into German-held territory, it seemed the German divisions remaining in Normandy were about to be trapped unless they retreated, but Hitler had other ideas. He instead ordered Kluge to defend the line between the Orne and the Vire Rivers with infantry units only, thus freeing four panzer divisions for a counterattack at Mortain, which he hoped would reach Avranches and sever the American supply lines fueling Patton's drive.

The senior German commanders knew that, with their scant resources and limited planning time, the attack's chances of success against prepared American positions at Mortain, protected by dominant Allied airpower, were virtually nil. Argument was futile, so they decided to cut their losses and attack as soon as possible, at midnight on August 6, before their positions worsened further.

The recently formed XLVII Panzer Corps was put in charge of the attack, which was code-named Operation *Luttich* (German for the town of Liege, in Belgium). It gathered elements of the 2d Panzer, 116th Panzer, 1st SS Panzer, 2d SS Panzer, 17th SS Panzergrenadier, and Panzer *Lehr* Divisions and hurled them against the 30th Division east of Mortain.

Although the panzer divisions could scrape together only 100 tanks between them, they had surprise and their own tactical abilities on their side. The armor of 2d SS Panzer broke through the outer U.S. defenses and thrust several miles into the American lines. It was stopped only by the intervention of the 35th Division, which had been ordered to Mortain from Fougeres by Bradley a matter of hours prior to the German attack, and by the steadfastness of 700 encircled troops. These were elements of the 30th Division that had been bypassed by the panzers. They gathered on Hill 317, a point of high ground that dominated the surrounding area. Supported by the divisional tank destroyer battalion, which accounted for fourteen precious panzers during the struggle,[51] they held out until relieved on August 12, by which time 300 of them had become casualties.

Several miles to the north, a 1st SS Panzer thrust made good initial progress, but then ran into 9th Division positions after dawn, and its attack also bogged down. The Germans failed to get the attack restarted down either axis during the day, as Allied fighter-bombers decimated their already threadbare panzer force. When, at a critical moment in the battle, the 116th Panzer Division commander declined to send his tanks forward as reinforcements, it was clear the attack had failed.

From that moment on, the *Wehrmacht* knew nothing but retreat and slaughter in Normandy. As the two pincers of the Allied advance began to close on the 80,000 men and over 630 tanks and self-propelled guns in the pocket of German resistance, Hitler refused to countenance a withdrawal. For a week, the Germans stuck to their guns. Their still-superior tactical skills kept the Allies at bay on the ground, but they were taking a terrible pounding from the air. Then on August 16, Hitler agreed to a retreat, but it was already too late for many of his men. The next day, the mouth of the pocket was only a few thousand yards wide, and three days later, it closed completely.

As retreat turned into a rout, only one German in four escaped the carnage within what became known as the Falaise pocket. An estimated 10,000 died, and 50,000 were taken prisoner. But the caution shown by the Allied commanders in closing the pocket so slowly as to allow 20,000 of their opponents to flee would come back to haunt them in December, when many of these survivors found themselves in panzer units gathered up by Hitler in the Ardennes for one final, desperate throw of the dice.

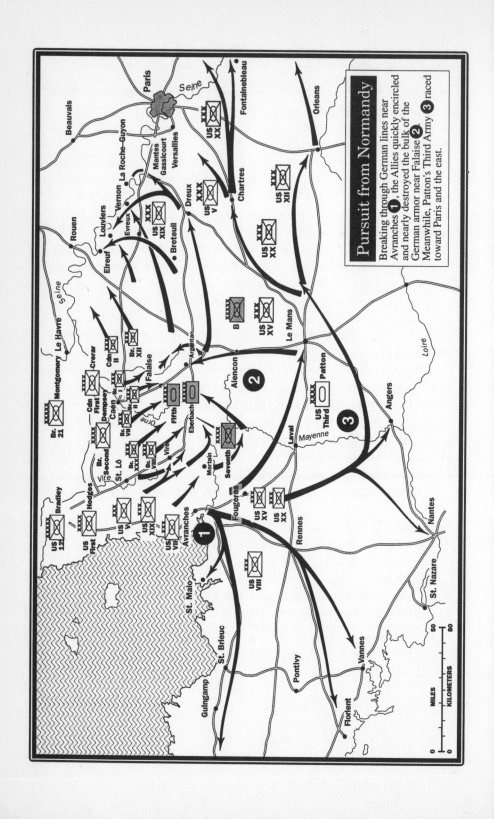

Pursuit from Normandy

Breaking through German lines near Avranches ❶, the Allies quickly encircled and nearly destroyed the bulk of the German armor near Falaise ❷. Meanwhile, Patton's Third Army ❸ raced toward Paris and the east.

MILES

KILOMETERS

0   50

0   80

CHAPTER FIVE

THE ARDENNES, 1944–1945

Death Ride of the Panzers

IN THE EARLY years of the war, when German armies surged forward in swift, decisive strokes, the term *Hitler weather* was given to the blue skies and good visibility that allowed the *Luftwaffe* to pave the way for the armored forces. Now Hitler weather was just the opposite: Hitler needed low clouds and bad weather to hide his forces from the omnipresent and virtually omnipotent Allied airpower.

It was through layered clouds of Hitler weather that German artillery shells rent the crisp dawn air of the Ardennes hills on December 16, 1944, shaking thousands of American infantrymen from their sleep and rousing their commanders from a false sense of security. The barrage was followed by the clanking, creaking sounds of panzers rumbling westward along the eighty-five-mile Ghost Front, which, since the summer, had been a relatively tranquil area thinly defended by a mixed bag of American troops. Some were veteran formations sent there to rest and recuperate. Others were inexperienced outfits deployed to the snow-shrouded woodlands to get a first taste of action in minor skirmishes along the front. None were prepared for a full-scale German offensive.

The Allied planners' belief that the Germans would not attack in the Ardennes was based less on their misreading of German strength on the Western Front than on their failed understanding of the German chain of command. The Allies believed that the aristocratic Field Marshal Gerd von Rundstedt, the nominal Commander in Chief West of Axis forces in Europe, actually held the reins of power. Rundstedt was a prototypical aristocratic Prussian officer who knew his only rational course of action was to preserve his strength while waiting for the next Allied offensive. The Allies therefore assumed that little in the way of a counterattack could be expected from his divisions manning Hitler's West Wall along the Reich's shrinking western frontier.

The Allied leaders were mistaken. The aging Rundstedt was in reality little more than a figurehead. Genuine power over all German forces resided in the Wolf's Lair, deep in the forested heart of East Prussia. The *führer* himself was calling the shots, and his moves were far harder to predict than those of his highly capable but conventional general staff. Although his strategy was often unorthodox, Hitler always demonstrated a keen sense of history.

As the Allied armies moved ever closer to the German homeland, the heart of the Third Reich, Hitler was reluctant to simply sit and await the inevitable, husbanding his forces for a final *Götterdammerung*. In his mind, there was still a chance for him to emulate his hero, Frederick the Great. Frederick, when similarly opposed by larger forces during the Seven Years' War, had taken the offensive and shattered the coalition ranged against him. Hitler knew he could amass enough reserves to launch one last major offensive against his enemies.

WHERE TO STRIKE?

Where would such an attack have the greatest impact? Not on the Eastern Front where a successful offensive might destroy between twenty and thirty of the seemingly inexhaustible supply of Soviet divisions, but would only delay, not halt, the Red Army's advance. If a gamble were to be made, it would have to be in the west, where a similar success could decisively alter the strategic equation.[1] Thus, by August 19, Hitler had decided to risk his reserves in a final all-or-nothing offensive against the Anglo-American armies in the west. By dealing the western Allies a serious reverse, Hitler believed he could get them to agree to a separate peace, thereby allowing him to focus all his energies on the climactic struggle in the east. But where to strike the decisive blow?

Hitler considered and dismissed two alternatives. One was an attack launched from the Dutch town of Venlo almost due west to the Belgian port of Antwerp, the key to Allied logistical supply on the Western Front. This plan had the advantage of cutting off the 21st British Army Group, but the ubiquitous canals and other waterways that marked the flat, sea-level terrain ruled out the swift panzer thrust Hitler envisaged. A second option was to attack at the boundary between the U.S. Seventh Army, which was marching north from the Mediterranean, and Patton's Third Army. However, not only was this section of the front too fluid for the planning of a major offensive, but behind it lay no strategic objective whose capture might influence the outcome of the war.[2] Hitler, his sense of destiny working overtime, finally settled on the choice successive German commanders had picked during their great victories in 1870 and 1940: the Ardennes.

The Ardennes is an area of low hills dotted with woodlands that lies at the intersection of the borders of Belgium, Germany, and Luxembourg. Although successive German invasions had broken into France via the Ardennes, it was hardly an ideal route for the panzers. It was the defenders' belief that no well-organized, mechanized assault could make it through the region that had caused them to leave it so weakly defended in 1940. The sparse network of paved roads in the region tends to run primarily along a north-south axis, and this factor, along with the lack of the wide-open spaces desirable for mechanized maneuver warfare, meant that any large-scale attack from east to west was bound to become channelized. Even without the challenges posed by the American defenders, it would take ruthless road discipline to avoid massive traffic jams as the 2,600 vehicles of a single panzer division crowded onto one of these narrow routes.[3] In addition, the forests, which were not all-covering, but rather spread over the hills in patches, with fields and firebreaks between them, meant that large unit actions tended to degenerate into smaller fights as subelements became separated from each other.

It was through this forbidding terrain that Hitler planned to thrust two panzer armies in a lightning armored thrust that would recall the halcyon days of *blitzkrieg* over four years previously. According to Hitler's plan, fleshed out by the OKW led by Colonel General Alfred Jodl, two panzer armies, protected by a third army to the south, would cross the Ardennes between Monschau and Echternach. Smashing through the thin crust of the American defense to break into the open country to the west, they would reach and cross the Meuse in two days and capture Antwerp within a week. The 21st Army Group and the 9th U.S. Army, cut off from the rest of the Allied forces to the south, would have no choice but to retreat across the Channel in a second Dunkirk—a humiliating withdrawal that would inevitably lead to a split in the Atlantic alliance, or so Hitler thought.

The German army was not the force it was in 1940, and Hitler's plan, while audacious, was seriously flawed. It is true that after Hitler ordered on August 19 that twenty-five divisions be moved to the Western Front in preparation for the offensive, his minions in the Nazi hierarchy scraped together such a force, pulling divisions from all over their shrinking empire and filling them with personnel culled from the Luftwaffe, the navy, and overstaffed rear echelons. While the Germans might have reasonably expected to achieve a breakthrough against the four U.S. divisions holding the Ardennes front, even a total force of over twenty-five divisions was not enough to guarantee victory against the five Allied armies in the north European theater.

Hitler's notion that a reverse in Europe, even a serious one, would cause a split in the Allied ranks was also suspect. Although the field commanders from different Allied nations frequently differed over how to wage their campaigns, they all deferred to Eisenhower as the final decision maker. Their political bosses, meanwhile, were firmly committed to forcing the unconditional surrender of Germany, no matter what the cost.

In addition, although the weakly held Ardennes seemed to Hitler the most promising section of the Allied line at which to hurl his last reserves of armor, the terrain that proved negotiable by Panzer IIIs and IVs in the spring of 1940 was to prove far harder going for the much heavier Panthers and Tigers driving through the waist-high snow of the winter of 1944–45.

All of these drawbacks occurred to the generals to whom Hitler gave the responsibility for prosecuting the attack, and they labored under no illusions about their chances of success. When told that the *führer's* ultimate objective was Antwerp, Rundstedt reportedly shot back, "Antwerp? If we reach the Meuse we should go down on our knees and thank God!" Field Marshal Walter Model, the recently appointed commander of the new, secret army group that was to mount the attack, was equally skeptical. The monocled field marshal, known as "the *führer's* fireman" because of his record of repeatedly restoring order to the Eastern Front when Soviet breakthroughs seemed inevitable, was fiercely loyal to Hitler, but even he was forced to admit that Hitler's plan "doesn't have a damned leg to stand on!"

Fearful that the *führer's* gamble would cost the Germans their last reserves of precious armor, Model and Rundstedt worked separately to persuade Hitler to scale back his ambitions for the offensive. Each proposed a more modest plan of his own, which together became known as the Small Solution. The two plans shared the objective of destroying the First U.S. Army but stopped short of making the dash for the coast that was the hallmark of Hitler's Big Solution. Submitted together on October 27, the plans were both immediately shot down by Hitler, who declared them "incapable of producing decisive results."[4] Valuable time had been lost during this haggling, and the original date for the offensive, November 25, was now unrealistic. Hitler therefore moved the deadline back to December 10, as the entire *Wehrmacht* girded for action.

Even if it was founded on shaky strategic ground, Hitler's final offensive was meticulously planned within the limits imposed by the Third Reich's shrinking resource base. Throughout Europe, divisions were pulled out of the line and maneuvered into holding areas that were cleverly located to look as if they were positioned to strike at an expected Allied offensive, rather than in preparation for a major German attack. Twenty-three new *Volksgrenadier*, or People's Infantry, divisions were formed from the last reserves of German manpower: Luftwaffe personnel, civilian workers who had hitherto escaped the draft, criminals who were formed into penal battalions, as well as the very young and the sick. Of the new divisions, which received no more than two months of hard training, eighteen were earmarked for the offensive in the west.[5]

Meanwhile, under the direction of Minister for War Production Albert Speer, the German war industry worked prodigiously to build up supplies for the offensive. Records were broken during the fall of 1944 in the production of ammunition and fighter aircraft, while figures for the manufacture of machine guns, rifles, assault guns, and howitzers also soared. Despite the attentions of the Allied air forces, which had targeted the Henschel works in Kassel where the Tiger tanks were made,[6] overall tank production peaked at almost 600 in December.[7] While overstretched *Wehrmacht* units on the Eastern Front were forced to make do with paltry replenishments for their wholesale losses of men and equipment, the vast bulk of the matériel was transported to the west by train.

The rail network upon which the trainloads of panzers, fuel, and other supplies reached the Western Front dated from World War I, but it had been improved for the 1940 *blitzkrieg*. Now it again proved its worth as train after train snaked out of the Reich's industrial heartland, moving only by night and hiding in tunnels during the day, to deposit thousands of wagonloads of supplies in the depots that were filling in preparation for the December assault. Despite the Germans' massive buildup of men and matériel on the Western Front, an elaborate deception plan kept senior Allied commanders unaware of the shock in store for them. No information about the offensive was transmitted using the Enigma encryption machine, which the Germans correctly suspected the Allies had cracked. The Allies were thus deprived of their most valuable source of intelligence on German maneuvers. Instead, all orders and plans were hand-delivered by officers accompanied by Gestapo bodyguards. Few German officers received more than two or three days' advance notice of the attack, and those who did were threatened with severe reprisals if they broke the code of silence about the operation imposed by Hitler. Even Hitler's code name for the operation, Watch on the Rhine, had a defensive tone to it.

The final, and possibly most effective, measure taken by Hitler to ensure the attack met with initial success was to order it postponed until his meteorologists could guarantee six days of uninterrupted bad weather. Rightfully distrustful of Goering's promises of 3,000 fighters to support Watch on the Rhine, and mindful of the destruction sown among German armored columns by Allied fighter-bombers over Normandy, Hitler knew the only way to shield his carefully hoarded panzer reserves from the same fate in the Ardennes was to attack when Allied aircraft could not take to the air. Having already been slipped to December 10, the date of the attack was then postponed three times as last-minute reinforcements and supplies were rushed to the front. Finally, Hitler declared there would be no more delays. He would stake his last card December 16.

GERMAN DISPOSITIONS

Responsibility for Hitler's do-or-die offensive fell on the shoulders of three German armies. In the northern section of the Ardennes front, between Monschau and the Losheim Gap, the Sixth SS Panzer Army was to provide the *Schwerpunkt* for the attack. With four elite *Waffen SS* panzer divisions, supported by five infantry divisions, the 140,000-strong army was easily the strongest of the three assembled on the German front. Nevertheless, giving this formation the leading role in the last great German offensive of the war was a decision based as much on political factors as it was on military common sense.

The fanatical Nazis of the *Waffen SS* were Hitler's favorite troops. In contrast to the regular army, of whom he had grown even more deeply suspicious since discovering that senior army officers had masterminded the assassination attempt against him, the *Waffen SS* were fiercely loyal, and in return they received the best equipment and most vital missions. For example, unlike regular army panzer divisions, the SS tank divisions were guaranteed two panzer battalions and an extra two panzer grenadier battalions.[8] Commanding the Sixth SS Panzer Army was *Oberstgruppenführer* Josef "Sepp" Dietrich, a barrel-chested crony of

Hitler's from the 1920s who knew little of combined arms warfare. Without distinguishing himself in his commands on either the Eastern or Western Fronts, and to the disgust of regular army officers, Dietrich had risen through the ranks of the *Waffen SS* due to his close ties to Hitler. Mellenthin was later to write that "it was a great misfortune that Hitler placed his *Schwerpunkt* with the SS Army, whose commander was a very gallant fighter but had no real understanding of armored warfare."[9] Hitler's bias did not completely blind him to Dietrich's failings, and so he assigned a respected army officer, Major General Fritz Kramer, to be Dietrich's chief of staff and to run the tactical operation.

The plan for Dietrich's army was for the infantry divisions both to hold firm the northern shoulder around Monschau and make the initial breakthroughs in the Allied line. Then the two divisions of I SS Panzer Corps, to be followed by two more in II SS Panzer Corps, would punch through the 99th Infantry Division's lines via the Losheim Gap, the same route used by the Germans in 1940. Although the strength of Dietrich's army made it a natural choice to make the main effort, Hitler's allegiance to the *Waffen SS* was to have serious repercussions later in the battle when their attack bogged down.

To the south of the *Waffen SS* lay *General der Panzertruppen* Hasso von Manteuffel's Fifth Panzer Army, comprising 90,000 troops and including four infantry and three panzer divisions. Unlike Dietrich, Manteuffel was a skilled tactician in the use of armor and had commanded the 7th Panzer and *Grossdeutschland* divisions on the Eastern Front. One of the *Wehrmacht*'s most highly decorated officers, the diminutive Manteuffel was promoted to the rank of full general from that of major general in the fall of 1944, without ever holding the intermediate rank of lieutenant general.[10] Manteuffel knew he faced weak opposition in his sector: the inexperienced 106th Infantry Division and two regiments of the 28th Infantry Division, which were battered from a vicious fight in the Hurtgen Forest. His plan was to use two infantry divisions to surround the 106th, dangerously exposed on a salient jutting into the Schnee Eifel range of hills, while pushing the rest of his force across the Our River farther south, toward Bastogne and beyond.

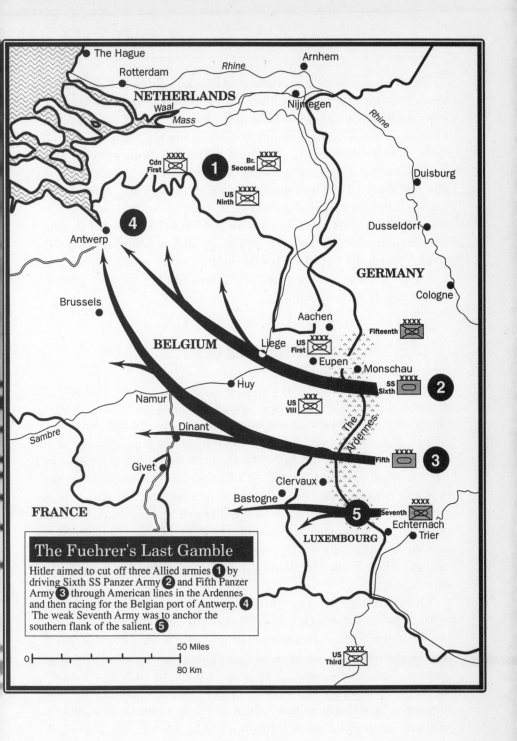

The Hague
Rotterdam
Rhine
Arnhem
NETHERLANDS
Nijmegen
Waal
Maas
Duisburg

Cdn First XXXX ➀ Br. Second XXXX
US Ninth XXXX

Dusseldorf

Antwerp ➃

Brussels

GERMANY
Cologne

BELGIUM
Aachen
Liège
US First XXXX
Eupen
Fifteenth XXXX

Huy
Monschau
SS Sixth XXXX ➁

Namur
US VIII XXX

Sambre
Dinant

Givet

Fifth XXXX ➂

The Ardennes

Clervaux
Bastogne
Echternach
Trier
Seventh XXXX ➄

FRANCE
LUXEMBOURG

The Fuehrer's Last Gamble

Hitler aimed to cut off three Allied armies ➀ by
driving Sixth SS Panzer Army ➁ and Fifth Panzer
Army ➂ through American lines in the Ardennes
and then racing for the Belgian port of Antwerp. ➃
The weak Seventh Army was to anchor the
southern flank of the salient. ➄

50 Miles

0

80 Km

US Third XXXX

The Seventh Army, the weakest of Model's three armies, barely deserved the name, being little more than a corps-sized formation. Led by General Erich Brandenberger, it had four understrength *volksgrenadier* divisions and one parachute division, which were almost uniformly understrength and poorly trained. Its mission was to advance to the Meuse and then face south, protecting the left flank of the German advance. Although the army faced only two infantry regiments and an armored combat command in its path, its lack of armor and motorized transport meant its rate of advance was limited to how fast its foot soldiers and horse-drawn transport could march through the snow. This rendered the army's chances of successfully accomplishing its mission slim in the eyes of its own staff.[11]

THE GAMBLE BEGINS

Almost from the moment the first gray-clad panzer grenadiers crossed the line of departure, things began to go wrong for the Sixth SS Panzer Army in the north. Evenly distributed along the army's twenty-five-mile front, the half-hour artillery barrage that preceded the attack did little but alert the well-dug-in U.S. troops on the northern part of the Ardennes front that something big was up. Nevertheless, morale soared among the German troops as the moment for them to surge forward approached. On the defensive in Western Europe since the Allied breakout from Normandy in July, they finally were being given a chance to throw the invaders from German soil and hurl them back into the North Sea.

The advantages in men and matériel conferred on them by their beloved *führer* were offset by his overly precise management of the battle plan. Against even Dietrich's wishes, Hitler ordered that the Sixth SS Panzer Army's infantry was to clear the first gaps in the Allied line.[12] The army's four SS panzer divisions were to be held in reserve, to exploit the grenadiers' breakthroughs by driving to the Meuse along five routes of advance, named *Panzer Rollbahnen A* through *E*. The flaws in this plan were quickly exposed. The infantry detailed to seize and hold the corner at Monschau were four battalions of the 326th *Volksgrenadier* Division. Poorly trained, the waves of German infantry were pushed forward by their officers into a hail of American artillery and machine gunfire. Few if any Germans lived to reach the first line of U.S. foxholes around the village of Hofen.

The 326th's colleagues in the 12th and 277th *Volksgrenadier* Divisions had no more luck to the south, where they were engaged in bitter fighting with the 393d Regiment of the 99th Infantry Division. The 393d was dug in along the forward slopes of the Elsenborn Ridge, a key series of hills that lay in front of the adjacent villages of Rocherath and Krinkelt. Seizure of the villages was essential to the Sixth Panzer Army's plan, as they lay astride *Rollbahnen A* and *B*, along which the *Hitler Jugend* Division's 25th SS Panzergrenadier Regiment and divisional antitank battalion were to pass.[13]

Under extraordinary pressure from the German infantry, the two battalions of the 393d, which held the forwardmost positions, bent but did not buckle. At one stage, the 1st Battalion, 393d Infantry's line, was held only by a desperate thirty-eight-man bayonet charge led by a lieutenant from the regimental antitank company.[14] This outstanding small unit action killed twenty-eight Germans and prevented a breakthrough that could have been fatal to Allied hopes of holding the Germans at bay. Both American and German corps commanders committed their infantry reserves to the fight on the Elsenborn that evening, but at dawn on December 17, the Americans were still in position, albeit at a cost of hundreds of casualties.

Farther south, the 12th *Volksgrenadier* Division was battering against the 99th Infantry Division's 394th Infantry Regiment. After some initial progress in which they took the town of Losheim, however, this attack also ground to a halt. Fierce fighting in the thickly wooded Gerolstein forest cost each side heavy losses, but the Germans failed in their objective of opening *Rollbahn C, Hitler Jugend*'s main avenue of advance.

South of Losheim lies the Losheim Gap where, more than anywhere else on the front, the force ratio favored the Germans. Yet, even here the 3d *Fallschirmjäger*, or Paratroop, Division failed to dent the line held by the 14th Cavalry Group. Thus, when darkness fell, the Sixth SS Panzer Army's infantry had nowhere advanced more than a few miles west. Behind them, Dietrich's 642 tanks and assault guns—the core of Model's combat power—sat idle, their frustrated crews waiting for the grenadiers to clear the panzers a path through the thin crust of American forces before them.

Manteuffel's Fifth Panzer Army found itself similarly unable to break through on the first day, but it nevertheless scored one of the greatest tactical successes of the offensive by encircling the two regiments of the 106th Infantry Division isolated on the Schnee Eifel. This the army accomplished after its commander elicited from Hitler permission to reduce the planned length of the artillery barrage, arguing that a prolonged pounding would only alert the American defenders to an imminent attack. By shortening the barrage, Manteuffel also gave himself time to infiltrate some of his grenadiers behind the American lines before dawn, bouncing searchlights off the clouds to light their way.

The pincer attack against the two 106th Division regiments took most of the day to complete, and so although the armorless German LXVI Corps had surrounded the U.S. forces and routed the U.S. VIII Corps artillery to their west, they failed to push on and capture the other principal first-day objective in that sector, the town of Saint-Vith. Meanwhile, the 106th Division's third regiment, located just south and west of its companions, avoided their comrades' fate by fighting off the inexperienced 62d *Volksgrenadier* Division and one of 116th Panzer Division's *panzer grenadier* regiments.[15]

South of the positions held by the 106th lay the 28th Infantry Division. Its northernmost regiment, the 112th Infantry, faced two German divisions, including the understrength 116th Panzer. From their prime defensive positions in a captured portion of Hitler's West Wall, the outnumbered Americans held the Germans at bay. Ironically, the dragon's teeth tank traps designed to hold back an Allied invasion of Germany prevented the panzers from outflanking the American-held pillboxes and forcing their way to the bridges across the Our River.[16]

Manteuffel's best hopes for a decisive breakthrough lay with the three divisions of the XLVII Panzer Corps, which included two of the finest armored divisions left in the *Wehrmacht,* the 2d Panzer and Panzer *Lehr,* as well as the 26th *Volksgrenadier* Division, the most accomplished infantry division in the Ardennes. Opposed as it was by only one regiment of the 28th Division, the corps enjoyed the greatest superiority in numbers of all German forces in the Ardennes. Realizing that the key to his reaching the Meuse quickly lay in seizing the crossroads town of Bastogne, twenty miles to the west of the front, before the Allies could reinforce it, Manteuffel was determined to capitalize on his numerical advantage by committing his panzers early to the fight. Hitler acquiesced, and 2d Panzer and Panzer *Lehr* moved forward on the morning of December 16.

Neither division got very far, however. In their preoccupation with reaching Bastogne and the Meuse, Manteuffel's planners had paid insufficient attention to how they would cross the first natural barrier, the Our River. Both panzer divisions spent the day fretting on the eastern bank while engineers struggled to erect bridges across the river. Once across, late in the afternoon, 2d Panzer and its infantry support tried to bypass the major centers of resistance and press on to Bastogne. Bitter fighting at the towns of Marnach and Hosingen, which blocked the major panzer-worthy roads, held up the German advance. The elite German troops were surprised to find themselves facing roadblocks fiercely defended by rear-echelon American soldiers who had been given a weapon and told to fight it out as long as possible before withdrawing. Lack of decent bridging equipment was also delaying Seventh Army's attempts to cross the Our. Deprived of armor and significant artillery support, Brandenberger's green troops penetrated nowhere more than a few miles beyond the river before becoming bogged down in house-to-house fighting against pockets of American resistance in village after village.

THE PACE PICKS UP

December 17 was to prove more fruitful for the Germans as the breakthroughs their commanders had expected the previous day came when American units, fatigued, outgunned, and outnumbered, began to fall back or surrender. Manteuffel, impatient with the first day's progress, had ordered his troops to press the attack during the night, when he rightly expected his infiltration tactics would enjoy greater success against the nervous Americans, many of whom were fighting their first battle.

By first light, the 2d Panzer Division was fully engaged against the 28th Infantry Division's 110th Regiment, defending the towns of Clervaux and Marnach, en route to Bastogne. At first the battle ebbed and flowed as meager U.S. armor reserves were committed. Marnach changed hands twice before the growing panzer strength inexorably forced the American defenders back. Colonel Hurley Fuller, the regimental commander, pleaded with his superiors for reinforcements as his outposts were overrun one by one, but all he received was one company of seventeen Shermans. This he divided into several penny packets of a few tanks each, which he dispatched to help those of his strong points still holding firm.

The practice of splitting armored units into small groups like this came in for criticism after the war and was particularly sneered at by the Germans, as it went against the notion that armored forces should be concentrated for a decisive strike, rather than divided into inconsequential subelements. In this case, however, it is difficult to see what else Fuller could have done, faced as he was by the entire armored strength of the most capable panzer division in the German army.

As his tanks got chewed up, Fuller knew that to save his regiment, he would have to withdraw, but VII Corps commander Major General Troy Middleton forbade any retreat. His orders to hold in place doomed the 110th, but the regiment's stubborn resistance gained valuable time for the reserves that the Americans were now rushing toward Bastogne. The regiment's last stand came in the twelfth-century castle that dominated the town of Clervaux. Out of all antitank ammunition, the defenders finally surrendered at midday on December 18 when a panzer broke down the castle's wooden doors.

Elsewhere on the Fifth Panzer Army front, German progress was steady at best and bore little resemblance to the untrammeled armored thrusts that had characterized the *blitzkrieg* through the same region four years earlier. Traffic jams at the Our continued to hamper Manteuffel's ability to throw his panzers into the fight. The 116th Panzer Division captured one bridge across the river, only to find it could not support the weight of the division's forty-five-ton Panthers. Manteuffel diverted the division south to the bridge at Dasburg over which 2d Panzer was crossing. The sparse road network in the Ardennes also slowed American attempts to buttress the creaking Allied line. Congestion on the road to Schonberg actually forced 7th Armored Division to cancel its mission to rescue the 106th Infantry Division, which was now completely encircled on the Schnee Eifel.

In contrast with their colleagues to the south and despite their disappointing progress on the offensive's first day, Dietrich's panzer grenadiers rested during the night of December 16–17. The cost in men and time due to their failure to pierce the American lines was becoming greater by the hour, however, and was a source of considerable frustration to their commanders, ever mindful that they were slipping farther behind Hitler's unrealistic schedule for the attack.

By dawn on December 17, Model and Dietrich had lost patience with their infantry's inability to push ahead and took the only logical step under the circumstances: they ordered the panzers forward. Ever eager for a fight, the *Hitler Jugend* Division surged ahead to encounter the U.S. 2d and 99th Infantry Divisions that had stymied the Sixth Panzer Army's *volksgrenadiers* at Rocherath and Krinkelt the previous day. The 2d Infantry Division commander, Major General Walter Robinson, earned a Bronze Star for his handling of his outfit during this tricky period, when he first pulled his division back from the Roer dams at night and established a new defensive line through which the 99th Division was to withdraw, before dispatching an infantry and a tank battalion to support the division in front of the villages. He then conducted an exceedingly complex maneuver known as a passage of lines, in which the battered 99th Infantry Division withdrew as the more experienced 2d Infantry Division moved into Rocherath and Krinkelt to take its place, all the time maintaining contact with the Germans.

For the remainder of December 17, fierce house-to-house fighting raged in the villages as the veteran American and German divisions grappled for control of the vital roads. That night, confusion reigned in the American lines, but the Hitler Youth were unable to break through either in the twin villages or farther south where the 99th Infantry Division was still holding the strategic crossroads at Losheimergraben. On December 19 the Americans pulled back to the Elsenborn Ridge, from where, backed by substantial artillery fire, they fought off increasingly weak German attacks for the remainder of the campaign. Dietrich's attempt to seize the northern shoulder had failed.

KAMPFGRUPPE PEIPER

At least one officer in Dietrich's army was not content to stew in traffic jams as his *führer*'s last-ditch offensive crumbled under the weight of unrealistic planning and unexpectedly stubborn American resistance. *Obersturmbannführer* Joachim "Jochen" Peiper, whose battle group comprised the 1st SS Panzer Division's main armored strike force, was not one to accept reverses fatalistically. A zealous Nazi, Peiper had already earned a reputation for daring, ruthless armored warfare on the Eastern Front, where his unit became known as the Blowtorch Battalion for its habit of burning Russian villages to the ground. Now he had been given the leading role in the Ardennes offensive; his mission was to deliver a knockout armored punch from which the Allies could not recover by driving his panzers forward at breakneck speed along *Rollbahn D*, with no regard for his flanks. ("Drive fast, and hold the reins loose!" Kramer told the handsome young SS officer.)[17]

Peiper followed Kramer's instructions to the letter, forcing slower German units into ditches as he powered his 100 Panthers

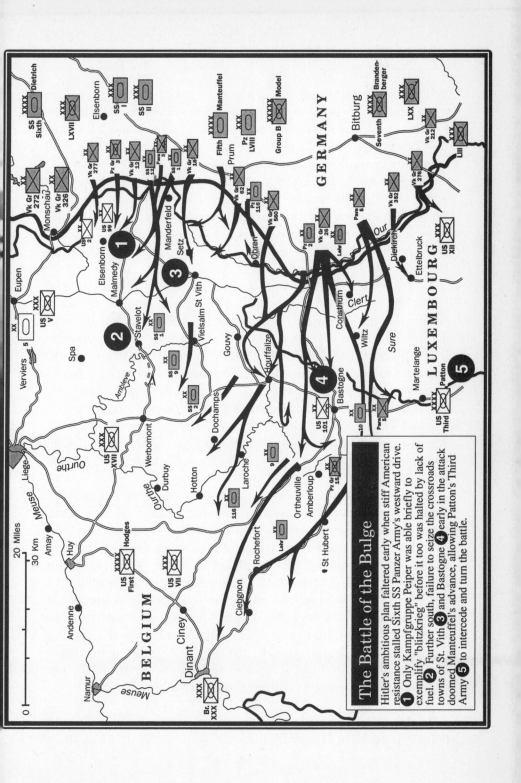

The Battle of the Bulge

Hitler's ambitious plan faltered early when stiff American resistance stalled Sixth SS Panzer Army's westward drive. ❶ Only Kampfgruppe Peiper was able briefly to exemplify "blitzkrieg" before it too was halted by lack of fuel. ❷ Further south, failure to seize the crossroads towns of St. Vith ❸ and Bastogne ❹ early in the attack doomed Manteuffel's advance, allowing Patton's Third Army ❺ to intercede and turn the battle.

and Panzer IVs through the Losheim Gap late on the afternoon of December 16. Brushing aside the feeble challenge of the 14th Cavalry Group patrolling the boundary between V and VII Corps that Peiper hoped to split with his thrust, the twenty-nine-year-old SS officer drove his armored *Schwerpunkt* forward with abandon.

Kampfgruppe Peiper's swift progress was all the more surprising given the shoddy nature of its prescribed route of advance. When Peiper first saw the partially unpaved *Rollbahn D* on the map, he exclaimed, "This route is not for tanks but for bicycles!" He was particularly jealous of the shorter, paved *Rollbahn C* assigned to the *Hitler Jugend* Division.

To cope with the treacherously narrow roads, Peiper placed his combat elements at the head of his fifteen-mile-long attack column in the following order: a pair of half-tracks led the way, with orders to press forward until fired upon, at which point the leading battalion, comprising Mark IVs and Panthers, would move up to deal with the enemy. A battalion of armored infantry came next, followed by part of a Tiger battalion that joined the battle group after it had begun its march. Peiper was not overly fond of Tigers, considering them too heavy and underpowered. The *Kampfgruppe*'s firepower was further strengthened by the inclusion of several enormous *Jagdtigers,* self-propelled 128 mm guns and some *Flak 88s.*[18]

As befitted an officer who demanded enormous self-sacrifice from his men and received hero worship from them in return, Peiper cleared the first obstacle in his path, a German minefield near Losheimergraben, by ordering his troops to drive through it. He lost ten vehicles this way, but little time. At midnight on December 16, he arrived in Lanzerath, only to find the 3d *Fallschirmjäger* Division stalled at the town, their commander complaining of a heavy American presence in front of him. Peiper needed infantry to protect his panzers during the coming night march, and after quickly divining that no German officer had actually scouted out this supposed American threat, Peiper ordered the paratroops to climb aboard his tanks.

As Peiper had expected, no American resistance materialized before he reached Honsfeld, through which retreating U.S. units were passing all night. Peiper cunningly attached his column to the rear of one of these retreating formations, a tactic that enabled him to capture over fifty vehicles, sixteen antitank guns, and a large number of prisoners. It was here, though, that *Kampfgruppe* Peiper showed the first signs of the cold-blooded brutality that had earned it such a fearsome reputation on the Eastern Front. In orders relayed to his troops by Peiper, Dietrich had directed that little time was to be wasted with prisoners. Peiper's troops took Hitler's SS henchman at his word and murdered nineteen American prisoners at Honsfeld, the first of several such massacres they were to commit in the following days. These widely reported atrocities had the short-term effect of motivating U.S. troops, who in turn grew more reluctant to take German prisoners, and the longer-term effect of canceling out any credit Peiper might have expected from history for the tactical *élan* he displayed during the campaign.

Peiper was now making good time, but the delays had cost him dearly in fuel. He veered northwest to Bullingen, where he knew there was an American fuel dump. Like all other German commanders, Peiper started the offensive without enough fuel to reach his objectives, partly because a promised fuel train from Germany never arrived. He was therefore expected to capture any additional fuel needed en route, and most American fuel dumps in the area were marked on his maps. At Bullingen he forced fifty captured American troops to pump 50,000 gallons of fuel into his vehicles, then had them shot.

Peiper, now so deep in the Allied rear that he had lost touch with his divisional headquarters, faced the first of a series of decisions that were to decide the fate not only of his battle group, but of the Germans' drive for the Meuse. He could continue driving west for the Meuse, or he could turn north and cut off the divisions on Elsenborn Ridge from their only route of withdrawal. But Peiper, out of touch with the rest of the battle, did not realize that simply by heading north he could seal off 30,000 American troops, and so he stuck to his orders and proceeded west. Ten miles west of Bullingen, his column captured several truckloads of surprised members of the 285th Field Artillery Observation Battalion as the two columns intersected south of

Malmedy. These men were herded into a field, where, two hours later, they, too, were butchered by Peiper's panzer grenadiers, the *Waffen SS* men firing casually into the pathetic mass of helpless, writhing figures. While several Americans survived by feigning death, at least eighty-six were murdered in the single most infamous atrocity of the war in the West.

Kampfgruppe Peiper proceeded on to Ligneuville, where another important decision awaited its commander. His orders were to follow poor secondary roads for the next fifty miles to the Meuse crossing at Huy, but by turning north toward Malmedy, he could put his column onto *Rollbahn C*, which ran for thirty-five paved miles to Liege. Peiper was mightily tempted to take this course of action, which would have saved his battle group a lot of time spent negotiating the muddy trails to which Jodl's plan had relegated it. Again, his loss of communications with the rear cost him dearly. Had he had radio contact with his higher headquarters, he would have known that 12th SS Panzer Division, to whom *Rollbahn C* had been assigned, was still engaged at Rocherath and Krinkelt, nowhere near close enough to interfere with his proposed race to the Meuse along the better road. In addition, by heading north, Peiper could have seized not only the tactical prize of Malmedy, but two large fuel dumps a couple of miles to the northwest. These would have changed the whole nature of his offensive, as he would not have had to worry about fuel again. Instead, fearful that the *Hitler Jugend* Division lay not far behind, he reluctantly stayed on *Rollbahn D* and headed for the bridge over the Ambleve River at Stavelot.[19]

At Stavelot, a lone battalion of engineers was hurriedly trying to set up a road block before Peiper's panzers could reach the bridge, which was neither mined nor defended by any armor or antitank guns. The engineers themselves could have offered only token resistance to Peiper had he made a concerted effort to gain the bridge, but instead, his three leading panzers, racing for the bridge with guns blazing, stopped short when one of them hit a mine laid minutes previously and threw a track. This caused some consternation among the panzer commanders at the head of the column, who were already slightly nervous after losing one of their tanks to a pair of Shermans in Ligneuville. They reported back to Peiper that Stavelot was heavily defended, and taking it would require infantry support.

Peiper, certainly as fatigued as the rest of his troops after thirty-six hours of almost nonstop driving, took the commanders at their word and decided to wait until his Tigers and grenadiers arrived before assaulting the bridge. It was now dusk on December 17, and the battle group settled in for the night. The respite might have seemed important to Peiper at the time, but it proved vital for First U.S. Army commander Lieutenant General Courtney Hodges, who used the pause in *Kampfgruppe* Peiper's advance to push the 30th Infantry Division south to shore up the defenses in Peiper's path. In some historians' eyes, this unnecessary delay marked the turning point in Sixth SS Panzer Army's offensive.[20]

The next morning, Peiper's attack got back on track when his newly arrived Tigers and panzer grenadiers forced the bridge at Stavelot, overcoming a company of American infantry that had arrived during the night. The rejuvenated battle group wheeled south toward its next crucial objective, the bridges across the Salm and Ambleve Rivers at Trois Ponts. Here his luck began to run out. American combat engineers demolished all three bridges just as Peiper's panzers were clearing a thin screen of engineers from the streets of the town. Denied a route out of the Ambleve valley, Peiper had no choice but to follow the path of the river north, using up precious fuel.

When he reached La Gleize, five miles to the north, one of his reconnaissance units found an undefended bridge at the village of Cheneux, a mile off the La Gleize–Stoumont road. A delighted Peiper led his battle group over the bridge, only to fall victim shortly thereafter to a flight of American fighter-bombers, which were taking advantage of a brief break in the weather. Ten of the leading vehicles were destroyed, blocking the narrow road and allowing U.S. engineers to blow a small bridge over a creek half a mile ahead. Peiper was forced to retrace his steps to the east bank of the Ambleve and head north toward Stoumont, which he expected to be well defended by now.

The next morning, December 19, he captured the town from the 30th Infantry Division's 119th Regiment with a well-executed combined tank and infantry attack. A last stand by ten American Shermans had been dispersed by one of Peiper's favorite tactics: sending groups of two or three Tigers charging straight down the road toward the enemy, supported by fire from self-propelled guns and other panzers.[21] The Americans retreated to form a roadblock across the route northwest to Liege, which they assumed was Peiper's immediate objective. However, the veteran SS officer had only one goal in mind: the Meuse crossing at Huy, which glittered like a mirage only twenty-five miles away. With the Americans obligingly defending the wrong route, all that remained was for Peiper to put his battle group back on the road, engage the American blocking parties with a small diversionary force, and drive on to Huy, which he could reach by nightfall. Like the *grand prix* driver whose engine sputters to a halt only a hundred yards from the checkered flag, Peiper now found victory snatched from his grasp by the cruelest of blows: his entire battle group was virtually out of fuel. Unknown to Peiper and the leading elements of his battle group, while they were wresting control of Stoumont from the 30th Division's 119th Regiment, the 117th had been similarly tearing Stavelot free from the grasp of Peiper's rear guard. When the bridge was finally blown that night, *Kampfgruppe* Peiper was cut off from its lifeline of fuel, food, and ammunition. This was the beginning of the end for one of the boldest, bloodiest panzer offensives of the war in the West.

Under increasing pressure from elements of the 30th Infantry and 3d Armored Division to his north and west and east, and with the 82d Airborne Division moving to cut off any escape to the south, Peiper's dwindling battle group fought a brilliant defensive battle in Stoumont. Five minefields, overlooked by dug-in panzers and well-positioned self-propelled guns and automatic weapons held off determined American assaults for two days before Peiper withdrew his defenses to La Gleize. There his troops repulsed repeated American armor and infantry assaults on December 23, but their position was clearly hopeless. Surrounded and low on all supplies—the Luftwaffe had managed one airdrop to them, but most of the fuel in the drop fell within American lines—and with all 1st SS Panzer Division attempts to reinforce them thwarted, there seemed no chance of escape. Speaking on a powerful Luftwaffe radio he had received before the supply lines were cut, Peiper at last received permission to withdraw. That night, he led the remaining 800 able-bodied members of his *Kampfgruppe* in single file into the woods, each man carrying a full pack, his weapon, and ammunition. Behind them they left 300 of their wounded colleagues plus almost all their American prisoners. Except for a brief exchange of fire with infantry from the 82d Airborne, they managed to evade the American troops drawing a noose around their positions, and on December 25 all 800 rejoined the rest of the 1st SS Panzer Division.

SAINT-VITH AND BASTOGNE

While *Kampfgruppe* Peiper was slicing through the American opposition on *Rollbahn D*, the German attack elsewhere was making much more fitful progress. The two isolated American regiments on the Schnee Eifel surrendered after making a vain effort to break out. Over 7,000 American troops fell into German hands, the largest surrender ever by American forces, excepting the debacle in Bataan. Ten miles behind the Eifel, the crossroads town of Saint-Vith was assuming great importance in the minds of both American and German planners.

A Fifth Army objective on the first day, it remained in American hands, and as the stubborn defense of the Elsenborn deprived the Sixth SS Panzer Army of its primary routes of advance, it began to search to the south for alternatives. Most that it found ran smack through the middle of Saint-Vith. As four divisions stacked one behind the other in traffic jams on the one good road west, the capture of Saint-Vith became imperative to the progress of both armies.

The town could have been captured during the first forty-eight hours of the offensive by an armored force of reasonable strength, but OKW's plans had assigned its seizure to an infantry division, 18th *Volksgrenadier,* that was already overstretched. Not for the last time, Jodl's failure to allocate forces commensurate with the mission assigned them held up the German advance. It was not until December 21 that two *volksgrenadier* divisions, supported by a small force of Tigers, took the town. However, the town's defense, anchored around four 7th Armored Division companies, had won crucial time for other American units to establish defensive screens to the rear.

Even more detrimental to the German cause was the failure of Manteuffel's panzer divisions to seize Bastogne during the first days of the offensive. Again, much of the blame lies with Jodl and OKW. They had given the objective of Bastogne to the 26th *Volksgrenadier* Division, but the veteran infantry unit had its hands full seizing the crossings over the Our and the Clerf Rivers. Nevertheless, by December 18, the 2d Panzer Division was clear of the fighting in Clervaux and had an excellent opportunity to capture the key communications hub, which was defended by only one combat command of the 9th Armored Division, split between two roadblocks. But 2d Panzer Division commander Colonel Meinrad von Lauchert was interested only in reaching the Meuse. After summarily dispatching the task forces at the roadblocks, he turned north to bypass Bastogne, which lay at his mercy.

Following hard on the heels of 2d Panzer was Panzer *Lehr*, commanded by Major General Fritz Bayerlein, who had learned his trade with Rommel in North Africa. That evening Bayerlein was to fall short of the aggressive, impetuous standard set by the late master of armored warfare. He allowed himself to be misled by a Belgian farmer into taking the worse of two roads toward Bastogne, and his vanguard soon found itself inching through a quagmire to Mageret, three miles north of Bastogne on the main road. There another Belgian farmer told him a large American armored force under a major general had just passed through en route to Bastogne. It was a lie, but fearful of running into an American armored division, Bayerlein chose not to press his attack and instead laid a minefield and waited until dawn. He did not know it, but the window of opportunity granted him to seize the most vital communications hub in the campaign was about to close.

The next morning, Bayerlein ordered his panzers to advance to Neffe, just east of Bastogne. There he again paused for no good reason, and by the time the attack restarted an hour later, units of the 101st Airborne Division, one of two airborne divisions that comprised the only American reserves in the theater, had reached Bastogne. The first battalion of paratroops raced east and struck Bayerlein's force with light 75 mm pack howitzers. Bayerlein was later to say that he mistook the sound of the howitzers for tank fire and called off the advance.

Whatever the reason for Bayerlein's reluctance to press home the attack, it cost the Germans dearly. Bastogne remained in American hands for the remainder of the Ardennes campaign and was to prove a significant thorn in the Germans' side. It sat astride seven roads, blocking the Germans' ability to push supplies forward to Manteuffel's spearhead panzer divisions. The latter were forced to use valuable combat power investing the town and making futile attempts to seize it.

Much credit is due the men of the 101st and Combat Command B of the 10th Armored Division, whose indomitable spirit through five days of siege has become legendary in the U.S. Army. Their never-say-die attitude was typified by the senior officer in Bastogne, the 101st's commander Brigadier General Anthony McAuliffe. When four Germans under a white flag appeared at his headquarters on December 22 carrying a message demanding Bastogne's surrender, his one-word written reply—sanitized in the record as "Nuts!" but in all probability a more colorful invective—earned him a place in the history books.

When the defenders' ammunition ran low on December 23, 241 Army Air Force C-47s took advantage of a break in the weather to air-drop supplies to them. The planes returned the next day, braving significant German antiaircraft fire to deliver their vital packages, in stark contrast with the Luftwaffe's abject failure to provide the same service for Jochen Peiper's beleaguered battle group.

Relief for Bastogne came, appropriately, on Christmas Day, with Combat Command R of the 4th Armored Division in the

207

role of Santa Claus. The division was the spearhead of Patton's Third Army, which the legendary commander had been driving north with his customary energetic enthusiasm since December 19. Although it had taken longer than expected for 4th Armored to break through Brandenberger's Seventh Army, its arrival at Bastogne marked a turning point in the battle. The vanguard of Manteuffel's leading formation, the 2d Panzer Division, lay only forty road miles from the Meuse, but its soldiers were exhausted from six days of combat, and its fuel tanks were running dangerously low. Had OKW not chosen to accord the Sixth SS Panzer Army priority with regard to supplies and reinforcements out of all proportion with its battlefield performance, such an outcome might have been avoided, but the high command's belated recognition that the main effort should be made by the Fifth Panzer Army could do little to alleviate the logistical problems facing Manteuffel.

A further setback for the Germans was that the poor weather that had allowed them to advance almost unhindered by the dreaded Allied air power was beginning to clear—the Hitler weather had abated. On December 25, the Americans used their aerial advantage to full extent when the 2d Armored Division delivered a devastating attack against 2d Panzer. Supported by fighter-bombers and tremendous artillery (the U.S. Army's single greatest strength in the Ardennes), the Americans killed over 1,000 men, captured a further 1,200, and wrote down over 600 vehicles, including 82 tanks. Together with the relief of Bastogne, this action snatched the initiative from the German hands permanently.[22]

Ironically, even as the chances of achieving *Wacht am Rhein*'s objectives on the ground were evaporating, the offensive seemed to be provoking just the sort of crisis in Allied command for which Hitler had hoped. On December 20, Eisenhower divided the Allied units (nearly all American) in the area of operations into northern and southern halves and appointed Field Marshal Bernard Montgomery to command the northern component. The decision infuriated several senior American generals with whom the imperious, condescending Montgomery had never gotten along. Montgomery further inflamed American tempers when he announced that the Germans had inflicted a great defeat on the Americans and were preparing another blow. This, at a time when the American commanders figured, correctly, that the Germans had reached their high water mark, caused a serious rift in the Allied command structure.

Montgomery had more on his mind than the tactical issues of the day, however. He was waging a campaign to have Eisenhower appoint him as supreme land commander of Allied forces in northwest Europe, but he pushed too hard, and Eisenhower prepared to give the Combined Chiefs of Staff a choice between him or Montgomery. Given the ratio of American troops to British in the theater, this was not a major risk on Eisenhower's part, but the sacking of Britain's most famous officer would have had very deep repercussions for the Anglo-American alliance. Fortunately, cooler heads prevailed. Montgomery's chief of staff, Major General Francis de Guingand, drafted an apologetic letter that Montgomery signed when it was explained to him that it was the only way to keep his job. The letter satisfied Eisenhower, and the moment of crisis passed.[23]

There was little left for the panzers to do but retreat. Further battles with the burgeoning Allied armor forces in the region, now supplemented by Patton's Third Army, "Lightning" Joe Collins's VII Corps, and the British XXX Corps, only served to grind down panzer strength even further. In the final analysis, the means at Model's disposal had never matched the ends his *führer* had set him. Nevertheless, but for want of some bridging equipment, fuel, and a little more dash and bravado at the right times from his subordinates, he might have come much closer to achieving the impossible.

CHAPTER SIX

THE MIDDLE EAST, 1967 AND 1973

Thunder in the Sinai

IN THE DECADES after World War II, the world was by no means a peaceful place, but the conflicts that raged and sputtered around the globe were almost uniformly guerrilla wars, where the AK-47 assault rifle, not the main battle tank, was the dominant weapon on the battlefield. Even those wars that were more conventional in character, such as the Korean and Indo-Pakistan conflicts, did not feature much in the way of tank battles of the scale or caliber of those examined in this text. It is one of history's greatest ironies that the nation whose army did as much or more than any other to keep the spirit of the great German blitzkrieg generals alive was Israel; the survivors of the Holocaust consciously adopted the blitzkrieg tactics of their tormentors.

The Israelis had good strategic reasons for doing so; like Germany, Israel was a land power surrounded by potential enemies. Born in conflict in 1948, the tiny nation found itself surrounded by Arab nations and peoples bent on Israel's destruction. Israel's small population and narrow confines meant any war would be a fight for survival, with little or no margin for error. Only the development of a highly motivated and innovative military was likely to ensure the nation's survival. These imperatives drove the tankers of the Israeli Armored Corps to become some of the world's most feared and respected practitioners of armored warfare.

IN THE BEGINNING

From inauspicious beginnings in the 1948 War of Independence, when the new country's tank force consisted of a motley collection of Sherman, Cromwell, and vintage French Hotchkiss tanks, the Armored Corps prospered during the mid-1950s. Crucial to its initial success in winning support and funds from Prime Minister David Ben Gurion's government was the performance of armored units in the annual military exercises of 1952 and 1953. On both occasions, the tanks of the blue force surprised both their green force opposition and the exercise planners by breaking through the front and effecting a spectacular envelopment of the green forces. Money started to flow the way of the Armored Corps, and by 1956, it had purchased about 250 Shermans of varying types and 100 French AMX-13 light tanks. These were to prove their worth in October and November of that year, when the corps came of age in the Sinai campaign. The Israeli tankers' performance in this operation is notable not only for its success, but because the stunning victory was achieved through the flagrant disobedience of orders.

The hero of the episode was Colonel Uri Ben Ari, commander of the 7th Armored Brigade, the only tank brigade in the regular Israeli army at the time. His superiors, who stubbornly believed that the tank was best used in an infantry support role—indeed, it was extraordinary how the creation of the Israeli armored forces reprised the debates of the previous decades about mobility, armor protection, and the proper tactical and operational role of the tank—had ordered him to follow the Israeli mechanized infantry units as they attacked Egyptian positions in the Sinai and to exploit any breaches the infantry made in the set-piece defenses. Instead, Ben Ari threw his brigade forward a day ahead of schedule, broke through Egyptian lines, and reached the Suez Canal in less than 100 hours, creating havoc in the Egyptian rear. The brigade's heroics were crucial to the Israeli victory, and the lesson was not lost on the leaders of the Israeli Defense Forces.

Israel's armored warriors had also proved, not for the last time, their mastery of the environment. The vast, sparsely populated triangle of desert that is the Sinai peninsula might have been designed as a battleground for armor, and it would again prove to be the principal theater in the wars of 1967 and 1973, each of which showcased the talents of individual Israeli tank commanders and broke new ground in armored warfare.

CONVERTS, PROPHETS, AND DISCIPLES

The startling success of Ben Ari's 7th Armored Brigade in 1956 made believers of those Israeli army leaders who had doubted the ability of armor to take the dominant role on the battlefield. The most important convert was IDF Chief of Staff Moshe Dayan, who until 1956 had been committed to the notion of infantry's preeminence. Dayan's dynamic influence ensured that the armored corps became the preeminent arm of the Israeli military, and soon promising junior and midgrade officers were transferring into it from the other branches.

Although Dayan kept the money and matériel flowing into the armored corps, his most far-reaching decision was one taken not regarding resources, but personnel: he appointed Colonel Israel Tal to the position as armored corps deputy commander. The thirty-two-year-old Tal was a diminutive man in stature, but one who would rise to become a colossus in the world of armored warfare. He brought to his new job two outstanding qualities: an abiding interest in military technology and a focus on discipline, training, and, especially, gunnery that had heretofore been missing from the Israeli tanker ethos. These, the hardest facts of all in armored warfare, were magnified in decisiveness in the desert environment, as Rommel had learned and preached in the 1940s; in the desert, he who shoots first also most often hits first, and most often lives to tell the tale. As technology progressed, small edges in equipment and individual and crew performance translated into greater and greater battlefield advantages.

Tal's fascination with hardware earned him the job of deciding which tanks would upgrade the armored corps' aging fleet of Shermans. After two years' study of the lessons of the Sinai campaign, he opted for the British Centurion. The decision went against the advice of most of his officers, who preferred the swift, lightly armored French AMX-30 to the fifty-ton Centurion, which had a top road speed of only twenty miles per hour. But Tal was convinced that mobility was useless unless paired with protection, and unlike the AMX-30, the Centurion's thick frontal armor could defeat all known antitank guns in the hands of Israel's Arab enemies.[1]

Israel eventually bought 250 Centurions and augmented its burgeoning tank fleet with 200 M-48 Pattons bought in secret from West Germany. Along with the remaining Shermans in the IDF inventory, these were all altered by Israeli technicians before being fielded. The Centurions and the Pattons received a British 105 mm high-velocity gun whose accuracy was much improved by its gyro stabilizer, and the Shermans were fitted with either an Israeli-designed 105 mm medium-velocity weapon or a French 75 mm high-velocity gun. In addition, the Pattons were given diesel engines to replace their highly flammable gasoline ones.

The influx of the new tanks also brought problems. Unlike the sturdy, simple Shermans, the Pattons and, particularly, the Centurions were complex, fragile mechanical beasts that needed rigorous care and attention if they were to function as designed. This sort of thorough, routine preventive maintenance went against the grain of the informal, individualistic IDF. However, when Israeli tankers were humiliated in a series of tank duels with Syrian units using vintage German *Panzerkampfwagen* Mark IVs on the Golan Heights, it was clear that changes were in order.

In 1964, Tal became commander of the Armored Corps and quickly instituted the changes necessary to raise the professional standards of its members. Tankers were required to become proficient in the maintenance procedures for their weapons systems as outlined in the vehicles' manuals. Particularly close attention was paid to gunnery. For the first time, Centurion crews learned to bore-sight their guns correctly, and tank units kept their gunnery skills at high pitch due to Tal's belief that in the next war, the ability to get a long-range kill with the first shot would be crucial. In all of this Tal led by example. He put himself through every technical course offered by the corps and was renowned as the top tank gunner in the IDF. While some of Tal's soldiers initially griped about the new emphasis on discipline, which extended to personal appearance, all soon had reason to thank him. In a few short years, he had reshaped the Armored Corps, giving it hundreds of modern tanks, greater tactical know-how, and a formidable *esprit de corps*. By 1967, it was an organization primed and ready for action.

THE SIX DAY WAR: OPENING SALVOS

The first decisive engagements of the 1967 war were not made by the tanks of the Armored Corps, however, but by the Mirage and Mystere fighter-bombers of the Israeli Air Force. Concerned at the buildup of Egyptian forces in the Sinai and alarmed by the warlike rhetoric emanating from Cairo and echoed in other Arab capitals, the Israeli government decided that war was inevitable. Faced with the likelihood of a war on three fronts, Israeli leaders felt they had no choice but to launch a preemptive strike against their enemies' air forces. Thus, on the morning of June 5, as Egyptian air force officials were still en route to work, Israeli jets suddenly appeared over Egyptian military airfields, having evaded early-warning radars by sweeping in at treetop height from the Mediterranean. In a matter of minutes, the fighter-bombers had smashed the core of the large Egyptian air force as it sat on its airstrips and in its hangars. Later that day, the young Israeli pilots repeated their exploits farther east, reducing much of the Jordanian, Syrian, and Iraqi air forces to heaps of tangled metal on runways throughout the Levant.

The Israelis' spectacular success—the result of faultless execution following years of meticulous planning for just such a strike—was crucial to the land campaign that followed. The destruction of the Arab air forces at a cost of only two dozen Israeli aircraft meant the IAF would enjoy air supremacy throughout the war, allowing it to concentrate exclusively on interdiction and close air support missions. This may not have been the difference between success and failure for the IDF, but it meant that only Israel was able to fight a joint air-land battle in the classic blitzkrieg style during the war, and it was certainly a factor in reducing Israeli casualties in the days that followed.[2]

As the first Israeli jets swooped down on their targets, tactical radios crackled to life in tank turrets and operations centers along the length of Israel's Sinai frontier, broadcasting the words "Red Sheet," the code phrase that was to begin the 1967 Sinai campaign. In rough outline, the Israeli goal was to repeat the successes of 1956 by forcing three division-sized task forces *through* the Egyptian defenses in the desert to reach the line of passes at the western edge of the Sinai. There they would turn and await the retreating Egyptians, who would have to fight their way through the passes to cross the Suez Canal.

On paper, it looked like a tough fight. The Egyptians had at least seven divisions in the Sinai, two of them armored, and a network of elaborate defensive systems modeled after the Soviet echelon "shield and sword" pattern; it was the tactics of Kursk translated to the Middle East. This entailed putting infantry divisions behind layers—shields—of minefields, trenches and antitank guns, covered by artillery and mortar fire, while small swords of 100 tanks per infantry division waited to pounce on any armored piercing of the defenses. The two Egyptian armored divisions formed a strategic reserve—big swords—to deal with any significant Israeli breakthroughs.[3]

To pierce the shield and neutralize the sword, the Israelis prepared a plan that inverted the tactics common to desert warfare in North Africa during World War II, where fixing attacks along the coastline combined with wide, flanking sweeps into the desert were preferred by both the Germans and British. By contrast, the Israelis prepared a feint into the desert, to be followed by a lightning drive along the coast toward the Suez Canal and into the Egyptian rear; the Israelis were determined to unhinge the Egyptians' prepared defenses and fight a mobile engagement where their advantages in training, equipment, and command would prove decisive.

Their opponents' tactics and operational plans were compromised by politics. Egyptian President Gamal Abdel Nasser played into the Israelis' hands by dismissing his own general staff's plan that relied on a more mobile defense of the peninsula, with the armor held well to the rear as a strategic reserve. Unwilling to be seen as ready to cede even a yard of the Gaza Strip, with its 400,000 Palestinian refugees to the Israelis, Nasser ordered his units to mass close to the front. From there, the Egyptians bought the Israelis' opening gambit, which was to move an armored brigade into the southeastern Negev desert, from where it threatened to cut off Egyptian forces in central Sinai. The Egyptians responded by stripping much of their armor away from the northern Sinai, where it would have caused considerable problems for the Israelis, and pushing it south to keep watch on the Israeli brigade, which mustered only sixty Shermans.[4]

Once in place, the unmotivated Egyptian troops sat in the sand and waited. Some were ensconced in well fortified defensive positions such as those at Rafa and Jiradi on the coast road, and in the Umm Katef and Abu Agheila complexes to the south. Others close to the front line were protected only by sloppily dug trenches and weapons systems in dire need of repair. All were unaware of the hurricane of steel that was about to engulf them.

TAL TAKES THE HIGHWAY

Arguably the most demanding role in the Sinai fell to Israel Tal himself, commanding a divisional task force whose job was to cut through prepared Palestinian and Egyptian defenses along the coastal road in what is known as the Rafa Gap. This was a vital mission: not only would it seal off two divisions in the northern sector and open the coastal highway for the Israeli drive to Suez, it would also set the tone for the remainder of the campaign. With this in mind, Tal's final briefing to his commanders on June 4 was somber yet stirring. He impressed upon them the necessity of driving forward at all costs, without any concern for their flanks or rear. "Whoever loses contact with our forces must continue to battle forward, knowing that the rest of his comrades—and all our formations—are doing the same," he told them.

> The success of the campaign hinges on our immediate battle. Thus, the fate of the State is bound up with what we now do, how we act and how we fare. . . . I must now add this very grave injunction: this battle must be fought, if necessary, to the death. There is no other course. Each man will charge forward to the very end, irrespective

216

of the cost in casualties. There will be no halt and no retreat. There will be only the assault and the advance.[5]

Such was his division's heightened state of readiness that when the word finally came to advance at 8 A.M. on June 5, his armored brigade, the 7th, was moving within fourteen minutes. Its mission was to strike north into Khan Yunis at the southern end of the Gaza Strip, which was held by a Palestinian brigade, then turn and assault the strongly fortified Rafa positions from the east, where the Egyptians would not expect to be attacked. Although briefly embroiled in a fight with Egyptian Shermans hidden in the trees of Khan Yunis, the brigade's Pattons and Centurions soon extricated themselves and pressed westward toward Rafa Junction. There the attack stalled, as the stunned Egyptian defenders came to their senses and opened up on the leading Pattons with an effective screen of antitank guns.

The Rafa defenses were divided into two complexes, Rafa North and Rafa South, by the highway that ran west to El Arish through Rafa Junction. Colonel Shmuel Gonen's 7th Armored Brigade was detailed to assault and reduce the northern part of the defenses, while Colonel Rafael Eitan's 202d Parachute Brigade was to take down the southern section. The intricate layers of bunkers, trenches, and minefields were prepared to a depth of several kilometers, and were defended by screens of antitank guns, dug-in tanks, and artillery. With heavy Egyptian artillery falling among them, the Israelis gritted their teeth and pushed ahead. Attacking from the northeast, the armored brigade's two tank battalions, one with Centurions and one with Pattons, traded fire with Egyptian T-34s and steadily ground away at the Rafa North defenses while reconnaissance troops dismounted from their jeeps and cleared Egyptian trenches with rocket launchers and Uzi submachine guns.[6]

The Egyptians put up dogged resistance, and soon several Pattons were hit by antitank fire from the well-camouflaged bunkers. The first Israeli breakthrough was made by Major Ehud Elad's 79th Tank Battalion, which circled around the northern tip of the defenses to attack from the west. The Pattons crashed into the rear of the bunker complex, firing as they went, the main guns accounting for at least a dozen T-34s and several antitank guns while their machine guns cut down any Egyptians foolish or brave enough not to throw away their weapons.[7] Meanwhile, three kilometers to the south, two squadrons of Centurions under the command of Lieutenant Colonel Baruch "Pinko" Harel frontally assaulted the main body of the Rafa North defenders. Here the Israeli crews learned the value of Tal's obsession with tank gunnery as they picked off dug-in SU-100 self-propelled guns and T-34 tanks while continuing to advance. One Centurion company cut right through the Egyptian positions without meeting much opposition, and it continued driving west on the highway, while the other fought its way through withering fire to subdue the defenses and seize Rafa Junction, effectively ending resistance north of the highway.[8]

South of the road, however, things were not going quite as smoothly for the Israelis. Eitan's parachute brigade had effectively been turned into a mechanized infantry outfit by putting the paratroops in half-tracks and giving the unit a Patton tank battalion crewed by the staff of the IDF Armor School, plus two additional tank companies, one of Pattons and one of AMX-13s. However, although the paratroops and tankers were elite troops within their own branches, they were given only a week to knit their skills together, hardly enough to mold the adhoc unit into a cohesive mechanized infantry brigade.[9]

As a result, when the brigade surged forward at 8:55 A.M. from Keren Shalom, just to the east of the Israeli frontier, the leading Patton companies promptly outdistanced the paratroops, whose ancient M-3 half-tracks could not hope to keep up with the tanks as they negotiated the sand dunes. Three times Patton companies were dispatched to accompany the lead paratroop battalion into battle at the southern tip of Rafa South, but on each occasion the paratroops were left behind. One company drove right through the Egyptian defenses, then, confused by a misleading radio order, headed due west and proceeded to cause mayhem in the Egyptian rear. Another company left the paratroops behind at the mercy of an Egyptian antitank screen through which it had broken, while the third company—the first to actually attack—stalled when its commander was killed in the lead tank. This last incident typified the high risk imposed upon tank officers by the Israeli

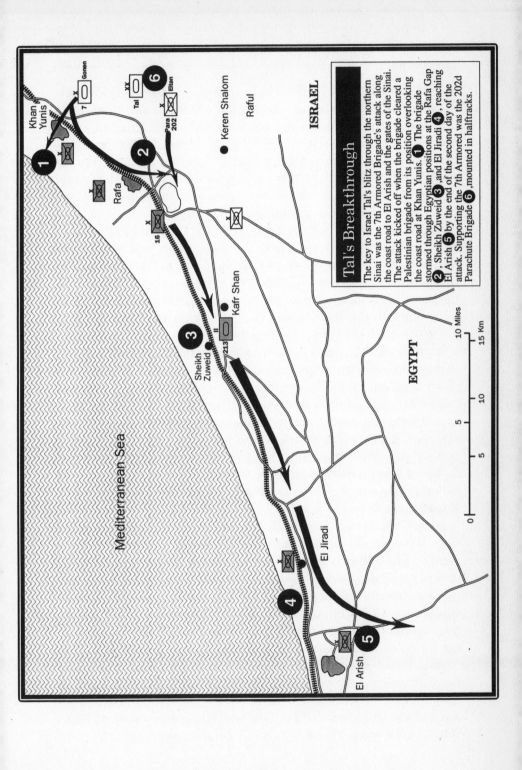

Tal's Breakthrough

The key to Israel Tal's blitz through the northern Sinai was the 7th Armored Brigade's attack along the coast road to El Arish and the gates of the Sinai. The attack kicked off when the brigade cleared a Palestinian brigade from its position overlooking the coast road at Khan Yunis. **1** The brigade stormed through Egyptian positions at the Rafa Gap **2** Sheikh Zuweid **3** and El Jiradi **4**, reaching El Arish **5** by the end of the second day of the attack. Supporting the 7th Armored was the 202d Parachute Brigade **6**, mounted in halftracks.

Mediterranean Sea

Khan Yunis

Rafa

Sheikh Zuweid

Kafr Shan

El Jiradi

El Arish

Keren Shalom

Raful

Gonen

Tal

Eitan

ISRAEL

EGYPT

0   5   10   15 Km
0   5   10 Miles

style of command. IDF officers, up to and including brigade commanders, were expected to lead from the front, rather than direct the action from behind their men, as is the case in many other armies. This has translated into 20 percent casualty figures for Israeli officers in battle, twice the average in other armies.[10] For Armored Corps officers, the risk was magnified by their penchant for riding with their heads out of the turret, even when under fire, the better to see the action unfolding around them.

The second paratroop battalion, led by yet another Patton company, successfully circumvented the Rafa South positions to the west and reached the village of Kafr Shan just to the northwest of the defenses. There it encountered the seventeen T-34s of the Egyptian 213th Tank Battalion. A fierce battle raged for half an hour between the Pattons and the T-34s, with casualties on both sides, before the Egyptian force withdrew shortly after 12.30 P.M.

A substantial Egyptian presence remained within the Rafa South stronghold, however. Organized around the Egyptian 16th Mechanized Brigade and led by the brigade's operations officer who had rallied his men when a rout seemed certain, it was putting up a valiant fight. Tal diverted all his available resources to deal with the obstinate Rafa South defenders, and for two hours, Israeli Pattons dueled with Soviet-built Egyptian JS-3 heavy tanks. Only after two flights of Israeli Fouga-Magister jet trainers fitted with rocket racks had swooped down on the Egyptians, could the Israelis claim the battlefield as theirs.

Meanwhile, Harel's Centurion force was approaching the next Israeli objective along the coastal route: the Jiradi Pass. A twenty-meter-wide defile that runs for fourteen kilometers between treacherously deep dunes to the south and the sea to the north, the pass was defended in depth by an Egyptian infantry brigade that included two dug-in Sherman battalions. However, led by Egyptian propaganda to believe Egyptian forces were on the offensive, invading Israel, the defenders were so shocked to see Israeli tanks that far west that they sat in stunned silence as the first Patton company swept through their positions. The next two companies made it through with light casualties, and suddenly Harel found himself advancing on the town of El Arish, sixty kilometers west of Khan Yunis, but he was perilously low on fuel and ammunition.

Harel's unexpectedly quick breakthrough posed a problem for senior IDF commanders, who had planned to reduce Jiradi with Tal's reserve armored brigade by circling south around the Rafa positions to strike into the Egyptian flanks. In reality, the brigade was stuck in the dunes, going nowhere fast, leaving Harel's force dangerously exposed deep behind Egyptian lines. The Jiradi garrison had meanwhile regained its fighting composure and when Elad's Patton battalion tried to follow in Harel's footsteps, it was violently rebuffed. During the vicious fighting, one Patton commander was set ablaze by burning fuel (he survived), another had a hand severed, and Elad himself was decapitated by an Egyptian round as he barked orders with his head out of the turret.

The remnants of Elad's battalion only made it through when joined by the Patton company that had headed due west by mistake in the midst of the attack on Rafa South. The Egyptians resealed their defenses behind the Pattons, and Tal was forced to commit a mechanized infantry battalion to reduce the Jiradi positions in a fierce night attack, backed up by IAF close air support. Following the war, some commentators used this episode to criticize Tal's belief that all-tank forces were the optimal type for breakthrough operations.[11] After four hours of fighting at close quarters, the last bunkers fell, and the 7th Armored Brigade command group and supply trains raced through to link up with their colleagues at El Arish in the early hours of June 6.

AT THE GATES OF THE SINAI

Tal's incisive thrust along the coast created the conditions essential for an Israeli victory in the Sinai, but at no stage did it go according to plan. Rather, it succeeded because of the IDF doctrine that allows each commander down to the lowest levels to use whatever means available to achieve broad goals set down by his seniors; again, this was an Israeli translation of German *auftragstaktik*—in English, *mission orders*. Thus, although units quickly became separated from each other in the chaos and confusion of the Rafa and Jiradi fights, majors, captains, and lieutenants who knew the division's objective was El Arish continued to urge their troops forward, shooting up whatever Egyptian vehicles were unfortunate enough to get in their way.

The breakthrough along the northern axis might not have enjoyed such success had the Egyptian big sword in the northern Sinai, the elite 4th Armored Division, been able to intercept Tal's division in a flanking attack. Instead, however, it was the Egyptian division that came under attack. Brigadier General Avraham Yoffe's two-brigade division, a reserve armored outfit, had anticipated the Egyptian move and raced through desert terrain deemed impassable by the Egyptians to cut the Jebel Libni–El Arish road at Bir Lahfan. The first Centurions reached Bir Lahfan at midnight, just in time to catch the initial wave of Egyptian T-55s heading north.[12] Firing by the light of their coaxial searchlights and the flames of burning vehicles, the Centurions knocked out nine T-55s that night, and over twenty more after first light, when the Centurions were joined in the fight by Israeli air force Dassault Mysteres and Ouragans. The Egyptian 4th Armored Division crews, considered the finest their nation had ever produced, fought valiantly, but the superior marksmanship of their Israeli counterparts swung the battle, and the Egyptians were denied the pivotal junction.

One major obstacle remained in the Israelis' path before they could complete their rush to the passes at the western edge of the Sinai: the massive Egyptian defensive complex at the Abu Agheila and Umm Katef crossroads. This division-sized position sat astride two road junctions that controlled the routes to the Mitla and Jiddi passes, as well as Bir Gafgafa and Ismailia. The Egyptian 2d Infantry Division had set up a formidable shield, in accordance with Soviet doctrine, defended by the usual layers of minefields, trenches, and bunkers, with dug-in tanks and antitank guns, as well as a mobile small sword of eighty-eight T-34 tanks and SU-100 assault guns. Battalion- and brigade-strength complexes protected the Egyptian flanks, and six battalions of artillery covered the approaches.

The division tasked with overcoming this impressive blocking position was commanded by Major General Ariel Sharon, a paratroop hero of the 1956 war. At Umm Katef, Sharon confirmed his reputation as one Israel's most capable commanders by orchestrating a complex set-piece frontal attack on the Egyptian positions. This nocturnal assault included the heaviest IDF artillery bombardment ever,

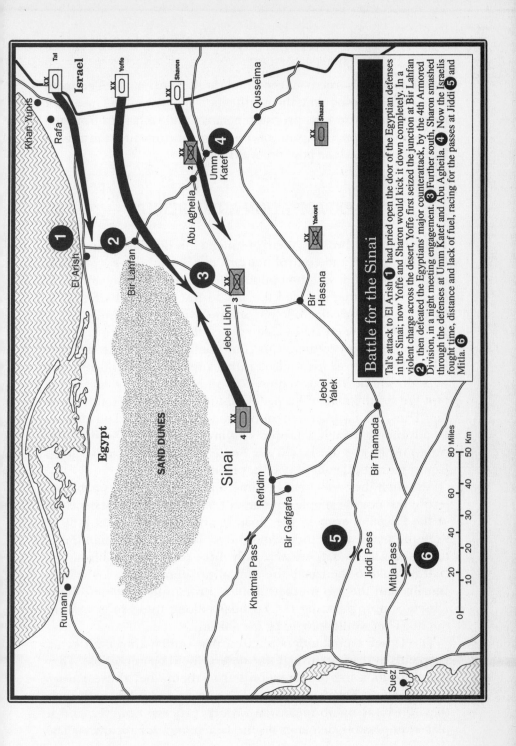

Battle for the Sinai

Tal's attack to El Arish ➊ had pried open the door of the Egyptian defenses in the Sinai; now Yoffe and Sharon would kick it down completely. In a violent charge across the desert, Yoffe first seized the junction at Bir Lahfan ➋, then defeated the Egyptians' major counterattack, by the 4th Armored Division, in a night meeting engagement. ➌ Further south, Sharon smashed through the defenses at Umm Katef and Abu Agheila. ➍ Now the Israelis fought time, distance and lack of fuel, racing for the passes at Jiddi ➎ and Mitla. ➏

Khan Yunis

Israel

Tal

Rafa

Rafa

Yoffe

Sharon

Egypt

El Arish

Qusseima

Shazall

Umm Katef

Abu Agheila

Bir Lahfan

Yakout

SAND DUNES

Jebel Libni

Sinai

Bir Hassna

Rumani

Jebel Yalek

Refidim

Bir Gafgafa

Bir Thamada

Khatmia Pass

Jiddi Pass

Mitla Pass

Suez

80 Miles

50 Km

0 10 20 30 40 60
0   20   40   80

as well as a heliborne paratroop raid on the Egyptian artillery positions and sweeping tank thrusts through the defenses. The attack never deviated from its precise timetable, and with help from the IAF, which dropped napalm on the Egyptian trenches, the Israelis had overwhelmed the position by first light.

EXPLOITATION AND PURSUIT

Their defenses broken, their premier tank division beaten, and their command and control network in disarray, the Egyptians in the Sinai were left with no option other than to turn tail and head for the passes that guarded the way to the canal and safety. The race for the passes that followed Sharon's victory at Umm Katef exposed one of the greatest weaknesses in the Egyptian army: the individual Egyptian soldier, who could be resolute in the defense, felt little loyalty to his unit or to his superiors. When the chips were down and he was required to show initiative or to risk his own life for the sake of his peers, all too often he was found wanting. Thus, the Egyptian retreat became a rout. Harried on all sides by advancing Israeli armored columns and from above by the swooping jets of the Israeli Air Force, few if any Egyptian units kept their tactical cohesion as they made for the canal.

Although they, too, were heading for the passes, the Israelis' objective was not the simple conquest of territory but the destruction of the Egyptian army in the Sinai. It would benefit them little to seize the peninsula if they allowed the bulk of the Egyptian forces to escape. However, there were only three routes that led from the central Sinai to the canal: the central axis through Bir Gafgafa to Ismailia and the two southern routes through the Jiddi and Mitla Passes. Simply pursuing the Egyptians along these routes would not do. They would have to be overtaken.

The Israeli commanders realized that outflanking the fleeing Egyptians by driving through the desert would be impossible. They therefore took the only solution left to them: they drove *through* the retreating Egyptian columns, at times side by side with their foes. This was by no means an orderly process, however, and it placed impossible demands on the Israeli logistics apparatus. The

1967 Sinai campaign saw the debut of the Israelis' conveyor belt system of supplying their frontline forces. Under this method, perfected by Tal, tank battalions attacking on their own made the first breach in enemy defenses and were immediately followed by mechanized infantry and a first echelon of supply columns equipped with cross-country vehicles. These were in turn sustained by road-bound wheeled supply vehicles bringing up the rear with truck-borne motorized infantry, who would clear obstacles bypassed by the initial breakthrough units.[13]

The speed required to beat the Egyptians to the passes worked against the conveyor belt system because, unlike the Israeli tanks, the soft-skinned supply vehicles were unable to fight their way through the Egyptian convoys that jammed the roads to the passes. The tanks of Colonel "Yiska" Shadmi's Centurion brigade—the same that had repulsed the 4th Armored Division at Bir Lahfan less than thirty-six hours earlier—were dispatched to the passes, one to the Mitla, the other to the Jiddi; they found themselves in a race against not only the fleeing Egyptians, but also the needles of their fuel gauges. In both cases, they won with nothing to spare.

The seizure of the Mitla Pass was particularly dramatic. Only nine Centurions, accompanied by a handful of half-tracks and self-propelled 105 mm howitzers, had enough fuel even to risk the journey to Mitla from the captured Egyptian camp at Bir el-Thamada. By the time they reached the pass in the late afternoon of June 7, four of the tanks were under tow. Another two sputtered to a halt as the Israeli task force was assembling in its blocking position overlooking the eastern approach to the pass, but fortunately, and for reasons never fully explained, the nearby elements of the Egyptian 6th Mechanized Division allowed them to set up their defense unhindered.[14]

The Egyptians paid dearly for their negligence. Only minutes after the small Israeli force had established its positions, the first of hundreds of Egyptian armored vehicles approached the pass from the southeast. With help from a pair of IAF jets, which destroyed the lead Egyptian vehicles in locations that effectively blocked the pass, the Israeli force held the Egyptians at bay until they were reinforced during the night by the rest of their battalion.

Other tank battles remained in the Sinai that week, but the crucial victories had been won. By the night of June 8, the Israelis had reached all their blocking positions, and the Egyptian army in the Sinai had disintegrated into straggling convoys of armor and trucks that were so relentlessly chewed up by the roving IAF jets that thousands of Egyptian troops threw away their weapons, removed their boots, and took to the desert.

ISRAELI AND EGYPTIAN LESSONS LEARNED?

It is a truism of military history that all too frequently armies victorious in one war try to repeat their success by using the same tactics in their next engagement, only to find their enemies have paid more attention to the lessons of the previous fight. Thus the French in 1940 placed their hope in the Maginot line of static defenses, expecting their next encounter with Germany to be another methodical war of attrition; the French were unable to respond to the German *blitzkrieg*. As the French found out to their cost, planning to refight the last war can have fatal consequences. For all their close study of German tactics and operational methods, after 1967, the Israelis followed the French path in believing the next war would be the same as the last.

This was most true at the strategic level, where the Israelis counted on being able to strike preemptive blows to avoid or at least control the pace of a two-front war; the Israelis' strategic thinking became too ossified to consider that their enemies' goals in war might change to a less predictable pattern. What was true of strategy also was true at the tactical level as well: to the Israeli military establishment, the stunning successes of the three tank-heavy divisions on the Sinai in 1967 seemed a validation of Israel Tal's all-tank doctrine, which had focused resources on the tank units at the expense of mechanized infantry. The valuable contribution of combined arms operations such as Sharon's reduction of the Umm Katef and Abu Agheila defenses notwithstanding, Israeli military leaders felt the Six Day War had proved that armor alone was the dominant element on the battlefield; indeed, the Israeli tankers became honored as national heroes. Before 1967, the neglect of the mechanized in-

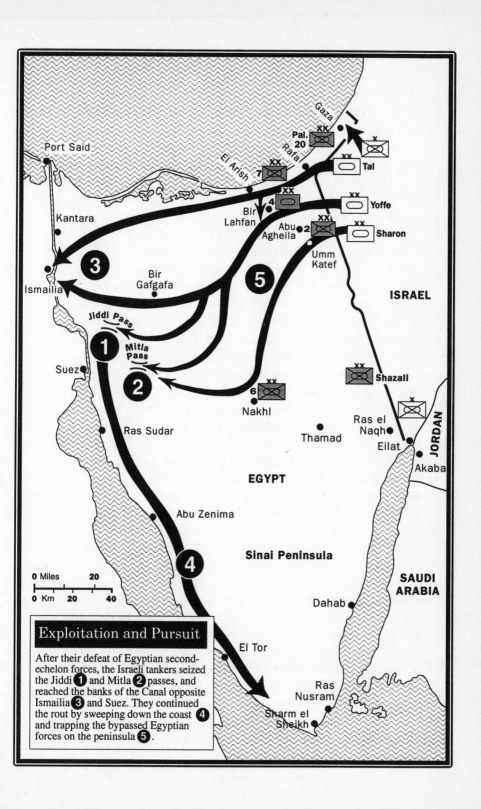

Port Said

El Arish

Kantara

Bir
Lahfan

Ismailia

Jiddi Pass

Suez

Ras Sudar

Abu Zenima

0 Miles   20

0 Km   20   40

Gaza

Pal.
20

Rafa

Tal

Yoffe

Abu
Agheila

Umm
Katef

Sharon

ISRAEL

Bir
Gafgafa

Mitla
Pass

Nakhl

Shazall

Ras el
Naqh

Eilat

Thamad

EGYPT

JORDAN

Akaba

Sinai Peninsula

SAUDI
ARABIA

Dahab

Ras
Nusram

El Tor

Sharm el
Sheikh

Exploitation and Pursuit

After their defeat of Egyptian second-echelon forces, the Israeli tankers seized the Jiddi ❶ and Mitla ❷ passes, and reached the banks of the Canal opposite Ismailia ❸ and Suez. They continued the rout by sweeping down the coast ❹ and trapping the bypassed Egyptian forces on the peninsula ❺.

fantry had been resource-driven. Not having the money to buy both modern tanks *and* armored personnel carriers, the IDF had chosen to devote their scarce cash to the former. After 1973, it was the result of the primacy of the all-tank doctrine; the British visionary of the 1920s, J. F. C. Fuller, had been resurrected in an Israeli uniform.

Israeli leaders decided the next war would be won by fast-moving wedges of tanks, picking off antitank missile and gun crews at long range before breaking through enemy lines to cause havoc in the rear. The commitment to the all-tank orthodoxy was so great that what little mechanized infantry there had been in the armor battalions was removed, along with the mortars previously organic to tank units. The IDF ground forces were reorganized into conveyor belt formations, with all other arms supporting the tank spearheads, which were to pull the other elements behind them as they advanced. The role of the mechanized infantry, still without an effective infantry fighting vehicle similar to the BMP models, which allowed infantrymen to move and to fire their antiarmor missiles while protected from artillery fires, supplied by the Soviets to their Arab clients, was relegated to slow-moving, dismounted mopping-up operations in the wake of the tanks.[15]

The Egyptians were under no such illusions about armor-infantry cooperation. One of the major lessons they had learned from the Six Day War was the importance of finding a means to cope with the Israeli tank thrusts that had sliced through their dug-in defenses and outmaneuvered their own armor formations. Egyptian generals hoped Soviet technology would provide at least a partial solution, in the form of the AT-3 Sagger antitank missile. The Sagger, a simple weapon that can be fired from vehicles, helicopters, or by an infantry team on the ground, has a range of 3,000 meters and is guided to its target by commands transmitted to the missile via a thin wire it trails behind it back to its launcher.

The Sagger and its American-made counterpart, the TOW (for Tube-launched, Optically tracked, Wire-guided) missile, shifted the fundamental balance between infantryman and armor. Since the battle of Cambrai, tankers had little to fear from foot soldiers. Antitank guns were large targets, far less mobile than tanks, and they required the infantryman to expose himself to artillery and tank gunfire; only the German 88 mm gun had enjoyed a long-term utility against armor, a range and versatility capability deriving from the gun's origin as an antiaircraft weapon. Short-range rockets such as the American bazooka and German *Panzerfaust* were notoriously inaccurate; they required near-suicidal courage to operate unless used in ambushes that further reduced their accuracy. Wire-guided missiles, on the other hand, had longer ranges than most tank main guns, let alone machine guns, of the time, and promised good accuracy as well when used with powerful sights that could even be used at night. When mounted in the BMP and other fighting vehicles, the launcher was protected from air-burst artillery; when dismounted, the infantryman was hard to see. Tanks could no longer operate with complete impunity, especially in the desert.

THE HOLIDAY SURPRISE

Perhaps the most important lesson learned by the Egyptians came from the Israeli air strikes that destroyed much of the Egyptian air force on the ground. Where the Israelis learned a tactical and operational lesson about the value of air power, these strikes quantified for the Egyptians the value of strategic surprise. On October 6, 1973, the Egyptians demonstrated how well they had absorbed this lesson by catching the state of Israel almost completely off guard with a surprise attack across the Suez Canal. The date had been chosen with care by the Arab forces, as it fell on Yom Kippur, the holiest day of the Jewish calendar, when almost all Israelis can be found at home (including most regular soldiers, who are given leave). Most importantly, the Israelis were incapable of grasping the Egyptian motives for attack: Egyptian President Anwar Sadat was willing to make war without the kind of air cover that Israel deemed essential in order to gain politically in negotiations to regain the Sinai. He was willing to take these great tactical and operational risks for a greater strategic purpose.[16]

The Egyptian attack was launched in coordination with an equally unexpected Syrian assault on the Golan Heights. Although the fighting on the Heights lies beyond the focus of this chapter, it is important to note that for the first week of war, the risk of the Syrian tank columns breaking through the Golan into the heavily populated valleys below prevented the Israelis from concentrating their aerial firepower on the Egyptians pouring over the canal.

The waterway itself was not well defended by the Israelis, who had counted on early warning and preemptive maneuvers to keep the Egyptians from a rapid breach of the canal defenses, and they had also relied upon the ability of their reserve armor formations to fight their way quickly to the canal and defeat the Egyptians, should the latter attempt a crossing. The only defensive positions on the canal were sixteen fortified installations along its western bank, which together were known as the Bar-Lev line, after the IDF Chief of Staff, Lieutenant General Haim Bar-Lev. These forts were five to seven miles apart and were never intended to beat off a concerted attack by themselves. Rather, manned by just an infantry platoon each, with support from artillery and a few tanks, they were designed to channel an Egyptian attack into killing grounds for reinforcing Israeli armor units. When the Egyptians attacked at 1:45 P.M., the entire line was manned by only 436 Israeli reservists and three tanks.[17]

The Egyptian attack opened Israeli-style, with an air strike by 240 aircraft that destroyed Israeli surface-to-air missile sites along the canal. This was followed by a massive Egyptian artillery barrage that rained over 3,000 tons of high explosives onto the Israeli fortifications in less than an hour, knocking out most of the Israeli artillery batteries that covered the approaches to the canal. Then the first wave of 8,000 Egyptian troops swept across the water in twelve-man dinghies. Bypassing the Israeli forts, they established a defensive screen two miles inland, where they were soon joined by antitank teams.[18]

In accordance with the Israeli plan for defending the Sinai, code-named Operation Dovecote, the Sinai Armored Division had only one armored brigade, the 14th, in position ten to fifteen kilometers behind the canal, ready to respond immediately to the invasion. The division's other two brigades were between thirty and fifty kilometers to the rear. The Israelis had built ramps along the canal from which the tanks were to fire at any invading force. As the 14th Armored Brigade moved forward toward its firing positions, it suffered the unusual experience—for Israeli tankers—of having several tanks knocked out by Egyptian fighter-bombers. Worse was to come.

As the Israeli tanks came within sight of the canal, they noticed groups of men standing before them in the desert, making no attempt to move out of the way of the charging steel behemoths bearing down on them. Puzzled, the tankers continued their race for the water, until, suddenly, tank after tank exploded in balls of flame. The men in the sand, of course, were the Egyptian Sagger teams, and their first volleys heralded a new phase in the history of armored warfare: the foot soldier at last had a mobile, effective, long-range weapon against charging armor.

The inadequacy of the all-tank doctrine in general and the Israeli plan to defend the Sinai in particular was now revealed for all to see. The scale of the Egyptian attack was far larger than the Israelis had anticipated: five Egyptian mechanized divisions stood on the canal's west bank ready to storm across the pontoon bridges that were quickly being installed. The 14th Armored Brigade commander, Colonel Amnon Reshef, was forced to divide his tanks up into platoon- and company-sized elements among the forts in the central section of the canal, the area he was supposed to defend. Instead of being able to take out the Sagger teams at long range, as called for in Tal's doctrine, the tanks found themselves easy prey for the Egyptian antitank crews, who guided their missiles onto the tanks while remaining almost completely hidden in the dunes. Bereft of any mechanized infantry or indirect fire support that might have killed the Egyptian infantry or at least harassed the missile crews enough to throw off their aim, the Israeli tanks were sitting ducks. Those tanks that were able to penetrate the Egyptian lines often found themselves at the mercy of another Soviet-supplied antitank weapon, the RPG-7, a shoulder-launched, rocket-propelled grenade weapon with which the Egyptian infantry was liberally equipped. Though no more accurate or powerful than the bazooka, the RPG was so cheap and small that their numbers made up for their other limitations; RPGs were most useful for attacking the sides and rear of tanks, resulting not in destruction but in blowing off a track or disabling the tank's automotive systems, earning a so-called mobility kill.

THE EGYPTIANS SEIZE THE INITIATIVE

The Egyptians followed a three-phase plan taught them by their Soviet advisers. The first phase was the crossing of the canal, to be followed by a steady buildup of forces on the eastern bank under the cover of a protective air defense screen. Only when the buildup was completed and the air defense screen could be moved forward would the Egyptians advance on their objectives: the Jiddi, Mitla, and Khatmia Passes, followed by the Israeli logistical center at Bir Gafgafa. Perhaps a little optimistically, the Egyptian leadership counted on the seizure of these objectives being enough to persuade the IDF to retire from the Sinai. There was some debate at the highest levels of the Egyptian army over this strategy, which was a compromise between the extremely conservative approach desired by some officers and the much more mobile campaign advocated by others.[19]

By midevening of October 6, the Egyptians were reinforcing their initial surprise attacks with heavier metal: armor was swarming over the canal on thirty-one ferries and several pontoon bridges, so that by 1 A.M. there were 800 Egyptian tanks in the bridgehead on the eastern bank; the Egyptians were fighting with professional competence. The few Israeli tanks that managed to fight their way through to the canal performed well, but their task was impossible. They briefly interrupted the flow of Soviet-built T-55 tanks across the water, but fire from other Egyptian tanks located on high ramps of their own on the west bank, plus the close attention they received from the antitank teams in the bridgehead, forced them to withdraw.[20]

Confusion reigned at the headquarters of the Israeli Southern Command. Frantic requests for assistance were coming over the radio from the isolated forts of the Bar-Lev line, but forming an accurate picture of where the Egyptian main effort lay that first night proved beyond the Southern Command staff. At first the officers in the rear believed the troops in the forts to be holding out well, and so made no moves to evacuate them, but as the realization dawned upon the staffers that many of the outpost garrisons had either surrendered or were on the point of doing so, packets of Israeli tanks were dispatched to relieve them, only to run into withering antitank fire. In their arrogance, the Israelis violated the principle of mass; their precious tanks were being lost piecemeal. Fierce battles raged the length of the canal, while beyond the bridgehead, Egyptian commandos complicated Israeli planning further by blocking many of the roads leading to the front.

Reshef's brigade was now heavily engaged and losing tanks fast. While it enjoyed some local victories, especially at the Purkan outpost opposite Ismailia, where one of its battalions destroyed dozens of Egyptian armored vehicles as they crossed a pontoon bridge, the brigade was spread far too thin to contain the Egyptian armor gathering in the bridgeheads. The brigade took particularly heavy losses that evening in a vain attempt to relieve the stronghold at Lituf, thirty miles west of the Jiddi Pass. In an attempt to stanch the flow of Egyptian armor between Lituf and Mafzeah, the Sinai Armored Division commander Major General Avraham "Albert" Mendler ordered his 460th Armored Brigade forward to counterattack south of Lituf. The brigade enjoyed initial success, its Centurions and Pattons destroying sixty-seven T-62s and T-55s without loss. The Pattons were the M60 model, a significant upgrade of the M48 with a new turret; the T-62 was the Soviet successor to the T-55, fitted with a powerful 115 mm main gun. However, once again as the Israeli tanks closed on the canal, the Egyptian antitank teams exacted a heavy toll, eventually forcing the brigade to retreat.[21]

By the next morning, a sense of crisis gripped the Israeli positions in the Sinai. Of the 279 tanks the Israelis had mustered on the peninsula when the Egyptians attacked, only 110 were in running order by first light on October 7.[22] Another Israeli armored brigade was pushed forward to mount what Edward Luttwak and Dan Horowitz term "a classic cut and thrust tank assault towards Kantara, as if nothing had changed." The brigade's mission was to cut off the northern section of the Egyptian bridgehead, but predictably, the tanks were rebuffed with losses by the Sagger- and RPG-7-toting Egyptians.[23]

With their depleted frontline armored forces stretched into a thin, fraying ribbon north to south along the canal, several factors prevented the normally reliable Israeli air force from relieving the pressure on the ground units. For a start, much of the air force was otherwise occupied during the first stage of the war with halting the Syrian armored advance on the Golan Heights, which seemed an even more immediate threat to Israeli security than the Egyptian invasion of the Sinai. Secondly, the infantry-heavy Egyptian bridgehead did not present the IAF with many promising targets. Dug-in, dispersed infantrymen are notoriously hard to dislodge with air strikes alone, and the Egyptians quickly replaced any bridge sections destroyed by IAF bombs.

The most significant factor inhibiting the deployment of Israeli air power over the canal, however, was the Egyptians' Soviet-designed screen of antiaircraft weapons. Since 1967, when they had suffered painfully at the hands of the IAF, the Egyptians had built an impressive air defense arsenal, every element of which they deployed along the banks of the Suez to protect their bridgehead. The air defense screen was layered with three different Soviet-built missiles—the SA-2, SA-3, and SA-6—covering the higher altitudes. These forced the Israeli pilots to choose between risking destruction from the lethal missiles or descending to run the lower-level gauntlet of the shoulder-fired SA-7 missiles and the Egyptians' antiaircraft guns. The network of these guns was centered around the radar-guided ZSU-4 gun, with four rapid-firing 23 mm automatic cannon; two or three of these located close to each other could throw up a virtually impenetrable wall of lead at low altitudes.

The Israelis were not ignorant of the Egyptian air defense screen—although the presence of both the radar-guided SA-6 with its twenty-five-mile range and the latest version of the SA-7 came as a shock—but they overestimated the ability of their tactically adept pilots and electronic countermeasure suites to defeat the missile threat. It was a costly misjudgment. The first waves of Israeli fighter-bombers flew into the teeth of the air defense screen with disastrous results. Several were shot down—the Egyptian claim for the day was eleven—and by 4 P.M. IDF Chief of Staff Lieutenant General David Elazar had suspended all air activity. Operations were resumed within an hour, the IAF now trying to stay away from the main missile belts, but losses continued to be heavy.[24]

The Syrians also had a Soviet-supplied air defense screen in operation, which exacted a similar toll on Israeli aircraft. By the end

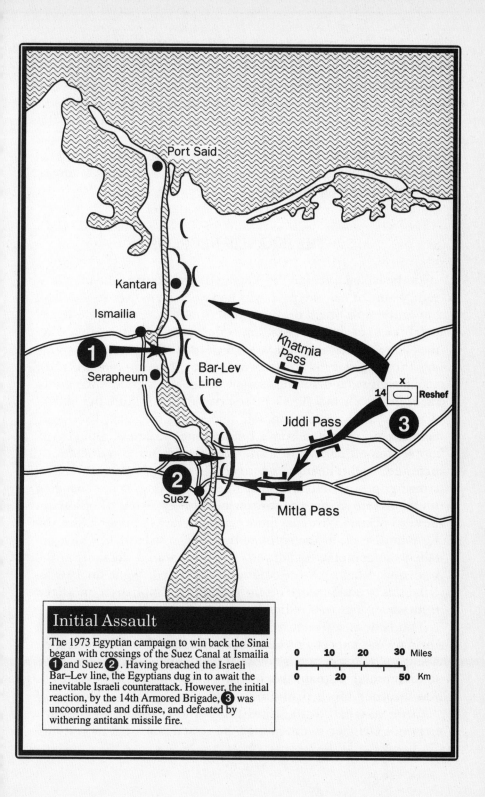

Port Said

Kantara

Ismailia

1

Serapheum

Bar-Lev
Line

*Khatmia
Pass*

Jiddi Pass

14 ☒ Reshef

3

2

Suez

Mitla Pass

Initial Assault

The 1973 Egyptian campaign to win back the Sinai
began with crossings of the Suez Canal at Ismailia
1 and Suez **2** . Having breached the Israeli
Bar–Lev line, the Egyptians dug in to await the
inevitable Israeli counterattack. However, the initial
reaction, by the 14th Armored Brigade, **3** was
uncoordinated and diffuse, and defeated by
withering antitank missile fire.

| 0 | 10 | 20 | 30 | Miles |
| 0 | 20 | | 50 | Km |

of the October war, the Israelis had lost a total of 109 aircraft, at least 77 of which were brought down by air defense missiles or guns.[25] Even allowing for the longer span of the 1973 conflict, this was a marked increase over the figures for the Six Day War, during which the IAF lost 46 aircraft, 43 of them to ground fire.[26] By contrast, the Egyptian air force rarely took to the air except to mount shallow attacks near the canal.

THE ISRAELIS REGROUP

With the Israeli forces in the Sinai in disarray during the first forty-eight hours of war, the Egyptians had won themselves an excellent opportunity to break through the crumbling crust of the Israeli defenses to reach the passes into the interior of the Sinai. Had they done so, they might have retaken the entire peninsula, avenging the loss of 1967 in its entirety, but they squandered their chance, sitting and waiting as their bridgeheads grew, while the Israelis frantically mobilized the reserves that constitute the bulk of their army and rushed armored units across the Sinai. The Egyptian hesitation resulted from a fundamental weakness of the Egyptian senior officers, who while able to execute a meticulously planned, well-rehearsed set-piece operation such as the canal crossing, proved much less capable of adapting to fast-changing situations and taking the sort of initiative expected of officers in western armies. Virtually ignoring the Israelis' vulnerability, the Egyptians stuck to their three-phase Soviet-style plan, which entailed the complete buildup of five mechanized divisions in the bridgehead before a breakout was attempted. Some analysts ascribe this to a reluctance on the part of the Egyptians to move out from under the cover of their air defense umbrella.

The Israelis suffered from no such rigid operational style. If their prewar expectations had been disastrously misguided, their ability to improvise and innovate at the moment of crisis remained undiminished; perhaps this mental agility and tactical excellence was another more profound—and ironically just—legacy of *blitzkrieg* inherited by the Israelis from the Germans. By the early hours of October 8, the first of the Israeli reserve armored divisions to mobilize—the 162d, commanded by Major General Avraham Adan—had reached the front, closely followed by another reserve division under the now-legendary Major General Ariel Sharon. Arriving via the coastal route, Adan was ordered to advance west to Kantara and then turn south, using long-range gunnery to pick off Egyptian tanks while avoiding the antitank teams on the ridge close to the canal. Adan's objective was the Firdan bridge. By enveloping the Egyptian forces in this part of the front, Elazar hoped to contain the bridgehead and give Sharon the opportunity to execute a similar mission south of Firdan.[27]

Initially, though, the Israeli tanks met with disaster yet again. Harassed by Egyptian air strikes and hampered by their lack of organic reconnaissance assets and Egyptian jamming of their radio nets, Adan's division fought its way south, only to find one of Sinai Armored Division's three brigades—the 460th Armored, under Colonel Gabriel Amir—already heavily engaged at Firdan. The gunners of the brigade's lead battalion had the Egyptian 23d Mechanized Division in their sights as the latter crossed the bridge, but being low on ammunition, they had to withdraw. The second battalion came forward at 10 A.M., straight into the Egyptian guns, and lost nineteen of its twenty-six tanks within minutes. Two more Sinai Armored Division battalions now arrived, under Lieutenant Colonel Natan Nir. Assessing the scene from a nearby hill, at 12:30 P.M. Adan sent Nir's fifty Centurions and Amir's brigade into the attack against the bridge positions, while circling one of the 162d's brigades south in an enveloping move.[28]

One of Nir's battalions stalled, and the other was cut to pieces 800 meters from the canal by hundreds of Saggers and Egyptian tanks, losing fourteen Centurions in three minutes and having its commander captured. Amir's brigade never left the ridge from which it had taken up overwatch positions. Meanwhile, the Israeli brigade to the south, barely managing to hold on to its position, let alone attack, was ordered to withdraw. That evening, the Egyptians launched a two-pronged attack from the Firdan bridgehead, which Adan repulsed with heavy casualties to both sides. By nightfall, he had lost 70 of the 170 tanks with which he had begun the day.[29]

That night, the divisional commanders held a tense meeting

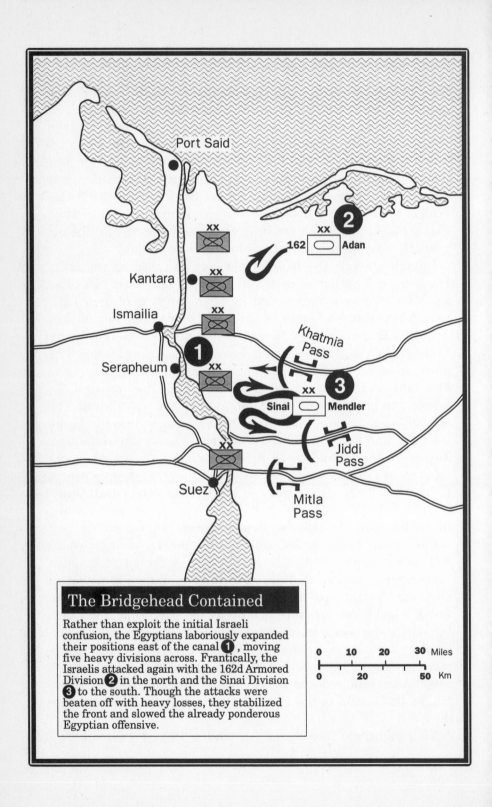

Port Said

XX

162 ☐ Adan **2**

XX

Kantara

XX

Ismailia

Khatmia
Pass

XX

1

Serapheum

XX

3

Sinai ☐ Mendler

XX

Jiddi
Pass

XX

Suez

Mitla
Pass

The Bridgehead Contained

Rather than exploit the initial Israeli
confusion, the Egyptians laboriously expanded
their positions east of the canal **1**, moving
five heavy divisions across. Frantically, the
Israelis attacked again with the 162d Armored
Division **2** in the north and the Sinai Division
3 to the south. Though the attacks were
beaten off with heavy losses, they stabilized
the front and slowed the already ponderous
Egyptian offensive.

0	10	20	30	Miles

0	20	50	Km

with Shmuel Gonen, now a major general and chief of Southern Command, as well as Elazar and Moshe Dayan, now Israeli Defense Minister, at the Southern Command's underground command complex at Um-Khusheiba. For men whose careers had been made winning the lightning armored victories of 1956 and 1967, the reverses of the past forty-eight hours had come as a debilitating shock. The tiny nation of Israel could ill afford the sort of losses in men and matériel it had suffered during the first two days of fighting, and it was immediately decided to go over to the defensive in the Sinai until the Golan front had stabilized.

Sharon, characteristically, disagreed with the decision, wanting to launch an offensive across the canal immediately. The Israeli government of Prime Minister Golda Meir was also less than pleased with the way Gonen had handled his forces, and so brought Bar-Lev out of retirement to serve as *de facto* commander in the Sinai, although his official title was Representative of the General Staff. Equally important was a realization by the senior IDF officers that the all-tank design of the divisions in the Sinai was seriously flawed. Characteristically, they did not agonize over the decision: a hasty reorganization of the units was ordered, with infantry and mortars being reattached down to battalion level and below. The Israelis were relearning the lessons of combined-arms warfare.

These decisions, combined with the growing Israeli strength on the peninsula, stabilized the front over the next forty-eight hours. The Egyptians had penetrated to a depth of between five and seven miles along the length of the canal's east bank, but their limited attempts to break out from this perimeter were firmly resisted, a Centurion brigade of Mendler's division destroying over fifty T-55s in one October 9 battle. In the space of a few days, the Israelis forced themselves to learn what it had taken the Soviets years to learn in 1941 and 1942: the tank could be as formidable a weapon in defense as in attack.

THE EGYPTIANS SHOOT THEIR BOLT

The turning point in the 1973 Sinai campaign came on October 14, when the Egyptians launched the long-awaited third phase of their offensive. Even then, the Egyptian high command would have preferred to wait a little longer, but they were pressured into attacking by their political masters, in an attempt to relieve the pressure on their Syrian colleagues, who were by now faced with Israeli armored columns bearing down on Damascus.

In preparation for the offensive, the Egyptians had gathered 1,200 tanks on the eastern bank of the Suez, opposed by 750 Israeli tanks in the Sinai; the thirty-minute Egyptian artillery barrage that ended at 6.30 A.M. on October 14 heralded the greatest single clash of armor since Kursk. The Egyptian offensive was mounted along six axes, each spearheaded by an armored brigade. Three of these, in the northern half of the front, were commanded by the Egyptian 2d Army Corps, while the remainder came under the 3d Army Corps, deployed to the south.[30] The Egyptian aim was for the northern spearheads to capture the Tassa junction while the southern elements took the Mitla and Jiddi Passes, before the lead elements of both corps rendezvoused at Bir Gafgafa, from where they could dominate the peninsula.[31]

The northernmost prong of the attack was also its most successful, although *least disastrous* might be a more apt term. Led by the highly regarded 15th Armored Brigade, it aimed to drive west along the Kantara-Baluza road, then south to the Tassa Junction from Baluza. Here it would link up with the corps' two more southerly attacks. As is the Egyptian style, the attack proceeded at a very deliberate pace, the T-62s advancing slowly toward the Israeli positions, which were strafed by two flights of SU-7 fighter-bombers. Egyptian infantry in antitank teams advanced with the armor. The thin force of Shermans and Centurions defending the route allowed the Egyptians to advance to within 1,000 meters of the Israeli positions before opening fire. As was to be the case throughout the front that day, the accuracy of the Israeli gunners made the difference. By 8.40 A.M. these part-time soldiers had accounted for thirty-four of the crack Egyptian brigade's T-62s, at a cost of only three Israeli tanks, two of which had hit mines. Faced with the loss of over half its armored strength, the Egyptian attack faltered and broke apart.[32]

The 2d Army Corps' main effort was a double thrust in the Firdan/Ismailia sector. At Firdan the 24th Armored Brigade came up against two battalions of Israeli T-55s commanded by Colonel Yoel Gonen, brother of the ill-fated Southern Command chief. The Israelis had captured the T-55s from the Syrian and Egyptian armies in 1967, and after refitting them with 105 mm guns had incorporated them into the Armored Corps.[33] At first the Egyptian armored juggernaut made good progress, knocking out about fifteen Israeli tanks in the first few minutes of battle. Gonen himself was blown out of his turret when a Sagger missile hit his tank, but, unhurt, he continued to direct the battle from another tank. Then an Israeli Centurion brigade arrived in the nick of time to reinforce Gonen. Tucked into a defensive position and firing from hull-down positions, the Israelis turned forty Egyptian tanks into just so many smoldering piles of blackened steel while the newly attached armored infantry and mortars kept the Egyptian Sagger teams from making any impact on the fight. What remained of the Egyptian armor withdrew by midday.[34]

The southern half of the effort met a similar fate. A desperate push toward Tassa by the 21st and 14th Armored Brigades ran up against Ariel Sharon's Pattons, the crews of which were thoroughly familiar with the local terrain from training exercises. Long-range Israeli sniping left sixty T-55s burning on the desert floor, and the Egyptians in retreat.[35]

Advancing on a twenty-five-kilometer front south of the Bitter Lakes, the 3d Army Corps pushed two infantry divisions plus three separate armored brigades forward toward the only Israeli division in the area. The northern and southern prongs were effectively repulsed, the former by hull-down Shermans and the latter by paratroops backed by one tank company, but the Egyptians were focusing their energies and resources on the central axis, where they threw a huge force up a *wadi* from which they hoped to assault the Mitla Pass from a flank. Up the dry riverbed came an armored brigade of ninety-four T-72s, backed by two battalions of 122 mm artillery and a large, mechanized infantry element.

Their hopes were short lived. Crowded into the gulley, the

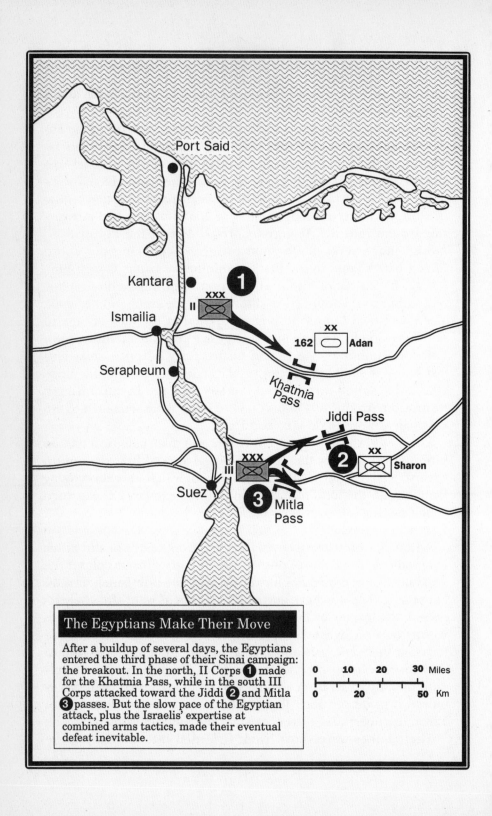

Port Said

Kantara

Ismailia

II XXX

1

162 ▭ Adan
XX

Khatmia Pass

Serapheum

Jiddi Pass

XXX

2
XX Sharon

III XXX

Suez

3 Mitla Pass

The Egyptians Make Their Move

After a buildup of several days, the Egyptians entered the third phase of their Sinai campaign: the breakout. In the north, II Corps **1** made for the Khatmia Pass, while in the south III Corps attacked toward the Jiddi **2** and Mitla **3** passes. But the slow pace of the Egyptian attack, plus the Israelis' expertise at combined arms tactics, made their eventual defeat inevitable.

0   10   20   30 Miles

0   20   50 Km

Egyptian column was soon set upon by small groups of Pattons. The steep walls of the *wadi*, made it difficult for the Egyptian tanks and Sagger crews to outflank the Israeli ambushes, and those that made it out of the *wadi* were easy prey for the IAF, which capitalized on the Egyptian departure from their air defense screen. By the time Israeli 155 mm artillery found the Egyptians' range in the afternoon, the attack had ground to a halt, and the remnants of the column were straggling west. They left 100 tanks—two-thirds of their force—in the *wadi*. The Israelis had lost only 2 tanks, both to Saggers.[36]

THE DECISIVE BLOW

Even in the relief of a desperate victory, the Israelis shifted tactics again. The failure of the Egyptian offensive paved the way for the Israelis to launch their counterstroke; conditions were now favorable for the kind of lightning armored operations the Israeli tankers knew best. They had been reluctant to cross the canal while there were still substantial Egyptian armored reserves on the west bank. The deployment of these to the east bank for the October 14 offensive, and their subsequent reduction, left the way open for Operation Stout-Hearted, the Israeli plan for a crossing to the west bank, drawn up by Sharon during his stint as Southern Command chief before the war.

The IDF high command established two provisional division commands for the purposes of Stout-Hearted. These were each given seventy-five tanks and the mission to oppose one of the Egyptian corps. This move freed up three Israeli armored divisions for the invasion, which began on the evening of October 15. Sharon's plan called for the Israelis to strike at the thinly defended juncture between the two corps. While a two-battalion force diverted Egyptian attention with an attack on the Tassa-Ismailia road, Sharon's division headed to the canal along routes south of II Corps. The first Israeli soldiers across were two battalions of paratroops who landed by ferry at 1:30 A.M. on October 16 near Deversoir, just north of the Great Bitter Lake. By 3 A.M., the lightly armed paratroops had established a bridgehead of 1,000 yards by

225 yards, and encountered little resistance from the confused Egyptians on the west bank.

On the east bank, however, things were heating up. Colonel Amnon Reshef's 14th Armored Brigade, now under Sharon's control, had blundered into a huge Egyptian supply dump at a vital crossroads about five kilometers from the water while on its way to the canal. The resultant battle—one of the fiercest of the war—raged through the night, as men and tanks traded fire at point-blank range, guided by the light of the infernos caused by exploding fuel and ammunition. For twelve hours the Egyptians fought ferociously as the Israelis pushed their bridging equipment through the chaos. By the time the battle ended, 60 of Reshef's 100 tanks were out of action, and 121 Israelis had been killed, over a third of them officers,[37] but by 9 A.M. the crossroads was in Israeli hands, and the first 30 Israeli tanks had made it over the canal.

At this stage, the Egyptians' rigid, Soviet style of command exacerbated their problems. No one had any idea of the situation on the west bank; it was no one's assigned task to react to the rumors of Israeli troops, and so nothing much was done. Sharon used the confusion he had sown in the Egyptian rear to good effect, taking his tanks and shooting up air defense missile and artillery sites. The Egyptians did manage two armored attacks on the bridgehead that morning. One, by two armored brigades, was fought off by the Israeli tanks on the west bank, while the other, by the 25th Armored Brigade, was decisively beaten off by Israeli tanks firing from east bank positions overlooking the bridgehead across the water. These engagements marked the first and last times the Egyptians threw tanks at the Israeli troops on the African side of the canal.

Not until October 18 did the Israeli 600th Armored Brigade open up the vital Tirtur route that ran between Artillery Road, seven kilometers from the canal, and Lexicon Road that ran parallel to the canal itself. Driving northward, the brigade linked up with the 14th Armored Brigade and swept the last Egyptian defenders from the Chinese Farm, an agricultural settlement that had been the focus of bitter fighting for the previous forty-eight hours.

From this moment on, the only question that remained was how

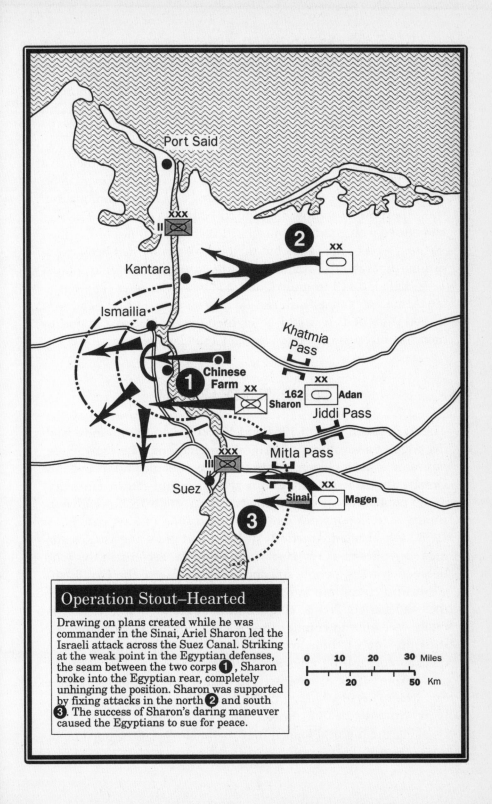

Operation Stout–Hearted

Drawing on plans created while he was commander in the Sinai, Ariel Sharon led the Israeli attack across the Suez Canal. Striking at the weak point in the Egyptian defenses, the seam between the two corps **1**, Sharon broke into the Egyptian rear, completely unhinging the position. Sharon was supported by fixing attacks in the north **2** and south **3**. The success of Sharon's daring maneuver caused the Egyptians to sue for peace.

long the Egyptians could allow Sharon's forces to run riot in mainland Egypt without suing for peace. A series of Israeli successes on the west bank, where the IDF now enjoyed a 420-to-250 superiority in tanks, settled the issue, although not without setbacks, including an ill-advised armored thrust into the town of Suez, which cost 80 dead and 120 wounded. With 45,000 troops of the Egyptian 3d Army Corps on the east bank surrounded and facing annihilation, the superpowers imposed a United Nations cease-fire. The war had ended with Israel in control of 1,000 square miles of Egyptian territory west of the canal, but the price of victory had been extraordinarily high. IDF Armored Corps losses in the Sinai totaled 1,450 killed, 3,143 wounded, and 232 taken prisoner. The Egyptian Army, of course, suffered far worse, with 11,000 dead and 25,000 wounded. It would be eighteen years before a major armored confrontation led to losses on a similar scale.

THE ULTIMATE LESSON

The Arab-Israeli wars of 1967 and 1973 marked the thinnest leading edge of a revolution in armored operations. The most telling indicator of such change was in the pace of battle and its lethality. Despite the Israeli ability to quickly repair and return tanks and other combat systems to battle, modern, high technology consumed matériel at rates that were impossible to long sustain; in 1973, only airlifted American supplies had given the Israelis adequate supplies of TOW missiles, for example. Second, in this joust between systems, people still counted. Many were the Israeli tank crews who ended the war in different tanks from those in which they had started. People counted most at the highest levels: the Israelis were able to counter their tactical mistakes—primarily, the squandering of their armor unsupported by other arms—by quickly reorganizing units and adjusting their operational preferences from attack to defense. The Israeli generals thought more rapidly and decided more quickly than did their Egyptian counterparts. However, at the strategic level, the Egyptians succeeded in breaking the political logjam over the Sinai. Sadat regained credibility with the world and with Egyptians; under the Camp David accords, the Sinai reverted to Egypt.

No military organization studied the 1973 fighting more thoroughly than did the U.S. Army. In Central Europe, American soldiers faced the same dilemma as the Israelis: how to fight outnumbered and win against an opponent with a rigid yet robust doctrine of armored operations. During the renaissance of the U.S. Army that followed the defeat in Vietnam and the accompanying Reagan defense buildup, the most thoughtful senior American tankers made the pilgrimage to the Sinai and the Golan Heights to talk to their Israeli counterparts about the changing face of tank warfare. How did the antitank missile really affect tank tactics? What were the real advantages of highly trained crews and sophisticated technologies? How did it all come together on the battlefield?

When they took their own turn in the desert two decades later, the Americans would test their answers to these and a thousand other questions. In doing so, they honed the thin edge of revolution into a lethal, cutting blade of killing metal.

CHAPTER SEVEN

IRAQ, 1991

Medina Ridge, the Killing Ground
of Desert Storm

BY 7:50 ON the morning of February 26, 1991, the U.S. 1st Armored Division was sitting on an empty piece of southern Iraq it called Phase Line Smash. The Old Ironsides division was a long way from its home in southern Germany, where it had formed part of the frontline defenses in the West's Cold War standoff with the Soviet Union. Now the Soviet empire was on its last legs, the Red Army was in retreat from Eastern Europe, and the American Army faced an entirely new and dimly foreseen challenge. The previous August, the troops of Iraqi dictator Saddam Hussein had staged a two-day blitzkrieg of its tiny but oil-rich neighbor, the emirate of Kuwait. Following, in local fashion, the script of armored warfare created by Heinz Guderian and the German *Wehrmacht* in 1940, the Iraqis had combined tank thrusts with helicopter airborne assaults to rapidly overrun Kuwait City and drive the Kuwaiti royal family into exile.

With masterful diplomacy—and to the shock of Saddam Hussein—U.S. President George Bush had cobbled together an unlikely coalition of Arab nations and European allies for the purpose of driving the Iraqis out of Kuwait and restoring the regional balance of power in the Middle East oilfields. The massive U.S. military commitment, hurriedly and haphazardly deployed to Saudi Arabia, was the glue holding the coalition together; its binding agent was the huge American armored force, of which the 1st Armored Division was the heaviest component, now poised for the decisive battle of the Gulf War, dubbed Operation Desert Storm by the theater military commander, General H. Norman Schwarzkopf.

The forces under Schwarzkopf's command represented everything that professional military excellence and the trillions of dollars spent on weapons during Ronald Reagan's defense buildup of the early 1980s could make of them. Units trained and equipped to fight the Soviet hordes in central Germany now faced a foe whose entire annual economic output was less than the yearly budget of the U.S. Air Force. Prior to any engagement of land forces, Saddam Hussein's army had been subjected to an intensive campaign of aerial bombardment; from the Iraqi capital of Baghdad to the pitiful frontline conscripts still manning the trenches in Kuwait and southern Iraq, the Iraqi soldier had learned to fear the power of the American military long before he saw the frontal slope of a U.S. tank. Still, Saddam would not withdraw from Kuwait until he had provoked "the mother of all battles," a ground war against U.S. troops; clearly, the Iraqi leader had no hopes of military victory, but he wished at least to inflict substantial casualties on the Americans. That, he felt, was within his power.

Had he paused to consider the order of battle of the U.S. 1st Armored Division or the half-dozen similar American heavy divisions or the massive British 1st Armoured Division, Saddam might have concluded otherwise, for the Western units were wholly unlike the kind of tank units he knew from his own army or, for that matter, the Soviet patrons who had supplied the Iraqi army. The mainstay of the U.S. 1st Armored Division, the M1A1 Abrams main battle tank, dwarfed the best the Iraqis had to offer, the Soviet T-72; standing side by side, the Abrams reflected the same solid engineering, precise construction, and crisp angles to be found in a powerful, top-of-the-line Western luxury sedan, while the T-72 looked like nothing so much as a Soviet-style econobox, with its rounded turret and poorly integrated sights and external fuel barrels pasted on to the humble chassis. The T-72 looked like a direct descendant of the World War II T-34.

Although the T-72 had its origins in the Soviet stalwart of

Kursk and the campaigns of 1944, the American Abrams was nothing like its Western predecessors. In the late 1970s and 1980s, Western tanks—the Abrams, the British Challenger, and the German Leopard—had undergone a revolutionary transformation in design. To begin with, the flat, sleek design of the Abrams was a matter not of aesthetics, but of practical engineering to accommodate a new kind of armor, a laminate design created by the British and called Chobham armor. Taking advantage of progress in material science and design, this armor offered exponentially improved protection if used in thick slabs. A further beauty of the design was its modular construction. As the balance of capabilities shifted between armor and antiarmor weapons, the Chobham recipe could be modified and the armor replaced easily; many of the American tanks in the desert were M1A1 heavy armor versions, whose laminate armor was laced with a mesh of depleted uranium.

This latest generation of Western tanks was as much an electronic weapon as a dispenser of cold steel. Their ballistic computers, thermal sights, and laser range finders made them all-weather, day-and-night, shoot-on-the-move platforms of stunning accuracy and lethality. World War II tank-on-tank engagements were most often short-range, daytime affairs where even the best gunners required multiple rounds to hit and kill their opponents. The thermal sights on the Abrams or the British Challenger allowed their crews to see their opponents from several kilometers away, at night or in dust or rain storms. The tremendous power of their 120 mm main guns, mounted in stabilized turrets, was monitored by sophisticated sensors all controlled by refined ballistic computers. In the desert, especially, these advantages were magnified by the conditions. Put simply, the coalition's tank crews could see the Iraqis and kill them almost always at ranges well beyond effective return fire.

Within the structure of the modern armored division, the tank was merely the centerpiece in an array of devastating weapons, all mechanized to move rapidly into enemy depths at speeds and distances far beyond the capabilities of World War II armies. The U.S. 1st Armored Division could call on masses of artillery, not only self-propelled howitzers but multiple rocket launchers. Infantrymen now rode in fighting vehicles that were a far cry from the half-tracks of World War II. The American M2/3 Bradley fighting vehicle, like its partner the Abrams tank, relied on a thermal sight and mounted a 25 mm cannon and antitank guided missiles that also outranged the Iraqi tanks. Close air support now was the province of AH-64 Apache attack helicopters, also with thermal sights and laser-riding antitank missiles with a range of ten kilometers. These fighting systems were supported by an impressive set of logistics organizations; even hundreds of kilometers inside Iraq and thousands of miles from their home station, the division's tankers were better provided for than their foes who were fighting on their home ground among massive supply depots. The American intelligence advantages, from spy satellites to forward observers, were also decisive.

Poised at Phase Line Smash after advancing into Iraq, 1st Armored Division commander Major General Ronald Griffith had kept his promise to his superior, VII Corps commander Lieutenant General Frederick Franks, that the Old Ironsides' 300-plus tanks would be ready for the decisive blows of the Desert Storm land campaign. The corps' leading edge, the 2d Armored Cavalry Regiment, was searching for the precise location of the heavy divisions of the Iraqi Republican Guard Forces Command, which Schwarzkopf had identified as the center of gravity of the Desert Storm land war. Behind the cavalry screen, Griffith and Major General Paul Funk's 3d Armored Division, to the south, were preparing to smash the prime tool of Saddam Hussein's attack upon Kuwait. Maneuvering his division for the kill, Griffith was leaving only the 6th Battalion, 6th Infantry Regiment behind to clear and secure the town of Al Busayyah, where the division had fought its first major engagement with the Iraqi army, and to secure the division's rear supply lines.

Though the 1st Armored Division was a long way from its prime target, the Iraqi army enemy was in disarray all across the theater, fleeing before attacks on every front. Schwarzkopf was trying to light a fire under Franks, getting him to attack as fast as possible before the Iraqis could flee to Basra and regroup. Franks's order to Griffith on February 26 was "to continue the attack without pause, to go after the Republican Guard." As a result, U.S. Third Army, the top Army headquarters in the Saudi capital of Riyadh, had placed a ruler flat on its maps of southern Iraq, drawing a boundary between VII Corps and its brother XVIII Airborne Corps to the north and extending all the way to the Persian Gulf. Thus, from Phase Line Smash, the 1st Armored Division began a sweeping turn that reoriented its attack from north to due east and shifted its formation to bring its three brigades abreast. Colonel Montgomery Meigs's 2d Brigade was in the north, Colonel Jim Riley's 1st Brigade in the center, and Colonel Dan Zanini's 3d Brigade in the south. While the division was shifting formation, Griffith sent his reconnaissance elements sprinting forward.

The division's battle for Al Busayyah had been a deliberate attack, with the Iraqi positions well templated, but the fight against the Republican Guard would be a meeting engagement. "We knew where their start positions are, but everybody was on the move," the division's intelligence chief, Lieutenant Colonel Keith Alexander, recalled. The Republican Guard's continuing movement into blocking positions made for a fluid situation.

MOVEMENT TO CONTACT

The division was huddled in what it called Attack Position Python, where it had expected to spend twenty-four to thirty-six hours as VII Corps gathered its combat power for its showdown with the RGFC. Here the division's rear support would remain. As it uncoiled from Python, the combat brigades began to move at full steam, the phase lines clicking by. Phase Line Texas was about thirty kilometers past Smash; another twenty-four kilometers brought the division to Phase Line Canada; ten more kilometers to Tangerine. Griffith expected to hit the Iraqis between Tangerine and Phase Line Poland. He told his commanders: "Let's don't let these bastards get out of here. . . . Let's press the attack as hard as we can."

To the division's north, one of the Joint Surveillance and Target Acquisition Radar System, or JSTARS surveillance aircraft—a heavily reworked Boeing 707 passenger jet jammed with sensors and other electronics—was tracking a brigade of the Adnan Infantry Division, one of the light infantry Republican Guard units. To the south, elements of the heavy Tawakalna Division had moved some thirty or forty kilometers. They were now mostly opposite the 3d Armored Division, but also had moved north into the 1st Armored Division's sector. An important Iraqi logistics site with enough ammunition, fuel, and spare parts to supply a corps-sized unit also lay in the southern part of the division's zone. Farther east, two brigades of the Medina Armored Division, Griffith's prime target, were trying to set up a line in the area around Phase Line Lime. To get to the Medina, Griffith would have to block any attack by the Adnan, then sweep aside the bits of the Tawakalna and stragglers from other units that lay in his path and clear the logistics site.

Early in the afternoon of February 26, the scout helicopters of the division's 1st Squadron, 1st Cavalry Regiment, reported through the 1st Brigade that they had located the northern brigade of the Tawakalna. Despite the impulse to press the attack at full speed, Griffith did not alter his tactical procedures. He still wanted to strike the enemy from long range before sending in his tanks for the kill. The divisional cavalry squadron had AH-1 Cobra attack helicopters—the predecessor of the Apache—accompanying its scouts. The weather had been miserable, and visibility was severely limited; forty mile per hour winds whipped up the desert. "By all means, we shouldn't have been flying," recalled warrant officer Christopher Louis, one of the Cobra pilots. Louis and the other gunships responded to the scouts' call, where they could make out a line of about seventy tanks snaking across the desert near the division's boundary with the Third Armored Division to the south. The weather had at last begun to clear, and at 2:30 P.M., eight Air Force air strikes were launched against dug-in tanks from the Tawakalna, with pilots claiming about thirty tanks were destroyed and reporting another twenty-five to thirty dug in. Division operations officer Lieutenant Colonel Tom Strauss would call for air strikes throughout the battle, sending the Air Force deep, twenty to seventy-five kilometers ahead the division. "We never had to slow the momentum of attack because of close air support," he said. The fixed-wing air battle was controlled by Air Force forward air controllers, who rode in the left seats of the division's OH-58 scout helicopters. Colonel Dan Petrosky, First Aviation Brigade commander, discovered that the perch provided better coordination of air strikes.

At about the same time as the air strikes began, the division completed its turn, now heading due east. At about 4 P.M., Griffith ordered Zanini's 3d Brigade to attack and destroy the Tawakalna elements in his path, allowing the rest of the division to bypass the Iraqi line to the north in pursuit of the other Republican Guard divisions to the east. Zanini's troops were about thirty-five kilometers from the Tawakalna's front line, just past Phase Line Poland.

The division's goal was to catch up to the cavalry squadron, about ten kilometers ahead of the three advancing brigades. Two of the squadron's ground troops, A Troop and B Troop, had moved forward to near the Iraqi frontline trace and spent anxious hours, worried mostly about friendly fire. "The problem was, there was stuff moving around out there," remembered 1st Brigade commander Riley. "There was an awful lot of concern about fratricide that night."[1] The scouts' fear was nightmarish. "We were so far ahead, [we were afraid] they'd see a hot spot at night [and] fire at us," said A Troop's Sergeant David Lane. "There were a couple of mistakes like that."[2]

The brigade's first ground contact with the Republican Guard came at about 7 P.M., when scouts from the 7th Battalion, 6th Infantry Regiment hit the Iraqi positions about a dozen kilometers ahead of the brigade's main body. From then until the cease-fire two days later, the 1st Armored Division would be in continuous contact with the Iraqis in battles that covered more than seventy kilometers.

Zanini's first action was to pound the Iraqis with preparatory fires from his artillery. As the 3d Brigade closed on the Tawakalna, evening began to turn to darkness and the weather turned foul again. Griffith could not tell whether the sun had set. When the ground scouts made contact, the artillery stoppped and began preparatory fires at a range of about thirteen kilometers; in the overcast, moonless night, artillery barrages substituted

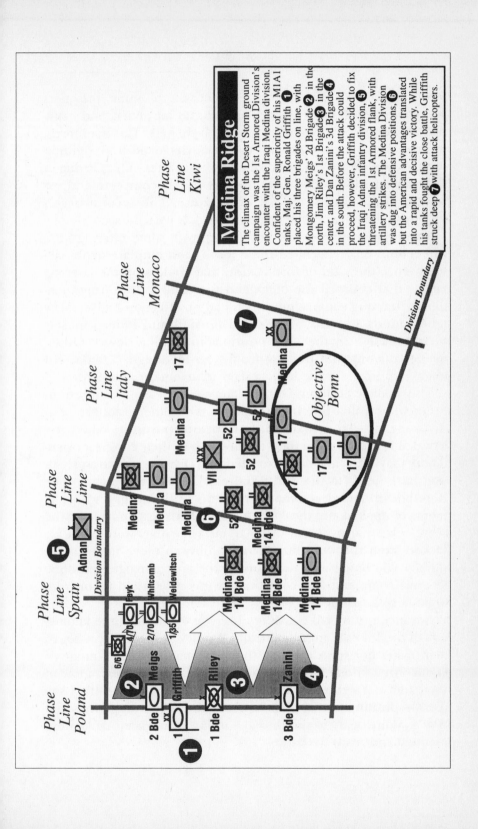

Medina Ridge

The climax of the Desert Storm ground campaign was the 1st Armored Division's encounter with the Iraqi Medina division. Confident of the superiority of his M1A1 tanks, Maj. Gen. Ronald Griffith ❶ placed his three brigades on line, with Montgomery Meigs' 2d Brigade ❷ in the north, Jim Riley's 1st Brigade ❸ in the center, and Dan Zanini's 3d Brigade ❹ in the south. Before the attack could proceed, however, Griffith decided to fix the Iraqi Adnan infantry division, threatening the 1st Armored flank, with artillery strikes. The Medina Division was dug into defensive positions, but the American advantages translated into a rapid and decisive victory. While his tanks fought the close battle, Griffith struck deep ❼ with attack helicopters.

Phase Line Poland
Phase Line Spain
Phase Line Lime
Phase Line Italy
Phase Line Monaco
Phase Line Kiwi

Division Boundary

Objective Bonn

Division Boundary

2 Bde
Griffith
Meigs
6/6
4/70
2/70
1/35
Bayk
Whitcomb
Weidewitsch
Adnan
Medina
Medina
Medina
Medina
VII
52
52
52
52
17
17
17
17
17
17
Medina
Medina 14 Bde
Medina 14 Bde
Medina 14 Bde
1 Bde
Riley
3 Bde
Zanini
Medina

❶ ❷ ❸ ❹ ❺ ❻ ❼

for air strikes. To the Iraqis, the effect was the same: prisoners later said they thought the artillery was an air attack, and many had abandoned their vehicles for bomb shelters. The Iraqi force, totaling about forty T-72s and twenty Soviet-made BMP fighting vehicles, was arrayed in two distinct but thin lines of hastily dug-in fighting positions. The first line was nearly complete and extended south out of the division's zone. The second began slightly to the north of the first and was only partially set.

The Iraqi positions varied in quality, with some offering little protection. Soldiers called these loose sand emplacements kill-me berms, the kind of fortification that could stop the laser-tag beams that counted the quick and the dead at the Army's maneuver training centers, but which had no effect on high-velocity tank rounds and antitank guided missiles and indeed merely served to identify the Iraqi positions in the flat desert. Other, deeper dugouts hid the low-profile, Soviet-designed tanks, but made it difficult for the Iraqi tankers to maneuver and fight.

This shallow position, Griffith later would learn, was meant to tie the Tawakalna line in with elements of other Iraqi armored divisions, but "they had not gotten into position. When the Tawakalna moved from their north-south to their east-west orientation they were not tied into Medina [Division, which was] sitting back here [to the north and east]. There was a gap." The Republican Guard commander tried to fill that gap with elements of the 52d and the 17th Armored Divisions, units from the regular Iraqi army. Clearly, the Iraqis knew they were being attacked from the west, but their inability to move large forces rapidly, combined with the damage the air campaign had done to their command and control networks, prevented them from organizing anything more than a hasty defense.

Advancing under the artillery barrage to within three kilometers of the Iraqis, Zanini's tank and Bradley crew members began identifying hot spots through their thermal sights at a range of about three kilometers and started firing. In the green glow of their thermal sights, the crews could see little specks—Iraqi soldiers—sprinting out of their bunkers and reboarding tanks and BMPs. Many of them didn't make it, but other Iraqi tanks were manned and ready for battle.

Zanini attacked with two battalions on line and the third, 3rd Battalion, 35th Armor, echeloned to the north; the brigade was separated from the rest of the division and Zanini needed to guard his flank. Soon the two lead task forces, 7/6 Infantry and 1st Battalion, 37th Armor, halted and opened fire, using the range advantage and superior optics of their tanks and fighting vehicles to methodically destroy the Tawakalna units. Iraqi tanks and personnel carriers erupted in columns of flame as vehicle after vehicle was hit. Both task forces reported sporadic return fire with no effect. "It turned into a horrendous night fight," recalled Major Chesley Harris, the brigade operations officer. "There was stuff going on all over the place." Again, the superior range and thermal optics of the M1A1s proved a tremendous advantage, allowing the Americans to shoot the Iraqis before the Iraqis could shoot them. Said Harris, "The fight kept going until all hot spots were burning that we could identify."

Adding to the confusion was the fact that the Iraqi positions straddled the division's boundary. To the south, attack helicopters in the 3d Armored Division's zone were attacking the Tawakalna line, too. Later, Harris wrote that the attack helicopters

> were too close for comfort, especially at night with our limited depth perception. With our moving hot tank engine turbines and surrounding burning Iraqi tank hulks we felt like potential fratricide targets. The sky was illuminated with red and green tracers, [high velocity tank round] ricochets, Dual-Purpose Improved Conventional Munition [artillery rounds] exploding like sparklers and streaking TOW and Hellfire missiles.[3]

After about forty minutes, the two battalion task forces reported that "the objective has been neutralized."

It was time to go forward.

At around 8:15 P.M., Brigade commander Zanini sent Lieutenant Colonel Ed Dyer's 1/37 Armor through the center of the hot spots: "Assault and take the objective," radioed Zanini.

The battalion's M1A1 heavy tanks, protected by depleted uranium armor, creaked forward, leaving the lighter-skinned vehicles behind. Despite the fearful pounding from aircraft, artillery, and then the tanks and Bradleys, some Iraqi tanks, fighting vehicles, and dug-in infantry lived on; Dyer found his battalion "right there amongst them. There were tanks and BMPs and ammunition exploding all over the place." Engaging the surviving Iraqis at ranges as close as 200 meters, Dyer's tanks broke between the two lines. "The Iraqis were in superb fighting positions," wrote Harris, "but their orientations limited the ability to traverse and fire completely into our attack."[4]

Three of the 1/37 Armor tanks were hit in rapid succession, and a fourth minutes later as the battalion passed through the second line. In the confusion, there were immediate suspicions that the tanks had been hit by Hellfire missiles or rockets fired by the 3d Armored Division attack helicopters just to the south. 7/6 Infantry reported seeing several rockets land among the tanks. Recalled Harris, "There was a mass scramble going through the battalion and brigade [radio] nets to order a cease-fire."[5] It took twenty minutes to sort out what was happening. The fight continued while the wounded were evacuated and the rest of the brigade refueled and rearmed.

Later investigation revealed that two of the tanks were hit by T-72 fire, one by a missile from a BMP, and one by an RPG rocket-propelled grenade. Six tankers were wounded by the fire, and only one of the tanks actually was destroyed. The likely explanation for at least some of the hits, concluded Zanini, is that his troops were six or seven kilometers ahead of the adjacent 3d Armored Division, and as Dyer's battalion advanced, skirting the division boundary, the backside of its tanks were exposed to Tawakalna tanks in the 3d Armored Division zone; he suspects that the fire may have come from Iraqis just over the line into the neighboring zone to the south.

Taking its first casualties unsettled the brigade slightly; radios crackled with heated exchanges. Initial reports attributed one of the tank losses to mines, a silent killer that tankers feared deeply. Despite losing the four tanks, Dyer and the rest of the battalion continued to take the objective. He decided that "there were no life-threatening casualties involved" and wanted to reassure his troops. "I got that out onto the net, and I think that made a big difference." Still, the brigade now knew how fast and deadly the action could be. Zanini remembered, "It raised the blood pressure a little, but the calm on the radio nets was almost eerie, from the [commanding general] down to the company nets." Zanini's men had destroyed twenty-one Iraqi tanks, twenty-two personnel carriers and BMPs, and many other vehicles. Most of the Iraqis had stood, fought, and died in their fighting positions, with only a handful attempting to retreat. Carefully, the brigade's support battalion picked its way among the flaming Iraqi vehicles, giving wide berth to the tanks and fighting vehicles, whose on-board rounds continued to cook off. The battlefield was also littered with unexploded munitions.

"The reality of death was everywhere—destroyed enemy tanks and their crews, catastrophic destruction," wrote Harris. "The caustic smells of burning metal and gunpowder and reports of dead soldiers kept the reality of death near. Everyone saw it as they moved forward—a burning U.S. tank. It lit the sky all night with secondary explosions."[6] The somber mood was reinforced by a report across the division artillery radio net that Iraqi artillery had shelled the cavalry squadron's command post, damaging vehicles and wounding a number of soldiers. Just before midnight, after a four-hour engagement, Zanini's brigade cleared the objective to the east, minus 1/37 Armor, which was making a last sweep of the objective. Griffith's intent had been clear: destroy all mounted enemy in the zone. It took the brigade about forty-five minutes to rearm and refuel. Within an hour, Dyer's task force also had refueled and rejoined the brigade.

After fighting wound down, by 11 P.M., the brigade was confronted with many prisoners. Again, the number of prisoners threatened to slow the attack: the brigade had but one platoon of military police, about thirty soldiers, to handle 442 prisoners. Neither did it have anywhere to put the prisoners, nor any transportation. Iraqi trucks were used to move some to collection points, and some of the division's engineers built a compound, digging large holes with Armored Combat Earthmovers—essentially, armored bulldozers—to use as holding areas. That made some prisoners nervous, thinking they were going to be executed. "They started talking like sons of guns," remembered Harris.

In the encounter, Griffith and his commanders had learned that they were more than a match for their Republican Guard foes. Indeed, they were surprised at just how much better they were: "We were more tentative than I would ever be if I were going to fight the Iraqis again," concluded division commander Griffith. "We envisioned counterattacks. We expected their positions would have a lot of depth to them. We envisioned minefields and obstacles. But it wasn't there."

Despite 3d Brigade's decisive victory, the intelligence picture to the east was unclear, at best. The Tawakalna units in the 1st Armored Division's zone had been dispatched, and no large units stood between the division and the Medina, but remnants of various Iraqi mechanized and armor units lay between the Old Ironsides and its prime target. The battlefield was chaotic, the weather lousy, and intelligence spotty. "The only picture I was getting of the tactical battlefield was from my Apaches and on the ground," said Griffith. Nobody knew precisely where the Medina was and what it was doing; the status of the final RGFC heavy division, the Hammurabi armored division, was even less clear. Nonetheless, from his conversations with corps commander Franks, hearing reports from the 3rd Armored Division to his south, and learning details of the 2d Armored Cavalry Regiment's fight to the south, he felt a growing sense of confidence. "The distinct impression that I had once we had started to fight the Republican Guard—within a matter of a couple of hours I said these guys are not very good. We've got a tremendous overmatch in our direct fire-systems, and their artillery, which really had us worried—they fired a lot of artillery but they couldn't shift it or mass it. When they would fire, our Firefinder [radars] were picking them up and we were getting counterfire within a matter of minutes and taking them out." What was clear was that the division was entering into a pursuit phase much sooner than it had anticipated.

TAKING IT TO THE REPUBLICAN GUARD

As the pace of the attack increased, Griffith tried to gather all his units for the big fight he knew was coming. The next day, February 27, would see the engagement his troops had traveled thousands of miles to keep: the rendezvous with the Republican Guard. Even as the division pressed relentlessly eastward, Griffith scrambled to assemble as much combat power as he could muster. First of all, he wanted to get his loaned Apaches back from the 2d Armored Cavalry Regiment; the regiment had been withdrawn into VII Corps reserve. At 6 A.M., the eighteen Apaches of the 2d Battalion, 1st Aviation Regiment pulled out of the cavalry's laager sites ninety kilometers to the south, and their ground support elements raced northward to prepare to support the division's attack. The battalion commander, Lieutenant Colonel John Ward, met with aviation brigade commander Petrosky to get the details of the division's plans for the day and set up his forward refueling points and command post. When Petrosky told him to take a break, that he wanted 2/1 Aviation on station at noon, Ward used the opportunity to fly a leader's reconnaissance of the likely battlefield. "I flew about 30 minutes. None of us had realized how fast the division was moving." Ward knew that his refueling points were set too far back, so he raced back and told his battalion to break down and push farther forward.

That night, the division also was reinforced by the 75th Field Artillery Brigade, which had begun the war supporting the 1st Infantry Division as it breached the Iraqi front lines, but it had been trying to catch the 1st Armored ever since. When the brigade did not show at a preassigned link-up point on the afternoon of February 25, Major Rick Anderson, the division artillery's assistant training and operations officer, searched the desert until he found the 75th Brigade. They caught up at 11 P.M. on February 26, after a 120-mile chase. The artillery brigade was immediately ordered to fire preparatory strikes on the logistics sites to the Iraqi rear. "Here we were, meeting in the middle of the night, in the middle of the war, and within 30 minutes, we had them decisively engaged in our division battle," said Major Ed Fagan, operations officer for 1st Armored's division artillery.

Also, 6/6 Infantry had caught up with the division after clearing Al Busayyah, linking up with rear support units at about 4:30 P.M. on the afternoon of February 26 and later rejoining the 2d Brigade. "By the time we reached the refuel at 12 o'clock that night, we were all pretty much zombied out," recalled Staff Sergeant David Crabtree, one of the battalion's Bradley commanders.[7] The continuous movement had taken its toll on the entire division as well. Almost twenty hours had passed since the division had halted to sleep; for most of the men, it would be another eighteen hours until the next rest. Lieutenant Colonel Steve Whitcomb, commander of 2d Brigade's 2d Battalion, 70th Armor, recalled that "guys were getting tired. Tank crews could circulate themselves through, so the tank commander could sleep and the gunner could TC for awhile. It was tough on the company commanders and battalion commanders and brigade commanders. This was about three to six hours into full time awake."

The division's intelligence staff worked through the night, too, struggling to piece together a detailed picture of the Iraqi dispositions, particularly where the Medina Division was located and whether it was on the move. The Iraqis were in a mess. Although the division did not know it, the Army's theater intelligence operation had picked up a conversation between two Iraqi commanders that revealed the desperation of their condition. The commander of the Medina Division of the Republican Guard, who had responsibility for the local defenses and was trying to tie parts of the 52d Armored Division and other units of the so-called Jihad Corps, into his position, was fighting with his subordinates over the radio on how to integrate the defense.

The first concern for Griffith, however, was the Adnan Division, part of the Republican Guard, but primarily light infantry with perhaps a battalion of tanks attached. To swiftly deal with the Adnan, Griffith went to his playbook of rehearsed maneuvers. He intended to swing his 1st and 3d Brigades to the south and fix the Adnan in place, then steamroller them with 2d Brigade's three armored task forces; with three tank and one mechanized infantry battalions, 2d Brigade was the heaviest brigade in the Desert Storm Army.[8]

Though he lacked hard intelligence, Griffith sensed it was

time to press the attack home. "I put everything in the fight and didn't hold the reserve back." His target for February 27 was a patch of desert dubbed Objective Bonn. As it happened, Objective Bonn included the forward elements of the Medina, again sprinkled with bits of the 10th, 12th, 17th, and 52d divisions, as well as an Iraqi corps logistics site. The Medina, like the Tawakalna, had been spared from the heaviest air attacks and still had about 75 percent of its tanks operating. Like the Tawakalna, the Medina was maneuvering to reorient against attack from the west. Though the Iraqi fear of radio communication made their job much more difficult—and even in the best circumstances they were slow to move large units—1st Armored intelligence chief Alexander anticipated "a very coherent defense. . . . These guys wanted to fight."

Before taking on the best the Iraqis had to offer, Griffith needed to prepare his forces. By the morning of February 27, his massive formations of M1A1 tanks and Bradley fighting vehicles were all reporting serious fuel shortages, as were the division's AH-64 Apache attack helicopter units. Zanini's 3d Brigade had raced to rejoin the division formation. After an all-night road march, D Company from the 1st Battalion, 35th Armor Regiment stopped around daybreak to bore-sight their guns and check equipment. Sergeant First Class John Scaglionne hoped the battalion would not be ordered to move soon. "Fuel was getting low," he recalled. "We were outrunning our logistics now and that kind of worried me." Major Jim Dwyer, executive officer for the 123d Main Support Battalion, was sent back to corps on an emergency resupply mission in an attempt to get fuel released to the division. On the morning of February 27, Griffith got the word that there were eighty-nine fuel tankers coming across the desert. Also, at about ten o'clock in the morning, Funk radioed Griffith that he would send another thirty fuelers.

As the night sky began to lighten on February 27, the 1st Armored Division was the sharp end of the spear that was thrusting into the side of the Iraqi positions in southern Iraq. The southernmost unit of XVIII Airborne Corps, the 3d Armored Cavalry Regiment, was about forty kilometers to the west and rear of 1st Armored. Because VII Corps was taking the Republican Guard in the flank and the Iraqi positions were better developed to the south, the division was also getting out ahead of the 3rd Armored Division to its south; by dawn, a gap of about fifteen kilometers had opened between the two huge formations. Franks's armored fist was becoming ever so slightly unclenched. Yet the initiative was clearly with the Americans, and the instructions were clear: exploit and pursue the crumbling Iraqi army.

As the division prepared for combat, a VII Corps intelligence report confirmed that a brigade of the RGFC's Adnan Division was moving against Meigs's 2d Brigade in the north. The report came from a JSTARS surveillance aircraft circling the battlefield to the south; the plane's radar systems had picked up the Adnan's movement. Attacking from across the boundary in the XVIII Airborne Corps sector, the attack threatened Griffith's northern flank just as the division was preparing to plow forward in search of the main positions of the Medina Division. Riley's 1st Brigade was encountering fragmented Iraqi defenses, with mixed units, including Adnan troops clustered around the Iraqi VII Corps headquarters farther to the west between Phase Lines Spain and Monaco. The brigade was swamped with prisoners of war. Because the Adnan was light infantry with little firepower or ability to hinder his progress, Griffith did not want to be diverted from the Medina Division, his prime target, to the east. Again, he "used a hell of a lot of artillery and Apaches against them," with little ground contact.

The attack helicopters also gave Griffith a good fix on the Adnan's movements; he realized they posed only a minor threat: "I had a good picture when we were in contact. They had not shown any great ability to counterattack. They had not shown good use of artillery. So as the fight goes on the confidence goes up and up." Griffith decided to swing the 2d Brigade around to sweep aside the last bits of the Adnan, thus bringing his three brigades on line again: 2d Brigade to the north, 3d Brigade on the southern flank, and 1st Brigade now in the middle.

The artillery and the Apaches prevented the Adnan Division from slowing Griffith's attack. Just after dawn, straying slightly out of its sector, the 4th Battalion, 70th Armor, 2d Brigade's northern flank unit, skirmished with elements of the Adnan, in about brigade strength, destroying several T-72s. Though part of the Republican Guard, the Iraqis did not give a very good account of themselves: 4/70 Armor destroyed an Adnan truck whose occupants were machine-gunning Iraqi soldiers in the back as they tried to surrender.[9]

On the southern wing, Zanini's 3rd Brigade was now out of radio contact with its right flank neighbor from the 3d Armored Division, so he shifted formation slightly to guard his open wing. At 7:15 A.M., the 3d Brigade made contact with an enemy tank company and two infantry companies defending the western edge of a large Republican Guard logistics base. Attacking with all three task forces abreast, the brigade quickly swept aside the defenders, with ten vehicles destroyed in the first minute of battle. The base included a huge ammunition and fuel dump. Giant secondary explosions followed engagements, in turn setting off more explosions. The base was littered with unexploded rounds, and many American vehicles set these off as they passed through.

Late in the day, brigade operations officer Harris stopped to work on a map overlay. "I needed to change my maps if we were to continue across Kuwait toward the Gulf," he later wrote.[10] Despite being in the midst of an engagement, Harris felt safe: "A tank company protected my front, another to both sides. Apache helicopters overhead provided deeper fire and observation. We found a small revetment for cover and concealment." Harris's driver, Specialist Chris Hamrick, and his operations NCO got out of the Bradley and walked around the vehicle. Harris heard an explosion that sounded like a mortar round. They had parked the Bradley among a dense field of air-delivered mines. The resulting explosion took off Hamrick's leg and cost the operations sergeant his foot. Hamrick had compound fractures and his femur artery was spurting blood. To Harris, the left lung appeared punctured. The operations NCO had no right foot and fragments perforated his legs and torso. "Blood was everywhere."[11] Combat lifesavers cared for them, inserting intravenous plasma bags, sealing the lungs, and controlling the arterial bleeding until medics arrived to take over. Quickly, the two casualties were helicoptered to a MASH site and within a week to a hospital back in Germany. Both lived.

However, the brigade had stopped. While clearing the logistics base, forward scouts reported Iraqi convoys and mixed units trying to escape to the north all across the brigade's front. Among them was a complete Iraqi tank battalion turned to attack into the gap between 3d Brigade and Colonel Montgomery Meigs's 2d Brigade to the north.

Again, the tactical situation—both enemy and friendly—was fluid and hard to grasp. Through their thermal sights, Abrams and Bradley gunners could locate targets up to three kilometers away, but could not distinguish friend from foe. "There was a great fear of fratricide," wrote Harris.[12] "If in doubt, no one fired. Commanders talked, trying to assess the situation. We were unsure if an offensive was developing; should we counterattack?"

THE MOMENT OF TRUTH

The staff's preparations were interrupted by tremendous volleys of tank fire to the north. "The flash and concussion from explosions pulsated through the air," recalled Harris.[13] "Everyone's senses heightened." What Harris heard and felt and saw was the thunder and lightning of Desert Storm's largest tank battle. To his north, Meigs's 2d Brigade was attacking a brigade of the Republican Guard's Medina Armored Division. The short, sharp tank fight became known as the Battle of Medina Ridge.

Colonel Montgomery Meigs's 2d Brigade had been through a rough night. As the 1st Armored's northernmost unit, they had traveled the longest road, moving in short sprints followed by pauses. At dawn, the brigade was on the move again, feeling for the outposts of the Iraqi line. Because his northern flank, on the XVIII Airborne Corps boundary, was open, Meigs's formation was led by two tank task forces, Lieutenant Colonel Steve Whitcomb's 2/70 Armor and 1st Battalion, 35th Armor Regiment, with the third tank unit, 4/70 Armor, traveling in a modified column echeloned to deny the left flank. The 6/6 Infantry was tucked in behind the tankers. Meigs was ready to crush any opposition in his path.

As they rolled past Phase Line Spain at about 7 A.M., calls of "Tanks, direct front. Engaging now!" came across Whitcomb's command radio net.[14] The battalion had hit Iraqi logistics units with small security attachments huddled in bermed positions. Attacking with his three tank companies on line, Whitcomb's men swept through the Iraqis, killing eight tanks, eleven BMPs, three BRDMs, and thirty-four trucks while suffering no casualties. The 2d Brigade pushed on another six kilometers, halting and rearming while the division paused to distribute badly needed fuel. Whitcomb's tanks were reduced to living off squirts of fuel; the battalion's support platoon had a full-time job feeding the thirsty M1s. Each operation required the platoon to travel thirty or more kilometers to find the supply, then retrace their tracks to distribute it.

Whitcomb used the refueling stop to give his men some rest; the division would not be moving again for a few hours. Even brigade commander Meigs was exhausted. As the fighting quieted around 9:30 A.M., he settled down for a nap in his Bradley, only to be roused by the sound of artillery.

"Hey, what's going on?" he called to Major Mark Curry, brigade operations officer.

"That's the Iraqis shooting artillery at us," Curry responded.

"Why the hell aren't we moving?" Meigs demanded.

Not necessary, the colonel was told. The shells were landing behind the brigade, and lacking the ability to shift their fire, the Iraqis pulverized the empty desert near Phase Line Spain with 200 rounds in twenty minutes.

Bone tired and disdainful of the Iraqis, Meigs went back to sleep.

After pinpointing the Iraqi batteries with Firefinder radar and getting clearance—the shots were coming from the XVIII Airborne Corps's zone— the divisional artillery silenced the guns with a thirty-six-rocket Multiple Launch Rocket System salvo. Just before 11 A.M., the 2d Brigade was ordered to move again, the division again attacking with its three brigades abreast. Likewise, 2d Brigade's Meigs brought his three tank battalions on line, with 6/6 Infantry trailing in reserve. His battalion did likewise: Whitcomb's 2/70 Armor advanced with its three tank-pure companies leading, using his scouts to maintain contact with 1/35 Armor on the south and his mechanized infantry in reserve.

At 11:40 A.M., the brigade began to roll. The intelligence picture remained cloudy, but expectation was that the Iraqi main defensive belt was still twenty to forty kilometers distant. Within minutes, the lead platoon of Whitcomb's B Company crested a small *wadi* created by the recent rains and running along a slight rise. "Around 12 o'clock, I remember distinctly we had come in a *wadi*," Whitcomb said.

> It was stretched across our front and remarkably it was like a fairly straight ditch. I recall watching the lead tank platoon that I was behind pull up. It stopped very quickly and they got down and almost immediately I got a call from [Captain] Mark Gurgis, B Company commander, and [Captain] Eric Williams, A Company commander, saying we've got something out in front of us. They weren't firing at us so we spent a good solid period of time making sure we knew where [1/35 Armor] was and what we had out in front of us. It was a far enough range; we were getting 3800 to about 3500 meters on our range finders. With the weather we couldn't make any visual contact. Relying on the hot spots we could pick out a fairly sizeable force.
>
> "By that time I had pulled up on line with the lead platoon. I couldn't see anything through my binoculars but I saw all of a sudden about eight flashes. The first thought I had was this looks like Hoffman charges [the pyrotechnic devices used to mimic the smoke of tank guns at Army training ranges], firing simulators. Obviously it wasn't. 1/35 [Armor] started engaging on the right. We started methodically engaging. That was what impressed me. It was not wild volleys of fire. We talked about fire control, who was going to fire where.[15]

The division at last closed upon its prey, the Medina Armored Division, one of the Republican Guard's two tank divisions. Sitting between the division's Phase Lines Spain and Lime, the Medina's T-72s tanks, with a sprinkling of T-55s from other units, BMP fighting vehicles, and MTLB armored personnel carriers were dug in for eight kilometers along the reverse slope of a slight ridge in a classic fishhook pattern. The Iraqis again were facing west, the Medina's 2d Brigade arrayed in a shallow, linear position bracing for the American attack.

After speaking with his company commanders, Whitcomb radioed brigade commander Meigs. "You've got the fight," he responded.

Meigs was trying to piece together a more complete picture of the Iraqi defenses. His two lead task forces were fully engaged. What was behind these positions?

The day was overcast and visibility was limited to about 1,500 meters. Brisk winds whipped up the loose sand from the desert floor. Through the haze, Whitcomb could see the muzzle flashes of Iraqi tanks as they fired and the fireballs created by the exploding ammunition and fuel when Iraqi vehicles were hit. Meigs told Whitcomb to have his tankers count the plumes from destroyed tanks as they burned; soon, Whitcomb had counted seventy. "He was trying to gauge the distances based on our reports," said Whitcomb of Meigs.

> It was a methodical shoot and you can see the explosions from the air. I don't want to say it was like a gunnery range, but it was. The fire commands were great. They were slow. There was a sense of doing business on the company commanders' part. We had fought at Al Busayah and had some combat and had this other one early in the morning, but nothing to compare to this.[16]

When Meigs realized he'd hit the Medina, he radioed Griffith. "It looks to me like I've got about 100 armored systems to the front; T-72s, BMPs. We're taking them under fire with the [M1A1s]. We've got the artillery going in. I'll keep you posted."

However, the division commander wanted a better feel for the decisive fight, and he moved forward. He viewed the battle from a position behind the 2d Brigade's tanks and in front of the artillery. "I went in on a ridge," he recalled.

> My command post was sitting about four kilometers to the rear of 2d Brigade's left flank. I got in a Humvee to go up there—which quite frankly was stupid—We came up on this ridgeline and there was the 2d Brigade's [direct support artillery] battalion and a reinforcing 8-inch battalion firing. We moved forward of the artillery

about four or five kilometers right up behind a line of tanks and Bradleys and artillery was coming in between us and the front line. The clouds were black, you had lightning flashing across the sky. You had tanks firing across the front for as far as you could see to include Iraqi tanks firing and the rounds falling short.[17]

As he watched his troops begin their work, lightning ripped through the clouds overhead, and thunder mixed with the sounds of the artillery rounds and then the tankers as they began to fire in volleys. To the division commander, "it was surreal. It was really an awesome spectacle which Mother Nature made even more spectacular."

VII Corps commander Franks also moved forward to get a feel for the battle. "In fact," recalled Griffith, "General Franks flew right across the top of the Medina Division. His pilot got a latitude-longitude location on us and misplotted. When he approached he almost got shot at because we thought he was a damn Hind [helicopter, built by the Soviet Union and sold to the Iraqis]. He was in a Blackhawk with the two external fuel tanks. He crossed the Medina Division and landed at my location."

Meigs now pressed home his attack, bringing 4/70 Armor forward, swinging it in on the northern flank of the brigade's line. Whitcomb's 2/70 Armor, now in the center of the U.S. line, hit many revetted tank positions and registered hits from more than three kilometers. Through their optical sights, the Iraqi gunners were unable to see the U.S. tanks through the haze and were reduced to firing on the muzzle flashes of the American tanks. "You'd see the [Iraqi] tanks fire back, and you'd see the rounds drop 1,000 meters short of [our] tanks," remembered Lieutenant Thomas Mundell, a platoon commander with A Company, 6/6 Infantry.[18] As in other engagements, the Iraqis were not aware of the American presence until the Americans began to fire.

The American tankers were now supremely confident of their superiority. The experience of Scaglionne's D Company, 1/35 Armor was typical. They spotted several BMPs at a range of 3,400 meters and opened up instantly. "The first tank fired, and it was kind of like every other tank fired within five seconds, fourteen rounds going downrange."[19] As they drew in to 2,800 meters from the Iraqi line, his tankers engaged the T-72s. In awe, Scaglionne watched Iraqi tank turrets flip forty feet into the air. "All along the ridge, you saw things that looked like blow-torches," said Lieutenant Mundell.[20]

The story was the same to the south, where Lieutenant Colonel Jerry Weidewitsch's 1/35 Armor manned the brigade's southern flank. "The first seven to 10 minutes were like no Grafenwoehr [gunnery exercise] I've ever seen, because each company as it came over the horizon began engaging targets to their front, and I could not at that time visualize the length of the target that would allow that many tanks to shoot," the battalion commander recalled." But then the smoke plumes started on the left-hand side and just continued across the front." [21]

Meigs's armor battalions were the focal point of the brigade and division's battle, but other units were also involved in the massive fight. Meigs had edged his reserve, 6/6 Infantry, from a rear position to one screening the brigade's left flank, filling in when 4/70 Armor had advanced on line with the other tank units. At about 3 P.M., C Company, 6/6 Infantry, on the extreme northern wing, ran into Republican Guard remnants, spotting BMPs on its left flank. Crabtree radioed his company commander and requested clearance to engage. Concerned about fratricide because his company was on the VII Corps boundary, Smithson asked if they could identify the vehicle.

The conversation was cut short. "About that time the first rounds hit," recalled Crabtree. One landed in front of Staff Sergeant Charles Yance's Bradley, another to the side.

Crabtree told Smithson, "They're firing on us!"

Smithson again asked, "Can you get positive ID it's not a friendly?"

"It's an armored vehicle, they're firing on us, I can't get the make."

"Hold fire," the captain ordered.

Finally, Crabtree's platoon made positive identification and opened fire with a deadly volley. "We're really not sure who took it out, but somebody did, because it went up in flames," Crabtree remembered. "The whole process probably only took about four minutes. It seemed like it took an hour and a half."[22]

The Iraqi position extended south out of the 2d Brigade zone. Colonel Jim Riley's First Brigade had cleared the Iraqi logistics site and in the north of his sector, 4th Battalion, 66th Armor Regiment was moving alongside 1/35 Armor. Lieutenant Colonel Philip Dow's task force surprised the Iraqis, a mix of Medina and other units, still facing to the south. Captain John Simmons's D Company, 4/66 Armor, came upon Iraqi tanks in the open, apparently refueling. A T-72 hit with a frontal shot exploded in sheets of flame.

In contact with the Medina at last, Griffith wanted to increase the pressure and get the division's Apaches into the fight. He first tried to cycle his attack helicopters into the close battle, but the tanks were taking out targets so rapidly that every time an Apache pilot would find a target, it seemed a tank would take it out first. Griffith had chopped a company of Apaches from the 3rd Battalion, 1st Aviation Regiment down to Meigs. They came on station about the time the division commander moved up to view the battle. "I could see the Apaches and they were having a very, very difficult time discerning friend from foe," Griffith remembered. "There was tremendous smoke and dust, typical battlefield confusion and inability to determine good guys from bad guys." The attack helicopters had moved north of the 2d Brigade's left flank, but pilots were frustrated "because every time they got ready to launch a missile a tank would blow up that they were locked on," said Griffith.

With all his tanks on line, 2/70 Armor's Whitcomb had "called up an infantry platoon to pull up on line and quite frankly because I wanted them to get a chance to fire, not because we needed them. It was about the same time an Apache came in and I remember a conversation from the Apache pilot saying call your TOW [missiles] off because we can't engage because of the wires."

The fight with the Medina had peaked after just ten minutes. Meigs's tankers now shot only when new targets presented themselves. After forty minutes of fighting, Medina's 2d Brigade was "pretty much gone," said Meigs.[23] Some sixty T-72s and nine T-55s had been destroyed. The 2d Brigade was untouched.

THE DEEP FIGHT

Even as Meigs's brigade was destroying the Medina brigade, Griffith was fighting a larger battle. Reports indicated a second line of Iraqi positions ten kilometers farther east. Unable to use them in the close fight, the division commander sent his attack helicopters deep, synchronizing their attacks with a massive Multiple Launch Rocket System strike the divison called an Iron Hammer. "There were two things on my mind," said Griffith.

Number one, I can't afford to waste this kind of combat power because [the Apaches] were getting off a missile about every two or three minutes. Second, I was still worried about what was out there in depth. So I wanted to start developing a situation deeper. I called up [aviation] brigade commander [Petrosky] and said this is not working. We're not getting good effect out of these Apaches so rather than use them up here let's send them deep. Because by now the feeling is starting to develop that these guys are not very good and we can take some risk here. So at this point I wanted to develop that situation in depth. I want to find out where the Hammurabi are or whatever that is out there. So let's send a battalion deep into the zone and see what we can do about it.[24]

The result was a classic, almost rote, exercise in U.S. Army doctrine. The close fight was tanks and Bradleys; Apaches and rocket artillery were working up to fifteen to twenty kilometers in front of them against dug-in or escaping forces. Still deeper in the division's zone, the Air Force was attacking against known positions. "You had artillery, Apaches, A-10s, tanks, Bradleys—the entire division, all the combat power we could muster—all firing and servicing the Medina Division at the same time," said divison artillery commander Corn.[25]

The deep attack by Apaches would fall to Lieutenant Colonel John Ward's 2/1 Aviation, which, by about 2 P.M., or about an hour after the Medina Ridge fight had slowed, began to replace the exhausted pilots and AH-64s of 3/1 Aviation, which had been on alert for thirty-nine hours. Arriving on station with his A Company, Ward looked down to see all three of the division's

brigades abreast. Ward had planned to rotate his attack companies in sequence, with B Company replacing A Company at 3:30
P.M., followed by C Company at 5:00 P.M. The deep fight would be
coordinated by Brigadier General David Hendricks, Griffith's assistant division commander for maneuver. Ward's mission was to
find and attack the second belt of Iraqi defenses while the division's ground forces rearmed, refueled, and moved forward.

Ward arrived to find a confused situation. "We were kind of
feeling our way up there because we couldn't see and we were
getting strange fire from here and there," he recalled.

> We were in front of bad guys and some were giving up and some
> weren't. Light rain was falling, and there was smoke from the oil
> fires. Really, it was a scene from hell. The smoke was so thick and
> lightning was striking. We landed, just sat down with the tanks and
> then we got our call to go forward.[26]

A Company had to wait thirty minutes for the artillery to lift. As
they at last began to move forward, the six Apaches in line, they
were caught in an Iraqi artillery barrage. "I'm sure there was
counterbattery fire from the Iraqis," concluded Ward. "One of
the aircraft was just covered on the side. All the panels got blown
open and he got holes in the blade and stuff. Had to replace the
canopy and that stuff but he finished the mission."

Moving beyond the Medina Ridge positions, the Iraqi defenses
at first thinned. A Company found only the stragglers from that
battle and other scattered vehicles, destroying a handful of tanks
and a like number of infantry carriers. Ward did not find his
main target until B Company arrived as planned at 3:30 P.M.,
about twenty kilometers forward of the division: "General Hendricks was on the radio. He was a real calming influence. He
said, 'Direct your fire a little to the south down in this area.'
That's when they really started shooting stuff up." Almost immediately, looming out of the smoke and rain, the Apaches found
their target: within twenty minutes, they bagged eighteen tanks,
fourteen armored personnel carriers, eight howitzers, and nu-
merous trucks in short-range engagements as close as 750 meters. The thick smoke from the oil fires attenuated the laser

engagement system on the Hellfire, making the missile ineffective over about 1,800 meters' range.[27]

Still, the destructiveness of the missile was awesome to Ward: the Iraqi reserves were "all lined up in those squares behind big berms. Hasty revetments. [B Company] just waxed them. They expended almost the whole fleet of ammunition, all their Hellfire [missiles]. They came back empty." The pilots had a field day against a wealth of targets. "We joked about it being a grab bag, because sometimes behind a revetment, you didn't know if it was a T-72, or a truck, or ammunition storage," said Chief Warrant Officer-3 Jack Bartol, an Apache pilot. "You'd lob a missile on it, and sometimes you'd get a fireball, sometimes just an explosion."[28] Ward's C Company arrived to take over the fight, but Griffith had started his ground forces moving again at 2:30 and the tanks were beginning to close on the Iraqis. Ward directed C Company to return to their forward rearming and refueling point. Fuel was again becoming a problem for the division.

Still, the 2d Brigade pressed on. The success of the Apaches made Griffith think he'd found either more of the Medina or perhaps the Hammurabi Armored Division of the Republican Guard: "I really thought we were hitting the Hammurabi at this point because [aviation brigade commander Colonel Dan] Petrosky reported that they were hitting lots of tanks, lots of BMPs, lots of stuff in zone. It turned out it was not the Hammurabi but elements of this Jihad corps that had moved up." As the brigade resumed its eastward march and passed through the Medina Division's lines, the troops of Whitcomb's 2/70 Armor were silenced by the devastation they had wrought. "It was a truly awesome sight as we passed the still-flaming hulks of the enemy," he later wrote. "Explosions continued, even over two hours after the fight, as tank rounds cooked off inside the vehicles, shooting flames skyward."[29] The charred remains of the Iraqi tankers who had tried to fight back were pitched out of their hatches; some bodies smoldered. While U.S. medical teams treated and evacuated the wounded and the prisoners, Meigs' brigade crept forward another six kilometers, halting for the night at about 5 P.M. The division's count for the whole battle was 186 tanks and 127

APCs destroyed that day, including 137 vehicles destroyed in less than an hour during the height of the Medina Ridge fight.

The Medina Ridge encounter and other Desert Storm tank battles such as the 2d Armored Cavalry Regiment's Battle of 73 Easting were remarkable not merely for the contribution they made to the victory of the American-led coalition in the Gulf War. Perhaps more important was how the victory was won and what it revealed about the evolving nature of high-technology land combat. Just as the nature of warfare had changed in the 1920s and 1930s when the large-scale production of the tank sparked the creation of panzer divisions and the ideal of *blitzkrieg*, the Gulf War strongly suggested that a new revolution was in its early stages. The tank was now a tool in information warfare, where what could be seen could be hit and what could be hit would be destroyed, but how would the tank, a steel beast from the mechanical age, even one as sophisticated as the Abrams, survive in this new age?

THE FUTURE

What Role for Steel Beasts in an Age of Information Warfare?

SINCE THE MOMENT of its birth in World War I, the tank has been a weapon to provoke controversy, either loved or hated or, in the hearts of cavalrymen, both loathed as the mechanical replacement for the horse and then celebrated for the same qualities. The United States Army's best-known tanker, George Patton, embodied this love-hate relationship within the span of his career: he first embraced the tank for its ability to quicken his promotion prospects, then as a polo-playing horse cavalryman, he sneered at the steel beast, and finally he rode his tanks to glory in the charge across France in 1944. A product of the mechanical age of warfare, the tank now seems an anachronism to many analysts of future combat, who, awed by the success of aerial bombardment in Operation Desert Storm or inspired by the promise of the dawning age of information warfare or impressed by the trend toward constabulary or peace-keeping operations, stand ready to drive the final nail into the tank's coffin. Thus, the kind of large-scale, blitzkrieg-style armored operations that concluded the Gulf War are a political as well as a technological anachronism. As one U.S. officer wrote in the Army War College journal *Parameters:* "America's proud regulars should put the Gulf War in its proper perspective. . . . Perhaps modern mid-intensity conventional war has become too terrible and costly to fight with ground troops, so it is just as well. Tactically, armored pursuits are exotic and exquisite things, but infantry legions on patrol are the stuff of superpower interventions."[1]

HEADS IN THE SAND?

Did the Gulf War sound the final bugle call for large, armored formations? Is the tank cavalry destined to go the way of the horse cavalry of the nineteenth century?

Even if information supersedes firepower and maneuverability as the currency in which future wars are transacted, there are good reasons to believe that the tank will find a major role on any high-technology battlefield and probably an increasing role in constabulary duties, as well. "I don't care whether you call it a tank or a bathtub," says Paul Funk, the general who commanded the U.S. 3rd Armored Division during the Gulf War. "I don't care if a future tank turns out to be a hovercraft. But if you think about the tank as mobile, protected firepower, and ask yourself what technological change in the next 25 years will take away the power of the tank and armored forces, what will take away their ability to take, seize and hold ground, the answer is: probably nothing."

Israel Tal, the legendary Israeli tank commander, sees two fundamental reasons why armor will continue to fulfill its role as the decisive force on land and why the tank continues to be the backbone of land forces. The first is continued dominance of the tank over countermeasures to the tank. "Those who question the central role of the tank and the leadership of armor think that the existence of new precision weapon systems that can hit the tank eliminate the chances of the tank and the armored fighting vehicle to survive. This assumption is wrong," he charges. "Nothing can replace the tank and the armored formation. No weapons system combines mobility, firepower, ballistic protection, [nuclear, biological, and chemical] protection and the ability to carry out breakthrough battles, advance and pursuit, reconnaissance, counterattacks and holding ground—and operates in all weather conditions, under fire and around the clock for sustained periods of time."

Tal also cites a second reason that large, armored forces will survive: there simply is no replacement on the horizon. "Not only is there nothing superior to armor which can replace it, there is not even anything equal to it. Armored troops are multi-purpose forces," he says. Since the German *blitzkrieg* into France in 1940, the best tactical and operational use of armor has been within the context of combined arms organizations. If Funk and Tal are to be proved correct, tankers must learn to survive and continue to dominate high-technoloy land warfare in a new age.

COME THE REVOLUTION

It is now a commonplace that the advent and widespread use of new computing and communications technologies will revolutionize the conduct of warfare, especially the kind of midintensity, conventional warfare in which large armored formations have played such a significant part. Certainly, Operation Desert Storm gave the world a glimpse of how powerful these new technologies might be. Will new technologies result in a completely new form of combat—"information war," as the enthusiasts call it? What kind of information weapon will the tank be?

Let us return to the four elements of revolutions in warfare outlined in the prologue to this book: technological change, the development of new weapons based on new technologies, the creation of new operational concepts to fully expoit the new technologies, and the building of new organizations to embody the new operational concepts. As Desert Storm was a war of transition, where some new bits of technology crept into weapons systems but did not result in radically new concepts of operation and new organizations, so, too, is the current generation of tanks in transition. Consider the American M1A1 Abrams, the workhorse of the Gulf War. From its introduction in 1980, it has represented a new wave of land combat systems, marked not only for its firepower and mobility but for its superiority as an information weapon. With the development of a new M1A2 version of the Abrams, the Army will be taking a second step toward a truly revolutionary new tank; if the technologies incorporated in the M1A2 pan out at all as the Army hopes, mounted land combat may be as much like air warfare as like the tank operations of World War II.

Beyond the excellence of the traditional elements of the M1's design—its main gun, automotive system, and armor—what pushed the Abrams a first short step toward the information age was the mounting of a thermal sight and a sophisticated ballistic computing system that allowed for new degrees of accurate gunnery under virtually all conditions. As the performance of the American tank fleets in the Gulf War revealed, neither darkness nor foul weather shielded the hapless Iraqis from attack. In many of the climactic tank battles of Desert Storm, the Iraqi tank crews first reacted when assaulted by VII Corps tankers as they had to air and artillery attacks; they could neither see nor strike back at their attackers.

These exchanges—they were so one-sided that they can hardly be called that—suggest how tank warfare has shifted to a new dimension. The struggle between weapon and countermeasure has expanded from the traditional contest between firepower and protection to include detection. For all the advantages enjoyed by M1 tankers over Iraqi T-72 crews—and they were considerable, from quality of ammunition to armor protection—the decisive edge came with the ability to see the enemy first and hit him with a first shot nearly every time. To put it simply, Gulf War battles like Medina Ridge emphasized that seeing an adversary is the first step toward killing him, as vital as hitting him with enough firepower to destroy him. Within the parameters of the Gulf War, the M1A1 was as much a precision strike weapon as was the Stealth fighter.

THE INFORMATION TANK

The Army's M1A2 program—being followed closely, and indeed imitated, by other advanced armies around the world—is an attempt to build upon these advantages by giving the tank commander an independent thermal viewer and incorporating a host of advanced electronic systems throughout the tank, the most important of which is the so-called intervehicular information system, which is designed to link the Abrams into a sophisticated communications network that could include information collected by satellite and in turn inform that communications and intelligence network. Soldiers now speak of the possibilities of complete knowledge of the battlefield. This, in turn, is leading the U.S. Army and others to reevaluate organizations and doctrines. While a full appreciation of the effects of new land warfare technologies will require years, if not decades, to work out, the limited field trials conducted to date suggest tantalizing possibilities. New, experimental organizations are planned; the 1920s Age of Experiments is returning.

THE ENDURING LURE OF *BLITZKRIEG*

Indeed, in many ways, the U.S. Army faces the dilemma of the British Army at the dawn of the revolution in armored warfare. By the end of World War I, the British were masters of large-scale, high-technology conventional warfare. The ideas for operational success in air-land warfare that informed the battle of Cambrai in 1917 and the final campaigns of 1918 were well enshrined within the Royal Tank Corps and its core of doctrinal prophets: J. F. C. Fuller, Basil Liddell-Hart, Percy Hobart, and the rest. After the war, the British army returned to the kind of colonial peacekeeping duties that maintenance of the empire required. Twenty years later, British armored forces were overmatched by the German *blitzkrieg;* the inital British advantages in tank warfare had been eroded by lack of funds, internal squabbling among soldiers, and the pull of worldwide missions.

The age of the tank, especially in Funk's larger sense of mobile, protected firepower, has yet to run its course. In an era of rapid technological change and uncertain politics, the tank retains its attractiveness as the best means of seizing and holding territory. The lure of *blitzkrieg*—the seizing of technological, organizational, and doctrinal advantage to gain rapid political advantage through the waging of offensive warfare—endures, even in the non-Western world: Iraq's invasion of Kuwait was, by regional standards, a *blitzkrieg* that would have had profound political consequences had it been allowed to stand. To achieve its full political effects, high-technology conventional warfare must have a substantial land force component, including the ability to close with an enemy, to shock him, to maneuver against him, and to control the ground in a decisive way. Just as this study has shown that the tank has never been such a dominant weapon that it could operate without support from other arms, so, too, has it shown the tank's enduring contribution: its mobility, its firepower, its shock effect, and perhaps, in the future, its potential decisiveness in an information war.

APPENDIXES

APPENDIX A: A COMPARISON OF OFFICER RANK STRUCTURES

Consistently rendering officer ranks without resorting to arcane designations is a challenge to the military historian. For ease of reading, the ranks in this book have been left in English, but some may still find them confusing, particularly ranks such as colonel general, which has no direct English or American counterpart. Also, we chose to make an exception in the case of the German SS; we felt the unique nature of these units demanded that we use their own nomenclature. Below are the formal titles for each of the armies discussed in this volume, with rough rank equivalency.

In general—or before casualties and the necessities of war begin to play havoc with things—2d lieutenants command platoons; first lieutenants often serve as company executive officers; captains command companies. Majors often are staff officers or junior battalion-level commanders; lieutenant colonels more often command at battalion level. Colonels usually command regiments or sometimes brigades, as do British brigadiers. Division commanders are most often two-star major generals, and three-star lieutenant generals command corps or field armies. German and Soviet colonel generals also hold such commands, but are perhaps more akin to British or American full, four-star generals. Field marshals and American generals of the armies are accorded five-star rank, the very highest, which is awarded only for command of huge formations or the conduct of major campaigns.

AMERICAN	**GERMAN**
2d Lieutenant	Leutnant
1st Lieutenant	Oberleutnant
Captain	Hauptmann
Major	Major
Lieutenant Colonel	Oberstleutnant
Colonel	Oberst
Brigadier General	Generalmajor
Major General	Generalleutnant
Lieutenant General	General der Infantrie, etc.
General	General-Oberst
General of the Armies	Generalfeldmarschall

BRITISH	**WAFFEN-SS**
2d Lieutenant	Untersturmführer
1st Lieutenant	Obersturmführer
Captain	Hauptsturmführer
Major	Sturmbannführer
Lieutenant Colonel	Obersturmbannführer
Colonel	Standartenführer
Brigadier	Oberführer
Major General	Brigadeführer and Generalmajor
Lieutenant General	Gruppenführer and Generalleutnant
General	Gruppenführer and General
Field Marshal	Oberstgruppenführer and Generalobserst
	Reichsführer

APPENDIX B: TANK TECHNOLOGY

This book has been about the development of armored warfare, meaning the mix of technology, tactics, and operations that made the *blitzkrieg* possible. Technology has been an essential element of the mix, but we have not dealt at length on the various incremental and radical advances in tank-making that have sometimes provided the edge of victory on the battlefield.

From World War I until the modern day, the tank has, in broad terms, undergone three generational changes. Prior to World War II, the technological struggle was to create a machine that would function reliably in battle, that did not break down repeatedly, that adequately protected its crew, and that delivered sufficient firepower in combat; in other words: the medium tank.

The medium tank grew to maturity during World War II. The German Panzer IV and V—the famous Panther—and the Soviet T-34 were the fully realized expressions of the dreams of the original prophets of armored warfare. Indeed, these designs were so successful that they survived for years after, with Panzer IVs and T-34s playing substantial roles in fighting two decades after the end of World War II. The tanks of the 1950s and 1960s were refinements of the same basic ideas.

Gradually, a third generation emerged, as new technologies—fast, accurate ballistic computers; laser range finders; and thermal sights—began to change the face of tank warfare. Tactical encounters became increasingly brief and violent. First-round hits are now the rule rather than the exception. Engagements occur at extended ranges, measured in miles rather than yards. Automation reduced crew size, yet gave each tanker more to do. Exotic new armor, turbine engines, and sheer size made modern main battle tanks look like steroid-inflated gladiators compared to the rickety, ninety-eight-pound weaklings who were their ancestors.

Still, the line remains continuous. For all their widgets, the American Abrams, British Challenger, Israeli Merkava, and German Leopard are, clearly, tanks, and they remain the big cats of the jungle. The charts on the following pages give a personal taxonomy of the big beasts.

The First Generation:
World War I and the Interwar Years

British, World War I	WEIGHT [TONS]	ARMOR	ARMAMENT	CREW
Mark I to III (male)[1]	28	12 mm	Two 6-pounder guns, 4 machine guns	8
Mark I to III (female)	27	12 mm	6 machine guns	8
Mark IV (male)	28	12 mm	Two 6-pounder guns, 4 machine guns	8
Mark IV (female)	26	12 mm	6 machine guns	8
Mark V (male)	29	14 mm	Two 6-pounder guns, 4 machine guns	8
Mark V (female)	28	14 mm	6 machine guns	8
Medium A "Whippet"	14	14 mm	4 machine guns	3
BRITISH INTERWAR				
Vickers Light Mark VI	5	14 mm	2 machine guns	3
Vickers Medium I	12	16 mm	47 mm gun, 3 machine guns	5
Cruiser Mark I (A9)	14	14 mm	40 mm gun, 3 machine guns	6
Cruiser Mark II (A10)	14	30 mm	40 mm gun, 1 machine gun	5
Cruiser Mark III (A13)	14	14 mm	40 mm gun, 1 machine gun	4
"Matilda" Infantry Tank Mark I	11	60 mm	1 machine gun	2
"Matilda" Infantry Tank Mark II	26	80 mm	40 mm gun, 1 machine gun	4
"Valentine" Infantry Tank Mark III	16	65 mm	40 mm gun, 1 machine gun	3
FRENCH WORLD WAR I				
Schneider	14	11 mm	75 mm gun, 1 machine gun	7
St. Chamond	25	25 mm	75 mm gun, 4 machine guns	9
Renault FT-17	7	22 mm	37 mm gun	2
FRENCH INTERWAR				
Renault R-35	10	45 mm	37 mm gun, 1 machine gun	2

Somua S-35	20	55 mm	47 mm gun, 1 machine gun	3
Char B-1 bis	32	60 mm	75 mm gun, 47 mm gun, 2 machine guns	4

GERMAN WORLD WAR I

A7V	32	30 mm	57 mm gun, 6 machine guns	18

GERMAN INTERWAR

Panzer IA	6	13 mm	2 machine guns	2
Panzer IIA	7	14 mm	20 mm gun, 1 machine gun	3
Panzer IIIA	15	14 mm	37 mm gun, 3 machine guns	5
Panzer IVA	17	20 mm	75 mm short-barreled gun, 2 machine guns	5

ITALIAN INTERWAR

M-13/40	14	40 mm	47 mm gun, 3 machine guns	4

SOVIET INTERWAR

BT-5	11	13 mm	45 mm gun, 1 machine gun	3
T-34/76	27	65 mm	76 mm gun, 2 machine guns	4
KV-1	47	75 mm	76 mm gun, 2 machine guns	5

AMERICAN INTERWAR

"Christie" T-3	10	13 mm	37 mm gun, 1 machine gun	3
"Stuart I" M-3 Light Tank	12	51 mm	37 mm gun, 3 machine guns	4

[1] The World War I designation of male and female tanks refers to the main armament. "Male" tanks mounted large-caliber main guns as well as machine guns; "female" tanks had machine guns only.

The Second Generation: World War II and Beyond

British, World War II	WEIGHT [TONS]	ARMOR	ARMAMENT	CREW
"Covenanter" Cruiser Tank Mark V	18	40 mm	40 mm gun, 1 machine gun	4

"Crusader III" Cruiser Tank Mark VI	20	51 mm	57 mm gun, 1 machine gun	3
"Cromwell Mark IV" Cruiser Tank Mark VIII	28	76 mm	75 mm gun, 2 machine guns	5
"Churchill" Infantry Tank Mark IV	39	102 mm	57 mm gun, 2 machine guns	5
Sherman VC Firefly	35	52 mm	76 mm gun, 1 machine gun	4

BRITISH POSTWAR

Centurion Mark 3	49	152 mm	83 mm gun, 1 machine gun	4
Chieftain 2	51	150 mm	120 mm gun, 3 machine guns	4

FRENCH POSTWAR

AMX-13	15	40 mm	75 mm gun, 1 machine gun	3
AMX-30	36	150 mm	105 mm gun, 2 machine guns	4

GERMAN WORLD WAR II

Panzer IIIE	20	30 mm	50 mm gun, 3 machine guns	5
Panzer IVF2	24	50 mm	Long 75 mm gun, 2 machine guns	5
"Panther" Panzer V	43	110 mm	Long 75 mm gun, 1 machine gun	5
"Tiger I" Panzer VI	56	110 mm	88 mm gun, 2 machine guns	5
"King Tiger" Panzer VI	69	150 mm	88 mm gun, 3 machine guns	5

SOVIET WORLD WAR II

T-34/85	31	75 mm	85 mm gun, 2 machine guns	5
JS-2	46	160 mm	122 mm gun, 2 machine guns	4
JS-3	46	200 mm	122 mm gun, 2 machine guns	4

SOVIET POSTWAR

T-54	36	105 mm	100 mm gun, 2 machine guns	4
T-55	36	170 mm	100 mm gun, 2 machine guns	4
T-62	40	170 mm	115 mm smoothbore, 2 machine guns	3
T-64	38	100 mm	125 mm smoothbore, 2 machine guns	3
T-72	41	100 mm	125 mm smoothbore, 2 machine guns	

AMERICAN WORLD WAR II

"Lee" Medium Tank M-3	27	50 mm	75 mm gun, 37 mm gun, 4 machine guns	6
"Sherman" Medium Tank M4A1	30	77 mm	75 mm gun, 2 machine guns	5
"Pershing" M26	43	102 mm	90 mm gun, 3 machine guns	5

AMERICAN POSTWAR

"Patton" M47	50	100 mm	90 mm gun, 3 machine guns	5
"Patton" M48A5	54	120 mm	105 mm gun, 2 machine guns	4
M60A1	53	100+ mm	105 mm gun, 2 machine guns	4
M60A2	57	150+ mm	152 mm gun/Shillelagh missile, 2 machine guns	4
M60A3	52	110+ mm	105 mm guns, 2 machine guns	4

THE THIRD GENERATION: MODERN TANKS

British	WEIGHT [TONS]	ARMOR	ARMAMENT	CREW
Challenger/ Challenger 2	69	composite	120 mm gun, 2 machine guns	4
GERMAN				
Leopard	40	spaced	105 mm gun, 2 machine guns	4
Leopard 2	60	composite	120 mm smoothbore, 2 machine guns	4
SOVIET/RUSSIAN				
T-80	47	composite/ reactive	125 mm smoothbore, 2 machine guns	3
AMERICAN				
M1	60	composite	105 mm gun, 3 machine guns	4
M1A1	63	composite	120 mm smoothbore, 3 machine guns	4
ISRAELI				
Merkava	56	spaced	105 mm gun, 2 machine guns	4+ infantry squad
Merkava II	56	composite/ reactive	120 mm smoothbore, 2 machine guns	4+ infantry squad

NOTES

PROLOGUE

1. Major General Heinz Guderian, *Achtung—Panzer! The Development of Armoured Forces, Their Tactics and Operational Potential*, translated by Christopher Duffy, Arms and Armour Press, London, 1992, p. 81.
2. Ibid., pp. 81–82.
3. Robert C. Johnson, *Breakthrough! Tactics, Technology and the Search for Victory on the Western Front in World War I*, Presidio Press, Novato, California, 1994, p. 201.
4. Ibid., p. 202.
5. Public Records Office, AIR 1/1510/204/58/10, 3d Brigade, Royal Flying Corps, quoted in Johnson, *Breakthrough!*, p. 203.
6. For some of the details of how units were organized for the attack on Cambrai, see Guderian, *Achtung—Panzer!*, p. 78.
7. Guderian, *Achtung—Panzer!*, p. 77.
8. Johnson, *Breakthrough!*, p. 204n.
9. Guderian, *Achtung—Panzer!*, p. 84.
10. Ibid., p. 85.
11. Ibid., p. 85.
12. Ibid., p. 87.

CHAPTER ONE

1. *Generaloberst* Franz Halder, *The Halder Diaries: The Private War Journals of Colonel General Franz Halder*, Boulder, Colo., Westview Press, 1976, entry for 29 September 1939, vol. 2, p. 18; also cited in Robert Alan Doughty, *The Breaking Point: Sedan and the Fall of France, 1940*, Archon Books, Hamden, Conn., 1990, p. 19.

2. Office of the United States Chief of Counsel of Axis Criminality, Nazi Conspiracy and Aggression, vol. 7, "Memorandum and Directives for Conduct of the War in the West," 9 October 1939, Document 1-52, p. 801, cited in Robert Alan Doughty, *The Breaking Point*, p. 20.
3. Robert Allan Doughty, *The Breaking Point*, chap. 1.
4. Erich von Manstein, *Lost Victories*, p. 70 passim.
5. Ibid., pp. 73–74.
6. von Manstein, *Lost Victories*, p. 103.
7. Guderian, *Panzer Leader*, p. 89.
8. von Manstein, *Lost Victories*, p. 122.
9. Doughty, *The Breaking Point*.
10. Ibid.
11. Hans von Luck, *Panzer Commander: The Memoirs of Colonel Hans von Luck,* Bantam Doubleday Dell Publishing Company, New York, 1989, p. 37.
12. von Luck, *Panzer Commander*, p. 38.
13. Hart, *The Rommel Papers*, p. 106.
14. von Luck, *Panzer Commander*, p. 39.
15. See Florian K. Rothburst, *Guderian's XIXth Panzer Corps and the Battle of France: Breakthrough in the Ardennes*. This is a superior study, thoroughly researched and clearly written, of German planning for the Ardennes attack.
16. Guderian, *Panzer Leader*, p. 98.
17. Rothburst, *Guderian's XIXth Panzer Corps* p. 57, note 32.
18. Guderian, *Panzer Leader*, p. 99.
19. Ibid., p. 101.
20. Rothburst, *Guderians' XIXth Panzer Corps*, p. 71.
21. Doughty, *The Breaking Point*, p. 103
22. Ibid., p. 133.
23. Ibid., p. 135.
24. Ibid., p. 143; see note 25.
25. Rothburst, *Guderians's XIXth Panzer Corps and the Battle of France*, p. 79; Doughty, *The Breaking Point*, p. 207.
26. Doughty, *The Breaking Point*, p. 209; see note 15.
27. Guderian, *Panzer Leader*, p. 105; Rothburst, *Guderian's XIXth Panzer Corps and the Battle of France*, p. 82; see note 36.
28. See Doughty, *The Breaking Point*, pp. 304–306.
29. Rothburst, *Guderian's XIXth Panzer Corps*, p. 85.
30. Guderian, *Panzer Leader*, p. 108.
31. Quoted in Doughty, *The Breaking Point*, p. 236; see note 25.

CHAPTER TWO

1. Quoted in Barrie Pitt, *The Crucible of War*, p. 23.
2. For a fuller discussion of British armor, see W.G.F. Jackson, *The Battle for North Africa*, 1940–43, pp. 39–40 and Pitt, *The Crucible of War*, especially pp. 87, 103 and 179.
3. Pitt, *The Crucible of War*, p. 190.
4. Jackson, *The Battle for North Africa*, p. 88.
5. Ibid., pp. 116–117.
6. Ibid., p. 119.
7. B. H. Liddell Hart, editor, *The Rommel Papers*, Collins, London, 1953, pp. 105–106.
8. Paul Carell, *The Foxes of the Desert*, Bantam, New York, 1962, pp. 7–8.
9. Pitt, *The Crucible of War*, p. 255.
10. Liddell Hart, editor, *The Rommel Papers*, p. 106.
11. Macksey, *Tank Warfare*, p. 148.
12. Jackson, *The Battle for North Africa*, pp. 136–137.
13. Perrett, p. 124.
14. Macksey, *Afrika Korps*, p. 33.
15. Macksey, *Tank Warfare*, p. 151.
16. Perrett, p. 126.
17. Macksey, *Afrika Korps*, p. 34.
18. Ibid., p. 35.
19. Pitt, *The Crucible of War*, p. 339.
20. Jackson, p. 182.
21. Liddell Hart, editor, *The Rommel Papers*, p. 153.
22. Perrett, *Knights of the Black Cross*, p. 127.
23. Jackson, pp. 178–179.
24. Ibid., pp. 182–183.
25. Pitt, *The Crucible of War*, pp. 304–305
26. Jackson, pp. 226–227.
27. See Macksey, *Afrika Korps*, p. 61; Jackson, p. 227.
28. von Mellenthin, p. 87.
29. Ibid., pp. 90–91.
30. Ibid., p. 91.
31. Perrett, p. 131.
32. Jackson, pp. 150–151.
33. Ibid., p. 250.
34. Perrett, p. 135.
35. Moorehead, quoted in Jackson, p. 305.
36. British Official history, quoted in Jackson, p. 302.

37. Jackson, pp. 302-303.
38. Ibid., p. 303.
39. Macksey, *Afrika Korps*, p. 94.
40. Ibid., p. 94.
41. Ibid., pp. 94–96.
42. Ibid., p. 100.
43. Ibid., p. 104.
44. Jackson, p. 319.
45. Liddell Hart, editor, *The Rommel Papers*, p. 298.
46. Ibid., pp. 299–300.
47. Jackson, p. 355.
48. Ibid., p. 332.
49. Ibid., p. 336.
50. Ibid., p. 365.
51. Ibid., p. 367.
52. Ibid., p. 368.
53. Liddell Hart, editor, *The Rommel Papers*, p. 308.
54. Jackson, pp. 368–369.
55. Liddell Hart, editor, *The Rommel Papers*, pp. 309–310.
56. Jackson, pp. 372–373.
57. Ibid., p. 372.
58. Ibid., pp. 374–375.
59. Ibid., p. 375.
60. Liddell Hart, editor, *The Rommel Papers*, pp. 318–319.
61. Ibid., pp. 318–319.
62. Jackson, p. 377.
63. Liddell Hart, editor, *The Rommel Papers*, p. 321.
64. Jackson, p. 379.

CHAPTER THREE

1. Adolf Hitler, Directive No. 21: Operation Barbarossa, December 18, 1940, quoted as Appendix XXII in Gen. Heinz Guderian, *Panzer Leader*, etc.
2. Earl F. Ziemke, "Military Effectiveness in the Second World War," in Allan R. Millett and Williamson Murray, editors, *Military Effectiveness: Volume III, The Second World War,* Unwin Hyman, Boston, 1988, p. 301.
3. Alan Clark, *Barbarossa: The Russian-German Conflict, 1941–45,* Quill, New York, 1965, pp. 17–18.

4. R.H.S. Stolfi, *Hitler's Panzers East: World War II Reinterpreted*, p. 18.
5. Albert Seaton, *The Russo-German War, 1941–45*, Presidio Press, Novato, California, 1991, p. 44.
6. Ibid., p. 44.
7. Ibid., p. 46.
8. *The German Campaign in Russia: Planning and Operations [1940–1942]*, Washington, U.S. Government Printing Office, 1955, p.4; quoted in R.H.S. Stolfi, *Hitler's Panzers East: World War II Reinterpreted*, p. 17.
9. Franz Halder, *Kriegstagebuch*, Vol. 2, pp. 32–3, 22 July 1940; quoted without further citation in Seaton, *The Russo-German War, 1941–45*, p. 52.
10. Seaton, *The Russo–German War, 1941–45*, p. 52.
11. Ibid., p. 56.
12. This odd disposition of forces—considering the importance of Moscow—is discussed both by Stolfi and Alan Clark. Writes Clark: "In the early 1930s, Marshal Tukhachevski had drawn up a master plan for the conduct of this defense, and this scheme, curiously, survived the execution of its author. . . . He had suggested a relatively light concentration in the north, with the bulk of the mobile forces to be placed on the Dnieper, where they could menace the right flank of the invader and, if all went well, undertake a rapid occupation of the Balkans." [see Clark, *Barbarossa, the Russian–German Conflict, 1941–45*, pp. 29–30.] Stolfi, too, mentions the offensive potential of this troop placement. However, the opportunity for counterattacks into the flank of an attack across the Orsha landbridge would certainly be impeded by the Pripet Marshes.
13. Seaton, *The Russo–German War, 1941–45*, p. 57.
14. Ibid., p. 58.
15. Ibid., p. 59.
16. All German formations detailed in Alan Clark, *Barbarossa: The Russian–German Conflict, 1941–45*, pp. 12-13.
17. Seaton, *The Russo–German War, 1941–45*, p. 62.
18. R.H.S. Stolfi, *Hitler's Panzers East: World War II Reinterpreted*, p. 21.
19. Seaton, *The Russo–German War, 1941–45*, p. 46.
20. Colonel David M. Glantz, "Soviet Defensive Tactics at Kursk, July 1943," CSI Report No. 11, Combat Studies Institute, U.S. Army Command and General Staff College, Fort Leavenworth, Kansas, 1986, p. 1.
21. Seaton, *The Russo–German War, 1941–45*, p. 91.
22. Ibid., p. 92.

23. Ibid., p. 93.
24. Ibid., p. 93.
25. Quoted without citation in Clark, *Barbarossa: The Russian–German Conflict, 1941–45.*
26. Clark, *Barbarossa: The Russian–German Conflict, 1941–45*, pp. 38–39.
27. Glantz, Soviet Defensive Tactics at Kursk, pp. 5–6.
28. R.H.S. Stolfi, *Hitler's Panzers East: World War II Reinterpreted*, p. 122.
29. Ibid., pp. 76–78, for more details.
30. Ibid., p. 78.
31. Ibid., pp. 138–149.
32. Ibid., p. 155.
33. Ibid., p. 165.
34. Armstrong, p. 30.
35. Guderian, *Panzer Leader*, p. 182.
36. Armstrong, p. 59, note 6.
37. Manstein, *Lost Victories*, p. 406.
38. Geoffrey Jukes, *Kursk: The Clash of Armour*, Ballantine Books, New York, 1969, p. 29.
39. Guderian, *Panzer Leader*, p. 288.
40. Jukes, Kursk, p. 36.
41. Quoted in Jukes, Kursk, p. 38.
42. Glantz, "Soviet Defensive Tactics at Kursk," pp. 24–25.
43. Quoted without further citation in Robin Cross, *Citadel, The Battle of Kursk: The Greatest Tank Battle of World War II*, Sarpedon, New York, 1993, pp. 108–109.
44. Geoffrey Jukes, *Kursk, The Clash of Armour*, Ballantine Books, New York, 1969, p. 88.
45. Cross, *Citadel, The Battle of Kursk*, p. 188.
46. Quoted without citation in Robin Cross, *Citadel: The Battle of Kursk*, Sarpedon Publishers, New York, 1993, p. 195.
47. Col. Frederick C. Turner, "Prokhorovka: The Great Russian Tank Encounter Battle with the Germans," *Armor*, May–June 1993, pp. 8–9.
48. Turner, "Prokhorovka," p. 9.
49. Estimates of II SS Panzer Corps' strength at the time of the Prokhorovka battle often have been overstated, due to the Soviet intelligence figures for the battle. Indeed, it is doubtful that tank strength for all of Fourth Panzer Army was much above the Soviet figure of 500 tanks for II SS Panzer Corps, although the German ability to recover and repair damaged tanks was quite good.
50. Turner, "Prokhorovka," p. 10
51. Ibid., p. 11.

52. Seaton, p. 435.
53. Ibid., p. 436.
54. Ibid., p. 436.
55. Translated from German by Joseph G. Welsh, edited by Richard N. Armstrong, *Red Armor Combat Orders: Combat Regulations for Tank and Mechanized Forces, 1944*, Frank Cass, London, 1991, pp. 15–18.
56. Ibid., p. 15.
57. Ibid., p. 67.
58. Ibid., p. 67.
59. Seaton, *The Russo–German War, 1941–1945*, p. 433.
60. Imperial War Museum, Führer Order No. 11; quoted in Matthew Cooper, *The German Army 1933–1945*, Scarborough House, Chelsea, Michigan, 1978, p. 473.
61. Alex Buchner, *Ostfront 1944: The German Defensive Battles on the Russian Front 1944*, Schiffer Publishing, West Chester, Pa., 1991, p. 150.
62. Seaton, *The Russo–German War*, 1941–1945, p. 438.
63. Quoted without further reference in Buchner, *Ostfront 1944*, pp. 153–158.
64. Seaton, *The Russo–German War*, 1941–45, p. 442.

CHAPTER FOUR

1. Stephen Badsey, *Normandy 1944*, Osprey Publishing Ltd., London, p. 45.
2. David Mason, *Breakout*, Ballantine Books Inc., New York, 1969, p. 9.
3. John Keegan, *Six Armies in Normandy*, Penguin Books USA Inc., 1983, p. 158.
4. Ibid., p. 142.
5. Hans von Luck, *Panzer Commander*, p. 179.
6. Badsey, *Normandy 1944*, p. 40.
7. Charles Messenger, *The Last Prussian*, Macmillan, New York, 1991.
8. Carlo D'Este, *Decision in Normandy*, HarperCollins, New York, 1991, p. 116.
9. Keegan, *Six Armies in Normandy*, p. 152.
10. Ibid., p. 153.
11. D'Este, *Decision in Normandy*, p. 177.
12. Ibid., p. 178.
13. Ibid., pp. 177–179.

14. Max Hastings, *Overlord*, Simon and Schuster, Inc., New York, 1985, p.132; see also Paul Carell, *Invasion—They're Coming*, London 1962, p. 169.
15. Gudgin, *The Tiger Tanks*, p.130.
16. Keegan, *Six Armies in Normandy*, p. 154.
17. Ibid., p. 154.
18. D'Este, *Decision in Normandy*, pp. 180–181.
19. Hastings, *Overlord*, p. 132.
20. D'Este, *Decision in Normandy*, p. 181.
21. Ibid., p. 182.
22. Ibid., p. 183.
23. Ibid., p. 178n.
24. Badsey, *Normandy 1944*, p. 47.
25. Ibid., p. 47.
26. D'Este, *Decision in Normandy*, p. 235.
27. Ibid., p. 240n.
28. Keegan, *Six Armies in Normandy*, p. 173.
29. D'Este, *Decision in Normandy*, p. 240.
30. Keegan, *Six Armies in Normandy*, p. 176.
31. Ibid., p. 177.
32. D'Este, *Decision in Normandy*, p. 246.
33. Ibid., p. 250.
34. Badsey, *Normandy 1944*, p. 53.
35. D'Este, *Decision in Normandy*, p. 356n.
36. Badsey, *Normandy 1944*, p. 53.
37. D'Este, *Decision in Normandy*, p. 315.
38. Ibid., p. 318.
39. John Man, *D-Day Atlas*, pp. 102–3.
40. Quoted in D'Este, *Decision in Normandy*, p. 362.
41. D'Este, *Decision in Normandy*, p. 364.
42. Ibid., p. 371.
43. Ibid., p. 360.
44. Ibid., p. 366.
45. Luck, *Panzer Commander*, p. 193.
46. D'Este, *Decision in Normandy*, p. 379.
47. Ibid., p. 379.
48. Ibid., p. 378.
49. Hastings, *Overlord*, pp. 251–252.
50. Keegan, *Six Armies in Normandy*, p. 237.
51. Ibid., p. 247.

CHAPTER FIVE

1. James R. Arnold, *Ardennes 1944,* Osprey Publishing, London, 1990, p.6.
2. Peter Elstob, *Hitler's Last Offensive,* The Macmillan Company, New York, 1971, pp.14–15.
3. Danny S. Parker, *Battle of the Bulge,* Combined Books, Inc., Philadelphia, 1991, p. 51.
4. Ibid., p. 22.
5. Elstob, *Hitler's Last Offensive,* p .9.
6. Ibid., p. 9.
7. Parker, *Battle of the Bulge,* p. 14.
8. Charles Messenger, *The Blitzkrieg Story,* Charles Scribner's Sons, New York, 1976, p. 210.
9. Major General F. W. von Mellenthin, *Panzer Battles,* University of Oklahoma Press, Oklahoma, 1956, p. 341.
10. Parker, *Battle of the Bulge,* p.37.
11. Ibid., p. 81.
12. Ibid., p. 71.
13. Ibid., p. 70.
14. Arnold, *Ardennes 1944,* p. 34.
15. Parker, *Battle of the Bulge,* p. 76.
16. Ibid., p. 78.
17. Ibid., p. 68.
18. Elstob, *Hitler's Last Offensive,* p. 150.
19. Ibid., p. 180.
20. Ibid., p. 182.
21. Ibid., p. 231.
22. Arnold, *Ardennes 1944,* p. 80.
23. Ibid., p. 84.

CHAPTER SIX

1. Eric Hammel, *Six Days in June,* Scribners, New York, 1992, p. 118.
2. Edward Luttwak and Dan Horowitz, *The Israeli Army,* Allen Lane, London, 1975, p. 230.
3. Ibid., p. 234.
4. David Eshel, *Chariots of the Desert,* Brassey's, London, 1989, pp. 77–78.
5. Major General Israel Tal's briefing as provided to the authors.

6. Eshel, *Chariots of the Desert*, p. 67.
7. Hammel, *Six Days in June*, pp. 186–187.
8. Ibid., p. 188.
9. Ibid., pp. 192–193.
10. Ibid., p. 134.
11. Luttwak and Horowitz, *The Israeli Army*, p. 240.
12. Eshel, *Chariots of the Desert*, p. 71.
13. Luttwak and Horowitz, *The Israeli Army*, pp. 292–295
14. Hammel, *Six Days in June*, pp. 257–258.
15. Luttwak and Horowitz, *The Israeli Army*, p. 363.
16. For a well-informed discussion of the strategic background of the 1973 war, see Eliot Cohen and John Gooch, *Military Misfortunes*, Macmillan, New York, 1990.
17. Samuel Katz, *Israeli Tank Battles*, Arms and Armour Press, London, 1988, pp. 59–64.
18. Ibid., p. 61.
19. Bryan Perrett, *A History of Blitzkrieg*, Stein and Day, New York, 1983, p. 262.
20. Eshel, *Chariots of the Desert*, pp. 126–127.
21. Katz, *Israeli Tank Battles*, pp. 64–65.
22. George Forty, *Tank Commanders*, Motorbooks International, Osceola, Wisconsin, 1993, p.182n.
23. Luttwak and Horowitz, *The Israeli Army*, p. 353.
24. Edgar O'Ballance, *No Victor, No Vanquished*, Presidio Press, San Rafael, California, 1978, p. 290.
25. Anthony H. Cordesman and Abraham R. Wagner, *The Lessons of Modern War, Volume I—The Arab–Israeli Conflicts, 1973–1989*, Westview, Boulder, Colorado, 1990, pp. 90–91.
26. Luttwak and Horowitz, *The Israeli Army*, p. 229.
27. Eshel, *Chariots of the Desert*, p. 128; see also Luttwak and Horowitz, *The Israeli Army*, pp. 353–354.
28. Eshel, *Chariots of the Desert*, pp. 130–131.
29. Ibid., pp. 131–133.
30. Katz, *Israeli Tank Battles*, p. 71.
31. Eshel, *Chariots of the Desert*, p. 138.
32. Ibid., pp. 134–135.
33. Katz, *Israeli Tank Battles*, p. 67.
34. Ibid., pp. 135–136.
35. Katz, *Israeli Tank Battles*, p. 71.
36. Eshel, *Chariots in the Desert*, pp. 140–141.
37. Katz, *Israeli Tank Battles*, p. 77.

CHAPTER SEVEN

1. Steve Vogel, "Metal Rain," *Army Times*, Nov. 11, 1991, p. 16.
2. Ibid., p. 16.
3. Maj. Chesley Harris, "Operation Desert Storm: Armored Brigade in Combat," unpublished monograph, p. 18.
4. Ibid., p. 19.
5. Vogel, "Metal Rain," p. 22.
6. Harris, "Operation Desert Storm: Armored Brigade in Combat," p. 19.
7. Vogel, "Metal Rain," p 22.
8. Lt. Col. Roy Whitcomb, "Personal Experience Monograph of Operation Desert Storm," unpublished monograph, p. 17.
9. Vogel, "Metal Rain," p 22.
10. Harris, "Operation Desert Storm: Armored Brigade in Combat," p. 21.
11. Ibid., p. 22.
12. Ibid., p. 22.
13. Ibid., p. 22.
14. Whitcomb., "Personal Experience Monograph of Desert Storm," p. 17.
15. Author interview with Whitcomb.
16. Ibid.
17. Ibid.
18. Vogel, "Metal Rain," p. 20.
19. Ibid., p. 20.
20. Ibid., p. 20.
21. Ibid., p. 20.
22. Ibid., p. 20.
23. Ibid., p. 20.
24. Author interview with Griffith.
25. Vogel, "Metal Rain," p. 61.
26. Author interview with Ward.
27. Lt. Col. John Ward, untitled, unpublished monograph, p. 19.
28. Vogel, "Metal Rain," p. 20.
29. Lt. Col. John Ward, monograph, p 15.

EPILOGUE

1. Lt. Col. Daniel Bolger, "The Ghosts of Omdurman," Parameters.